MOZART

GENIUS OF HARMONY

MOZART

GENIUS OF HARMONY

by ANN M. LINGG

Illustrations by Helen Frank

NEW YORK: HENRY HOLT AND COMPANY

To the Memory of Charles

CONTENTS

[v i i]

CONTENTS

ACKNOWLEDGMENTS

I wish to express my sincere gratitude to Miss Helen K. Taylor for editorship of the book. I cannot thank her warmly enough for her understanding and tactful guidance.

Grateful acknowledgment is also made to the editors of Henry Holt and Company for their co-operation and efficiency. I am particularly indebted to Miss Siri Andrews and to Miss Alice Torrey.

MOZART

GENIUS OF HARMONY

PROLOGUE

"LOOK, Mamma, Wolferl is so tired!"

The little girl glanced sympathetically at her two-year-old baby brother whose tiny hands were vainly trying to close on Mother's hand.

This was one of his first long walks. He was a lively, healthy child, and his cheeks were reddened by the strong wind that was sweeping winter out of the land and making it clear and clean for the coming of spring.

It was late on a February afternoon, and Anna Maria Mozart had taken her two children for a stroll along the bank of the Salzach, the gray-green river which came roaring down from a distant mountain range. Even here, where it passed the old and picturesque town of Salzburg, with its bed growing wider and its course smoother, irregular, foaming waves showed that huge stone rocks were breaking the water as it thundered northward. Many bridges of stone spanned the river, and at the head of one of these bridges Anna Maria interrupted her walk and lifted little Wolfgang in her arms.

As she looked back, and forward, and across, her eyes roamed absent-mindedly over the seemingly endless rows of small houses that flanked the river. Built with many arches and vaults, painted in various shades, brightened by multicolored window shutters, this cavalcade of stone and color has always seemed unreal, like a stage setting of indescribable beauty to tourists of later days. But Frau Mozart had not stopped to admire. Instead, she thought of the war of which the men were talking, and wondered what it was all about;

of her husband the hard-working musician; of high living costs; and of her children whom she had to feed and clothe. Finally, she turned with a sigh to where mountain meadows, still barren and only partly covered with snow, swung upward, high into the fog. And as she proceeded, she seemed to walk right into the hill which carried the proud fortress on its top, into the rocks that pressed close to the river, herding, as it were, the houses like frightened sheep.

Stone and color gradually dissolved in the twilight. Candles flickered up, dimly lighting scattered windows. Bells began to ring from all sides. They came from Salzburg's many churches—silvery, joyful tunes sounding above mighty, hollow ones.

The little girl stood still, fascinated. "Why do all the bells ring together, just now?"

"It's praying time," Mamma answered. "All their voices, high and low like those of human beings, join in praising God. It's His time now, not man's. . . ."

"And Wolferl can't hear it," the girl complained. "Look, he's asleep."

Anna Maria looked at her baby tenderly. He was leaning heavily against her body, with his fat little arms tightly around her neck. "Maybe he doesn't hear them," she said, "but they are ringing for him just the same. For every human being, little or big, awake or asleep, wherever he might be . . . Remember this, Nannerl, every time you hear the bells. . . ."

But Wolferl was not fully asleep. With his eyes half closed, he had seen the houses gradually fade in the oncoming twilight. The roar of the river lulled him, and as if from far away came the sound of the bells and Mamma's words, although he was too little to understand what she meant. The water, the bells, the suddenly grave voice of his mother, united for the tired baby into a revelation of melody as his consciousness vanished . . . and the song went on, and on . . . and on. . . .

CHAPTER I

SALZBURG

EIGHTEENTH-CENTURY SALZBURG, where the Mozart family lived, was a town rich in history. Long before the Christian era, Roman emperors sent out their legions from the peninsula which is now Italy, to establish strongholds beyond the mountain wall of the Alps. The soldiers fought their way across snow, ice, and rocks until one day the gray-and-white wilderness gave way to gentle, wooded slopes and a friendly river valley strangely like the countryside of their native South. Here, where North and South seemed to melt into each other, the Roman legions built the city of Juvavum.

Along the road the legions had explored, Roman goods, law, and culture came across the Alps. In the fifth century, barbaric tribes from the North set out to conquer the South and Roman imperial might vanished. But in the seventh century came other heralds from Rome. They carried neither sword, nor shield, nor helmet; they brought the Cross and the message of Christian salvation.

At the foot of a steep, rocky hill, they built their first monastery, St. Peter. Juvavum had ceased to be a Roman military outpost, but in its place, proudly and splendidly, grew Salzburg, the Eternal City of the North.

The rich salt mines in the surrounding mountains gave the name to the expanding city and to its river, the Salzach. They brought prosperity to its inhabitants. Salzburg's overlords were Bishops of the Roman Church, and became Princes of the Holy Roman Empire

—proud, courageous, and militant. Their fortress, built on the hill above St. Peter's monastery, gave the Salzburgers protection to live in faith and security and in their natural gaiety.

The Southern element in the Salzburgers is responsible for their infatuation with everything theatrical. Since early days, church

students acted Latin and German plays during the Carnival season; peasants dramatized scenes from the Scriptures; and it was in Salzburg and the surrounding countryside that the jolliest character of all stages was reborn in a new guise; the Italian *Arlequino* received the German name of *Hanswurst* (meaning John Sausage), a nutcracker's face, and the attire of a Salzburg peasant. He was Comedy personified and ever-present, peeping through the curtains even in religious plays. The Salzburg popular theater was a mirror of the Salzburgers' character.

And the town itself, shaped by imaginative Prince-Bishops, became a mirror of its history. With the exception of fashionable hotels and modern traffic, the Salzburg of today is the Salzburg of Mozart. Yet it took a thousand years to develop; it took a thousand years for its squares to widen, for its pompous palaces in and outside the city to emerge, for its magnificent gardens with box hedges, fancy fountains, and natural theaters to grow, for its monasteries, convents, and twenty-seven churches to be built.

Because of the clever policies of its Archbishops, Salzburg had remained an island of peace in a continent of wars. While the rest of Europe was aflame with strife, lavish processions and breathtaking spectacles after the Italian fashion took place in the city streets. Clergy and nobility, burghers and peasants freely mixed on any occasion that offered an excuse for celebration. Grandiose symphonies of music and color and rhythm were becoming part of the Salzburg tradition.

To bolster Catholic morale after the Reformation, a *Gymnasium* was founded as a "sanctuary of true faith," and "for the fight against the evil of heresy." In 1623, the *Gymnasium* was made a University. Processions and performances now took place there; dignified professors turned playwrights; the cultivation of music became an important feature in education. And there was plenty of music besides, at the Archiepiscopal Residence and in the churches.

The University files for 1737 show the registration of one Leopold Mozart, aged 18, of Augsburg. In 1738 it is recorded that said Mozart was officially honored for unusual achievements, and in 1739, that he was officially—expelled. Obviously the young student from Augsburg had been too enamored of the city's artistic attractions to apply himself to his studies with sufficient care. Ever since his early years as a choir boy, when he was still destined for the priesthood, music had been his major interest.

He left the University; now music was to become his profession. In 1740, a Canon of the Church engaged Leopold Mozart as musi-

[5]

cian and valet—a customary combination of jobs in the upper circles of the time. Leopold played, composed, and bowed. Three years later, he joined the Archbishop's Court orchestra as a violinist, and soon he was entrusted with the instruction of the chapel boys. In 1757, he received the title of Court Composer, and the next promotion would raise him to Court Conductor, so he hoped.

Leopold Mozart was as content as his pessimistic nature let him be. He was the only member of an artisan's large family to work himself up to a higher social level. He was intelligent, well read, and he had a wide range of interests. He was proud of his self-taught knowledge, however, and his simple colleagues in the orchestra resented his air of superiority. Leopold grumbled about them, but did not really care. Salzburg society thought well enough of him, and he was on good terms with the present Archbishop, Sigismund von Schrattenbach, a kind and pious gentleman, fond of music, children, and dogs. In time, Leopold's reputation spread beyond the city limits: in 1753, he was offered membership in the respectable Society for Musical Sciences in Leipzig, and his *Violin School,* published in 1756, was widely used. For a bookbinder's son who had started out as a valet, he had done well enough.

He wanted children who would become musicians. And they in turn would have children who would be musicians. They would all make music together, like the Bachs. Who knew but that in a few generations there might even be a Philipp Emanuel? (In Mozart's day, the Bach sons were far more famous than their father, Johann Sebastian.)

In 1747, Leopold had married Anna Maria Pertl, a native of nearby St. Gilgen. Anna Maria was by no means well read or even educated; but always laughing and singing, deeply devoted to her husband, and profoundly religious, she proved the ideal wife for the grave, suspicious, and sometimes difficult Leopold. At the time of their marriage the young Mozart couple was considered the handsomest in town. They settled down in the busy Getreidegasse, in one of those bourgeois houses in which apartments were rented to not-so-rich but respectable people. Their landlord was Herr Hagenauer, a man of artistic inclinations who later was to prove a true friend and helper to the Mozarts.

They occupied the entire third floor—four rooms and a neat kitchen. The rear outlook was a typical Salzburg courtyard with double tiers of balconies, their pillars hung with flowers and the bulging tower of a church in the background. Here the children were born. Of seven only two survived: Maria Anna, called Nannerl, born in 1751, and the youngest son, born on January 27, 1756. He was given many names, but he used only two. He was called Wolfgang after the lake whose waters lap the shore of his mother's native village; he became Amadeus when he traveled in Italy, adopting the Italian version of Theophilus.

CHAPTER 2

"THAT IS MUSIC, WOLFERL!"
[1759-62]

LITTLE WOLFGANG sat on the floor with his toys spread out before him. His small face had a serious expression as he chose carefully among the bricks which should build a house just like the one in which he lived. It was a bright and quiet Sunday morning. "Herr Canari" was singing his song; the puppy slept peacefully in his corner, and Mamma Mozart sat by the window with her sewing.

Bells began to ring; Salzburg's churches called people to Mass. Perhaps little Wolfgang had heard these sounds before, but they had never spoken to him so vividly as on this beautiful Sunday morning. Presently the door of a nearby church opened, and organ tones floated into the room. Wolfgang stopped playing and listened.

"What's that, Mamma? It's so pretty."

"That is music, darling."

"Where does it come from?"

"From Heaven, Wolferl. Everything beautiful is made by God and for God, and it comes from Heaven and goes to Heaven."

"But Papa is making music, too, isn't he?"

"Certainly, Wolferl—that's how he earns the money we live on."

"So Papa comes right after God. . . ."

Wolfgang gradually came to be intoxicated with music. He could hardly wait for the ringing of the chimes. The voices of his parents,

[8]

the street noises, the tapping of the puppy's paws, or the famous Salzburg rains which go on for days without interruption—everything, for him, became meaningful sound. When Nannerl had her music lessons, he sat quietly in a corner, listening.

"One-two-three—one-two-three—one-two-three!" Nannerl was at the harpsichord, Papa standing beside her. "You must be very careful, Nannerl, to play strictly in time. Remember, this is a minuet and people will want to dance . . . For Heaven's sake, what's the matter with you, Wolferl?"

"Nothing, Papa."

"But your cheeks are hot. What have you been doing?"

"Nothing, Papa. Just imagining I was dancing."

"And you like it—this music?"

Wolferl nodded eagerly.

"That's good. But now you'd better run along and play."

"I want to play the harpsichord, Papa, please."

"No, Wolferl, not yet."

"Why?"

"Why! You're much too young. Just look at your hands. You must wait until they grow. Toys are much better for you. Now be good and let me finish with Nannerl."

Wolfgang was an obedient child. With his cheeks still flushed and his eyes cast down, he turned toward the door. "But the harpsichord is the finest toy of them all," he muttered to himself.

Papa called him back, sternly. "What did you say, Wolferl?"

"That the harpsichord is the finest toy there is."

"Never say that again, Wolferl. The harpsichord is no toy, and music is no game! You see why I told you that you are too young? Music is something very serious; it requires hard work and study, and it means a lot of responsibility. Don't think that it is easy—and don't mix it up with hobby-horses! Now run along."

In the other room, Wolfgang looked at his toys. He did not feel like playing. He looked at his pink and yellow bricks, which he had not touched for days. Finally he drew his little chair near the window, knelt on it, put his elbows on the window sill, and rested his small head in his hands. From the living room came the sound of Nannerl playing the minuet, to her father's sharp "One-two-three—one-two-three," and in the kitchen Theresa, the maid, was humming a folk tune. The boy looked down into the yard, and suddenly his eyes filled with tears.

But Wolfgang could not resist the temptation to try that "finest of all toys," the harpsichord. Music came from far away, from Heaven, Mamma had said; it was difficult and cumbersome, said Papa—and yet Papa could make even Nannerl bring it out of this handsome piece of furniture in the corner of the living room. You just had to push down one of these dainty keys, and there it was. Why did grown-ups always exaggerate the simplest things in life?

So he began pushing down the keys himself, experimentally, just to see what it sounded like. And then, one day, he accidentally hit on that simple chord known as a "major third"—and with shouts of joy he ran out to the kitchen, stormily embraced Mamma and Theresa, and forced them to come and listen and admire. Wolfgang Mozart had discovered the miracle of harmony. From that day on, he spent many hours at the instrument. No more toys for him!

Gradually Leopold began to change his mind on the subject of the boy's desire to play. At first he merely kept a sharp ear on Wolfgang's strumming. "It is amazing," he said to his wife one night, "what a fine ear he has and how sensitive he is. Other children of his age beat the keys with their fists and enjoy the noise. But when Wolfgangerl strikes a dissonance, his face twists as if in pain. Strange!"

"He has your talent, Leopold."

"Sometimes I think that he has more," Papa replied thoughtfully.

So, though Wolfgang was only a little over three years old, Leopold no longer had to be persuaded to teach him to play the harpsichord. Starting out with casual "lessons" planned for mere fun, he discovered, in addition to Wolfgang's sensitive ear, a no less astounding speed of musical memory.

It was the custom at that time for the teacher of music to assemble or compose the material for his pupils' instruction, since there were no music stores in which simple collections of pieces could be bought. For Nannerl, their father had made up a handy sketch book into which he copied pieces by himself or others, and Wolfgang was given *his* book on his sixth name-day, in October, 1762. Until that date he was taught Nannerl's lessons, and in her book the proud father noted some stages of the boy's progress. "The above minuet Wolfgangerl knew by heart when he was not yet four." Or: "On January 26, 1761, the day before his fifth birthday, Wolfgangerl learned this minuet and trio within half an hour, at 9:30 P.M." These notes and others can be read in the fragment of Nannerl's book that is kept today in the Salzburg Mozarteum.

Now Wolfgang had become acquainted with the language of music. Notes were his friends—a part of the household, like Theresa and the pets. Here were the small black notes running around quickly, waving their pennants or holding hands. And here were the bigger ones with white faces, carrying a cane like grown-ups and walking at a slow, dignified pace. Finally, there were the stout gentlemen in white with neither pennant nor cane, looking on quietly at the bustle around them. If, until then, everything had dissolved itself for Wolfgang into vague waves of sound, it now began to take definite shape in musical notes. Inevitably, he would sooner or later try to put them down on paper.

One day he had been left alone, in the care of Theresa who was preparing supper out in the kitchen. For a while he sat at the harpsichord, practicing. Then—"I am going to write a concerto," he told himself. He got up, went for some paper, a bottle of ink, and a quill pen. With these he seated himself at the table and began doing what he had so often seen his father do—dip the quill deep down into the ink and then draw on the paper with it. So—

There, a blot! "Never mind," thought Wolferl and wiped it away with the palm of his hand. Across the ink smudge he drew a few lines for the staff. Another blot. Wipe that one off and begin again.

A few more lines. Still another blot—this time a big one that ran all over into the other smears. By this time the work didn't really look much like Papa's, but the boy kept on. For hours he sat at the table, patiently wiping off each black, smeary blot, using his sleeve when both hands had got too inky, and gradually filling the sheet with notes.

The door opened, and Papa and his friend Schachtner entered. Andreas Schachtner was a trumpeter in the Court orchestra, a skillful violinist and a good all-round musician. He had long been particularly fond of Wolfgang and was usually greeted with happy cheers. But today the boy seemed not to notice him at all.

"What are you doing here, Wolferl? What *is* this mess?" Papa asked.

"I am writing a concerto for the clavier; the first part is nearly finished."

"Let me see."

"It isn't ready yet."

"Let me see it just the same. This must be *something!*" The father took the sheet away from Wolferl and laughed at the mixture of circles and lines, blots and smears. But suddenly Leopold Mozart stopped laughing and studied the sheet of paper closely.

"Schachtner," he said quietly, "will you come here for a moment?"

To his amazement, Schachtner saw that the sheet in Leopold's hand was trembling and that his cheeks were wet with tears.

"Look here!" said Leopold. "Everything is set properly and symmetrically. Almost perfectly. Only it's too difficult for anyone to play."

"But that's why it is a concerto," Wolfgang interrupted. "One must practice it until it goes well. Listen, like this. . . ." And he ran to the harpsichord and played. He couldn't really play what he had written, but he did it well enough to make the two men understand that he knew what he wanted. For the rest of the evening, Leopold was very thoughtful.

[12]

Though musically mature far beyond his age, Wolfgang remained a normal child with normal pleasures and normal reactions. But, since music was the center of his life, his pleasures had to be accompanied by it and his reactions expressed in it.

"Come, Papa, come. I won't go to sleep before you come. So. Now put me on the chair. So. And now *I'll* teach you music." The boy in his nightgown standing on the chair and Papa Mozart holding his hands were singing with a serious expression:

"*O-ra-gna fia-ga-ta fa ma-ri-na ga-mi-na fa. . . .*"

"From now on we are going to do this every night."

"All right, Wolferl," Leopold said. "But what is it?"

"Don't know. I heard the melody somewhere."

"But what does it mean?"

"Don't know. Just made it up. To me it means that I love you. Here!" And he kissed the tip of Papa's nose.

"I love you too, Wolferl, but now lie down and sleep."

"Good night, Papa."

As Leopold left the room he heard the child murmur to himself: "Papa comes right after God."

Wolfgang learned to compose while learning to play. His own nature seemed to unveil to him the mysteries of melody, harmony, rhythm, and structure. After he finished practicing, he would remain at the instrument for hours. Often Leopold sat by him and wrote down on music paper what the child invented during this most fascinating of all games.

His friends saw Leopold grow pale, thoughtful and nervous, and heard him complain of sleepless nights. Once, when they were playing chamber music at the Mozart home, he missed a cue. They glanced at one another, then at him, and put their instruments aside.

"What's the matter with you, Mozart? Something is worrying you."

"It's Wolferl," Leopold sighed.

"Wolferl? But he seems all right." And Schachtner added: "I

talked to him a little while ago and told him to take his toys into the other room because we were going to have music in here. He asked me to go with him and while he carried his box of bricks or whatever it was, he made me play a little march on the fiddle, and he sang, and then he put his arms around my neck and asked me 'Do you love me?'—you know, the way he always asks. And I said 'yes,' and then we both laughed, and now he is sitting on the floor with Nannerl and they are building a palace for themselves and a dog house for the pup. I don't think the boy is sick. I really don't."

"I am not worried about his health," Leopold Mozart said somberly. "But what am I going to do with him?"

"Why, he likes music all right," said one of the men. "And he has talent. He'll play in the orchestra sooner than you think."

"That's just it," Leopold sighed.

And, upon the astonished silence that followed, he broke out vehemently: "Don't you understand? This isn't talent. This is a miracle. God has chosen me, the humble musician, to perform a miracle right in my own simple house. Listen. There is nothing I could teach Wolferl which he wouldn't already know. If I start to explain a musical principle to him, I don't have to finish the sentence. He demonstrates it almost as perfectly as any grown-up who has worked for years. It's just *in* him. We all like music, but with him it's different. And I am scared—scared to death. The responsibility is too great."

"Will you let him appear in public?"

"Yes, but not here."

"Why not?"

"Because Wolfgang belongs to the world. God has not put this miracle into my hands to have me bury it between mountains!"

"Bury between mountains!" one of the men said indignantly. They all resented deprecatory remarks about their hometown coming from a man born elsewhere. "Bury between mountains," the man repeated, shaking his head. "Salzburg has had great men, Mozart, and they did not feel buried at all." And they went on

talking of Salzburg's glorious history. Leopold listened patiently
to their often-told stories; of the "Wolf in Purple," Archbishop
Wolf Dietrich, who was enamored of Italy and had eliminated
entire districts of old Salzburg to make room for his own "little
Rome"; of Markus Sittikus, his melancholy successor, who had
brought in the splendid Italian theater to get cheered up; of other
Archbishops of even older generations who had defended Salzburg from their fortress against worldly and spiritual foes. "Salzburg is a great town, Mozart," they said. "Good enough for any
gifted child. Where else would you want to take him?"

"All over Europe. And Nannerl will go, too."

"Be careful, Mozart. All that traveling, with the war on?"

"I'm not going to spoil my children's future merely because
England and France haven't been able to decide which owns
America!" Leopold retorted impatiently.

"I don't know about America," said Schachtner. "But for
Wolferl's sake, take it easy."

On the street, one of the men said to Schachtner: "Our Mozart
seems to have grown rather dramatic lately. What, exactly, is he
planning to do? Exhibit his children like acrobats and pass the
hat?"

Schachtner didn't reply.

"What's to become of his job?" the man insisted.

"He'll get a leave of absence, I suppose. If he doesn't, he'll just
have to quit."

"What? He must have lost his mind!"

"I wouldn't be surprised if he had," Schachtner said quietly.

And now Leopold Mozart's plans took shape quickly. He
wanted to show Wolfgang and Nannerl the great world: Vienna,
their fascinating capital; Paris, the center of good taste; and, finally,
Italy, the Eldorado of musicians. His son would be announced as
a virtuoso and would introduce himself as a composer at the same
time. He would play alone or with Nannerl, and as soon as they
knew how, the children would sing. Sometimes Leopold himself

would accompany them on the violin. Mamma would go along to look after their clothes and have a good time. That much he told them at supper, emphasizing the seriousness of the decision.

The children were overjoyed. Mamma kept silent. Later she cried a little. At this, Leopold was surprised and a little angry. He was not used to this reaction to his suggestions.

"You surely know what you are doing," said Anna Maria. "But I am worried. The children have never been away from home. The roads will be bad, the inns will be bad, food will be bad, the weather will be bad, and Wolferl is so young! He can't be treated like a mechanical doll. You have no idea how sensitive he is."

"Haven't I?"

"Leopold, I watch him when he doesn't know he is being watched. And I can tell you that he is a normal child like all the rest, only with much more imagination. The other day I saw him making the *Hanswurst* for Nannerl and the dog—it was comical! And a minute before he had been sitting at the harpsichord with the most serious expression in the world."

"Oh, you Salzburgers with your *Hanswurst!* Anna, you are the dignified mother of two child prodigies and you still fall for that nonsense?"

"Surely I do," she said, smiling. "I always will. And so will Wolferl. That's *my* heritage. It isn't very much, but it might help him in life."

They both laughed.

"You haven't changed, Anna," Leopold said tenderly. "You haven't changed a bit. I wouldn't know what to do without you. But now I must tell you something, quite in earnest! Child prodigies of ten, twelve, fourteen, are nothing out of the ordinary. But never before have I heard of a boy of six playing the way he does." And he held forth again on his responsibility and on Wolfgang's abnormal talent, and on the boy's career, which couldn't start early enough.

But Leopold finally decided to start with a short trip, to see how it worked out. There was no harm in taking the children the eighty-three miles to Munich to play for Elector Maximilian III, a connoisseur and generous patron of music, and a first class 'cello player himself. Upon their return, they would make further plans.

CHAPTER 3

SCHÖNBRUNN AND THE EMPRESS
[1762 - 63]

MUNICH did work out. The children played without stage fright, and the Elector was very kind. Everybody came to see the two pairs of small hands that moved so quickly, and the surprise was great when their performance was not merely sensational but also artistically perfect. Leopold returned to Salzburg in high spirits. A few months later the four Mozarts set out for Vienna.

Salzburg and Munich were just ordinary Courts—residences like many another in eighteenth-century Europe, from which a King, Prince, Duke, or Elector ruled many thousands of subjects. But Vienna was different, for it was the capital of the Empire to which they all more or less loosely belonged and to whose Emperor all owed allegiance. This was a legendary atmosphere of power into which the Mozarts were now entering, and Leopold felt quite dizzy at the prospect.

The center and symbol of imperial power was the Queen-Empress Maria Theresa, descendant of the 500-year-old Habsburg dynasty, and the only woman ruler ever to represent it. Female succession was not provided for in the ancient family laws, and her father, Charles VI, had to pay with political concessions for his neighbors' formal recognition of Maria Theresa's rights, and their promise to leave her unmolested. She was a handsome and spirited young woman, a daring horsewoman, and a devout Catholic.

[18]

When her father died in 1740, Maria Theresa had been married for four years to Duke Francis of Lorraine, who was, in 1745, to be elected King of the Romans and German Emperor. He was tall, broad-shouldered, and handsome. Maria Theresa loved him dearly and bore him sixteen children. Care for their health and education preoccupied her to the same extent as matters of politics. She was a housewife and mother if there ever was one. She would not permit in her country what she would not permit in her own family. Austria, with its complex system of provinces and underlings, seemed to her an over-sized household with many millions of children and a vast staff of none too reliable servants. An Empress and Queen by law and title, but with little money and no experience, Maria Theresa found herself in the position of a young woman who has suddenly been placed in charge of a huge estate loaded with debt and surrounded by greedy neighbors, bent on exploiting her weakness.

Contrary to the promise given to her father, these neighbors challenged her rights to the throne in a series of wars. The ringleader was Frederick II, young King of Prussia, ambitious, unscrupulous, and personally detestable to the conservative Empress. Austria's traditional rival had always been France, but the cultural ties between the two countries were strong, with the Austrian aristocracy copying the ways of the brilliant French courts. The favored language of the Austrian Court and of high society was French, and many never learned to speak German flawlessly.

Maria Theresa realized at once that Austria's arch-enemy was not France but Prussia. "If we don't check him [Frederick] now, it will mean the doom of the Empire, and of Europe!" she once wrote prophetically. Frederick, bent on adding to Prussian territory at the expense of Austria, attacked without so much as a pretext. When, in 1740, he launched the First Silesian War, it was primarily the chivalry of the Hungarian nobles toward their young Queen, who had come to them asking for an army with her newly born infant son (the later Emperor Joseph II) in her arms, that had saved the country. Since then Russia, too, had entered the picture, and there had been alternations of war and peace, all equally indecisive.

Through all these troublous times, the Empress stood practically alone, advised only by a few men she trusted. Her husband was of little help to her, and if Austria survived the ever-recurrent crises, it was due to Maria Theresa's religious belief in her mission, the full devotion of her subjects, and the assistance of Chancellor Prince von Kaunitz, one of the greatest statesmen in Austrian history. Now England and France were starting to fight on the American continent, and the tension in Europe once more exploded. The French and Indian War in the North American colonies, and the Seven Years' War in Europe had both begun in 1756, the very year of Mozart's birth, and were still going on when Leopold took him to Vienna.

Maria Theresa found herself growing wearied by her responsibilities. She saw no point, however, in depriving the pleasure-loving Viennese of their customary entertainments. War might prevent the Court from keeping up its balls and hunting parties, but private concerts were still being given and the Imperial family continued to attend the opera. Music was the traditional family recreation of the Habsburgs. Some of the Emperors had themselves been good composers and excellent performers. Their fondness for Italian opera, and their readiness to spend large sums for it, had had no small share in the growing reputation of Vienna as the most musical city on the continent. The example of the Imperial Court stimulated imitation among the minor rulers and wealthy nobles, many of whom maintained their own musical establishments.

Until the early nineteenth century, the salons of town and country palaces were the anterooms to world success. Without them, Haydn might have starved, Gluck might have remained a violinist in a dance hall, and Schubert a dissatisfied schoolteacher with an inferiority complex; without them, Beethoven might have forever ignored the inspiring charm of Vienna and its suburbs. Despite the desire for independence natural to the creative mind, much of the very best music that was written before and during the classical period was commissioned by some patron for performance at his home.

With many letters of introduction in his pocket, Leopold Mozart supervised the loading of the luggage and their small clavier, while Anna Maria gave her last instructions to the servants, and the children tried to find a convenient place in the carriage for Wolfgang's little violin. Their friends the Hagenauers had come to say good-by and the two families promised to pray for each other. When the horses pulled away, Wolfgang gave a cry of joy. He liked riding, and now, Papa had told him, he would get a lot of it.

It was a tiresome journey, punctuated by bad weather and irregular meals. By the time they reached Vienna, Wolfgang had a bad cold. But Leopold was full of hope. The undertaking had proved moderately successful so far. Wolfgang had played in Passau, and both children had played in Linz; though poorly paid, they had been enthusiastically received. And there had been a number of pleasant experiences. At the border custom-house, Wolfgang had made friends with the officers, showing them the clavier and playing for them on his fiddle, and the Mozarts had been allowed to go through with almost no examination. In the monastery at Ybbs the boy had strummed on the organ, making such beautiful sounds that the monks had interrupted their meal and rushed in to listen with amazement and delight.

Leopold noticed that, even at this early age, Wolfgang was not affected by the presence of strangers when he played. Nor did he show signs of becoming spoiled by their praises; indeed, he never cared for applause at all unless it came from experts. The one thing he demanded, however, was the undivided attention of his hearers.

The Mozarts' reputation had preceded them to Vienna, and they were soon being welcomed in the aristocratic and diplomatic salons. Their invitations would be sent four to eight days in advance, to make sure they would be free. Wolfgang often had to play two,

three, four times a day, and the patrons put gala carriages at the Mozarts' disposal before and after the musicales.

Sooner than Leopold had ventured to hope, the command came for them to present themselves at Schönbrunn. This was the summer palace of the Imperial family and had been completed just twelve years before the Mozarts' visit. It was the favorite residence of the Empress. Only four miles outside Vienna, it boasted a picturesque park with winding paths, blooming flowers, fountains and hedges, chalets and statues—all laid out after the pattern of Versailles, Louis XIV's magnificent palace near Paris. The royal carriage that had called for the Mozarts turned into a broad drive lined with chestnut trees, whose leaves were already turning red, gold, and brown and whose ripe fruits in their half-open shells covered the ground. Before them, on a wide square, lay the vast yellow castle.

At the time, neither of the Mozart children had yet grasped the immense distance that separated them socially from their hosts. The minute Wolfgang was presented to the Empress he jumped on her lap, put his arms around her neck, and kissed her: "Do you love me?" He had taken at once to the imposing woman with the kind blue eyes who lived in this splendid house and whose children wore such nice clothes.

"Wolferl!" exclaimed Mamma, blushing. And Papa made a gesture of hasty apology.

"Never mind, Mozart," the Empress said simply. "I like children."

Leopold rubbed his hands with relieved pride and said to himself, "Now if I told that story in Salzburg, they'd think I was bragging."

Wolfgang was less impressed than his father by the informality of the visit. When it came time for him to play, he looked around critically. "Is Herr Wagenseil here?" he asked. "He knows music."

The Court Composer was summoned. "I am going to play your concerto," the boy told him. "Will you please turn the pages for me?"

After he had finished the Wagenseil piece, the Emperor told

him to play with the keyboard covered with a napkin. Then he must play with one finger only; still no mistake. . . .

The Mozarts were summoned to Schönbrunn repeatedly. The Princes and Princesses—the oldest son, Archduke Joseph, was already married while the youngest was exactly Wolfgang's age—enjoyed the unusual treat immensely. There is a famous anecdote that Wolfgang once proposed to seven-year-old Marie Antoinette, the future Queen of France, because she helped him to get up when he slipped on the polished floor.

The Vienna visit was turning out far better than Leopold had expected. His dreams threatened to run away with him; already he was picturing Wolfgang as Europe's star performer, with Her Majesty herself as his sponsor. Humble and bowing, he gradually assumed the attitude of a puffing advertiser of wonders and miracles, not realizing the poor impression such noisy "publicity" methods were bound to make at a conservative court.

The Empress—although it did not occur to her to plan a career for that Salzburg boy—was undoubtedly very much impressed by the Mozart team, pleased at the pleasure they gave her own children, and ready to pay well for it. Two days after the first visit in the Castle, the Privy Paymaster drove up to the house where the family had their modest lodgings and delivered to the children the gala costumes that the Empress was giving them. Wolfgang's was of the finest purple cloth, with a moiré waistcoat of the same color edged with wide gilt braid; it had originally been made for the youngest Archduke, Maximilian. Nannerl's was of white taffeta beautifully trimmed. Then, a few days later, the same emissary appeared again, this time with a message from the Emperor: Could the Mozarts stay a little longer? And he handed Leopold the sum of one hundred ducats.

At this juncture, however, luck turned against them. Two days afterwards Wolfgang came down with scarlet fever. Fortunately it was only a light case and the boy was up in ten days. But since epidemics were frequent in Vienna, everybody feared any type of rash, and the Mozarts had to wait patiently until the last traces of Wolfgang's had disappeared. This meant a serious loss of time and money.

Leopold was worried about his own future, too. In June, the Court Conductor at Salzburg had died; the Vice-Kapellmeister Lolli had been promoted to his place, and now Leopold was hoping to get Lolli's old position. He felt that he deserved the honor, and—as he hinted to Hagenauer in a letter—he *could* make a living in Vienna now, in case Salzburg proved to be unappreciative. Leopold eventually got the job; but he remained Vice-Kapellmeister to his dying day.

The family's schedule, halted by Wolfgang's scarlet fever, was revised again when the report of smallpox in Salzburg postponed their return "until Christmas." They did not get back to Salzburg until the early days of the new year.

CHAPTER 4

"KINGDOM RIDGE"

[1 7 6 3 - 6 6]

A LETTER from Paris," said the postman at the Hage-nauers' door. "For you, Madam," he added with a grin. "For *me?* Lorenz—look, a letter from Leopold Mozart! Quite a long one."

"Let me see it."

"No, it's for me. Isn't that nice?" And she broke the seal and unfolded the letter.

"What does it say?"

"Well, Mozart is disgusted because the women in Paris are so much painted . . . and are having such a good time. He says that 'if God is not especially gracious, the French state will suffer the fate of the ancient Persian Empire.' I wonder what did happen to Persia. . . ."

"Couldn't say. Go on. I want to know what's happening to *them.*"

"Oh, yes—here it is." And she read aloud:

If the recognition we receive equals the pleasure that my children have given this Court, we ought to do very well. It is not the custom here to kiss the hands of royal persons, or to bother them with a petition, or even to speak to them *au passage,* as they call it—that is, when they are walking through the gallery and the royal apartments on their way to church. Nor is it customary to do homage either by inclining the head or by genuflection to the King or to members of the Royal Family. Instead, one stands erect and motionless and just lets them pass close by.

So you can imagine how it impressed and amazed these French—so infatuated with their Court etiquette—when the King's daughters, not only in their apartments but even in the royal gallery, paused when they saw my children, came over to them, and not only let them kiss hands but gave them innumerable kisses. And the same thing happened with Madame la Dauphine.

But what seemed most extraordinary to these French was that at the *grand couvert* on the evening of New Year's Day, not only were we all bidden to go up to the royal table, but Wolfgang was graciously allowed to stand beside the Queen the whole time, to talk with her, entertain her and kiss her hands repeatedly, besides partaking of dishes that she handed him from the table. The Queen speaks as good German as we do, and —as the King knows none—she translated for him everything our gallant Wolfgang said. I was standing beside the King, and on his other side were my wife and daughter. . . .

"I can imagine how proud he was," said Hagenauer. "But why doesn't he mention Pompadour at all? Remember what he called her in his last letter? Powerful and haughty."

"Patience," replied Frau Hagenauer. "Here she comes."

You surely would like to know what Madame la Marquise de Pompadour is like? She must have been very beautiful, for she is still good-looking. In figure she is tall and stately, stout, or rather well-covered, but very well-proportioned. She is fair and extremely like our former Therese Freysauf . . .

"Does he mean the shopkeeper's daughter?"
"Guess so."

. . . while her eyes are rather like those of Her Majesty the Empress. . . .

But Leopold had not bothered to mention the rebuff which poor little Wolfgang had suffered from the Pompadour. Standing on a table before her, he had been drawn to her by his natural tenderness, with his "Do you love me?" already on his lips.

[27]

Madame de Pompadour had shrunk back in disgust at bodily contact with poor people. Common folks had contagious diseases, hadn't they? Wolferl, unaccustomed to such treatment, had turned around: "Who is she, that she doesn't want to kiss me? The *Empress* kissed me!" She had it coming to her, Leopold had told himself, though he did not see why this story should make the rounds of the Salzburg taverns. He had more pleasant things to tell.

Four sonatas of M. Wolfgang Mozart are now being engraved. Just picture to yourself the furor they will arouse when people read on the title-page that they were composed by a seven-year-old child! And when the skeptics are challenged to test him (as they already have been), imagine the sensation when he asks someone to write down a minuet or some other tune and then—immediately and without touching the clavier —he writes in the bass and, if it is needed, the second violin part. . . . Indeed, I tell you that God performs fresh miracles every day through this child. . . .

They had left Salzburg on June 9, and arrived in France by way of Germany and Belgium, playing at many courts and in many salons en route, and sometimes putting on their own concerts. Gifts had been given them, in money or—not at all to Leopold's pleasure—in trinkets. On their long rides Papa would count and figure aloud, while Wolfgang played a game he had invented for himself. Early in life he had come to think in terms of kings, princes, and subjects; and now the wide world became his imaginary kingdom of children whom he ruled and for whom he did the nicest things. He called it Kingdom Ridge—*Königreich Rücken* —and their valet Sebastian, who traveled with them, had drawn a map of it.

The journey had been an incessant pursuit of Electors, or other potential patrons, a continual waiting, first to be asked to play, and again for remuneration. It was quite normal for eighteenth-century musicians to introduce themselves in this manner. The children performed in ceremonial grown-up clothes, with wigs, and Wolfgang had a sword at his side. Wolfgang played the harpsichord, the organ, or the violin, and went through all his little tricks.

In one of their audiences in Frankfurt-am-Main sat a tall, blond, freckle-nosed youth of fourteen: Johann Wolfgang Goethe. As an old man, decades after one of his tenderest poems had become virtually a folk-song through Mozart's setting of it, Goethe still talked about this concert. But even if Leopold had been told that a budding genius, due to become one of the greatest literary fig-ures of all time, was present in the hall that day, he would have been more impressed by the smile or nod from some titled gentle-man. For such salutations meant money.

As for Wolfgang, he was genuinely happy. Truly this was his world, his kingdom. People spoiled him and said the nicest things to him. At table he sat with princes and princesses, and they talked to him as though he were a grown-up. When he played, they listened attentively, and when he had finished, they applauded. Between concerts, he went about the churches with Papa and was allowed to try their organs. In Heidelberg his name was inscribed on one, at the request of the Magistrate. Life was wonderful, indeed, when people loved you so, and there were so many excit-ing things to see, and all you had to do in return was to make music. . . .

Then for the first time, the Mozarts had arrived in a country not politically linked with their homeland. In France they really were foreigners. Leopold knew some French and saw to it that the children learned to speak it. But Mamma was afraid of it—as of everything in Paris—and never learned it. Most of the time she stayed home with their hostess, friendly Countess van Eyck, the Bavarian Ambassador's wife.

The streets of Paris were unpaved and filthy. The Mozarts could not go about without soiling their clothes. So Papa hired sedan chairs, and the three strangers made the rounds of the fashionable private mansions, called *hôtels*. Leopold presented letters of intro-duction from high personages—ambassadors and ministers, princes, counts, and dukes. He bombastically asserted that his son, the little blond boy in the tiny French suit and hat, would, if graciously permitted, perform miracles on the harpsichord, and that the pretty thirteen-year-old girl was a mature virtuoso. He received many pleasant words, astonished smiles, and a promise or two—and the doors closed behind the three as politely as they had been opened.

It was not long before Leopold detected the underlying reason. French society was corrupt, and the masses were impoverished. The nobility lived in strict segregation, and their own lives were full of contrasts. Ladies of rank—with thick layers of powder and rouge on their pretty faces, dressed in what they thought were the craziest costumes imaginable—entertained writers, philosophers, musicians, or mere interested amateurs, and indulged in an imaginary picture of a better world. Men and women of society were rich, decorative, and absolutely idle. After sessions of debates full of sentiment or sparkling with wit, cavaliers and their ladies danced the minuet, always to the same old tunes, gathered round the gambling table, or played daring games. Children were out of fashion. They were usually sent to the country to foster parents. And now this society was supposed to sit still and listen politely to a couple of young foreign provincials, who—according to their father—played as well as adults. No, the Paris of the 1760's had no use for "wonders of God."

Leopold was disgusted. But finally one of his letters did bear fruit. Unexpectedly, he found doors being opened to him as by a magic wand. Friedrich Melchior Grimm, a graduate of the University of Leipzig, had for some fifteen years made his home in Paris. He was now the secretary of the Duc d'Orléans, a friend of Rousseau, and a recognized authority on music and letters. Grimm and Leopold took to each other immediately, proudly considering themselves two "solid Germans" struggling in a nation which they held in fundamental contempt.

Grimm was tall, with an indolent carriage and prominent eyes in an attractive face. He knew much, and talked about more. An easy conversationalist, he was extremely popular. His criticism was sharp and amusing, and created an illusion of profounder knowledge than he really possessed. Called "the classic among the critics" by a courteous colleague, he was nicknamed by his intimates, "the white tyrant," because he painted his cheeks with white lead.

Grimm introduced the Mozarts to a few salons, carefully at first, limiting himself to selected intimates. But when Wolfgang, accompanying a singer, rapidly invented ten variations of the piano part to a song he had heard only once, Grimm knew that all the boy needed was publicity. And he also knew that he would add to his own prestige by presenting such a sensation to this blasé society.

So, the December 1, 1763, issue of the *Correspondence Littéraire,* of which Grimm was co-editor, began with an article on the Mozart family. "True miracles," the startled Parisians read, "are rare enough to deserve mention if you have witnessed one. . . . I fear that this child will make me lose my head if I hear him very often. The children of M. Mozart have aroused the admiration of everybody who has heard them. The Emperor and the Queen-Empress have showered them with favors; they were given equal reception at the courts of Munich and Mannheim." He appealed to the Parisians' pride: ". . . It is a pity that in this country, people know so little about music . . ." and to their jealousy: ". . . The father intends to go to England from here, and then to take his children to lower Germany. . . ."

As a result, the Mozarts' first concert in Paris was sold out. Grimm helped sell the tickets and paid for the minor expenses. Then they spent Christmas and New Year's at Versailles, and thereafter became the "must" entertainment of the season. Wolfgang, greatly stimulated by the enthusiasm of his audiences, often improvised in public now and so began to develop this talent which was to make him later a pianistic celebrity.

The strongest musical impressions, however, came from a number of German composer-virtuosi living in Paris, Johann Schobert in particular. Schobert was an eccentric, dark young man who played the keyboard with new and fascinating results and was the favorite of the salons just then. Leopold and Grimm were highly suspicious of his personality, but Wolfgang, at this early age, already displayed an independent musical judgment. The poetic and emotional side of Schobert's music appealed to him in particular, corresponding as it did to a strong, though still undeveloped, natural disposition.

It was under the abundance of new impressions that the child Mozart wrote a group of sonatas which were to become his first printed work (K. 6-9). In imitation of Schobert, he added a violin obbligato to the piano part.

When Lorenz Hagenauer got a letter from Leopold asking him to have eight masses read for himself and his family beginning on April 10, he realized that his adventurous friend was up to something unusual and perhaps dangerous. Until now, Leopold had shrunk from the idea of taking the children across the Channel; but everybody in Paris kept telling him that he ought to do it, his friend Grimm advised it, and there was plenty of money.

On April 13, the Mozarts arrived in London, seasick but happy. As usual, Leopold carried a bagful of introductions. Before presenting these, he thought that the most important thing to do was to give himself and his family a genuinely English appearance. To the Mozarts, the English seemed to be perpetually dressed for a masquerade, their custom still being to dress according to trade or social position. The French clothing was therefore put away temporarily, and Wolfgang—who cared little what costume you put him into, so long as it was pretty—set forth again to conquer royalty.

George III, the bad boy of American colonial history, was then twenty-seven, an agreeable young man with simple habits. His Queen shared his taste for informality and, like him, was devoted to music. She both played and sang fairly well, and her one demand after marriage had been the weekly visit to the opera—much to the annoyance of non-royal opera subscribers, who had grown accustomed to using their boxes in privacy and without ceremony.

The two young people on the English throne were sincerely

delighted with the unusual diversion provided by the handsome children. Wolfgang appeared as virtuoso, sight-reader, accompanist, and organist—the last talent winning him almost greater fame than did his performance on the harpsichord. After the first concert, he seized the violin part of a Handel aria that happened to be lying at hand and, using it as a bass, invented a lovely tune above it. Nannerl, too, was much admired. She had made such progress on the clavier that she hardly suffered by comparison with the boy.

Leopold felt much more at ease in England than he had in France. People seemed to be ascending with firm steps toward a sound prosperity. The acquisition of colonies, commercial expansion, and industrial progress made them sure and proud of themselves. And they were gay. Gambling, dancing, and other sorts of entertainment were in full swing. They took pleasure in lavish

spending. Through unpaved, muddy streets that were poorly lighted and made permanently unsafe by pickpockets, whom the authorities were unable to manage, fashionable crowds flocked wherever there was something to see and hear: to concerts, musicales, ballad opera, and Italian opera. Interest in music was as active as it had been in the days of Purcell, and their full purses permitted the English to import the best that could be had from the Continent.

Above all, the spirit of Handel was still vividly alive. The King, as a boy, had been very fond of him. He used to watch the great man silently. Once, when Handel came over to ask whether he liked his music and the young Prince replied eagerly in the affirmative, Handel had put his hand on his shoulder and said: "So you will watch over my work when I am dead!" Now the young Prince was King of England, and Handel had been dead for five years. "By order of the King," Handel's work was constantly performed. Wolfgang had many opportunities to hear it, though the seed of this experience was not to ripen until much later.

Wolfgang was entranced by opera. He was always talking about one which he was going to write for the children of Salzburg, with an orchestra made up of Papa's friends. His dream-land—*Königreich Rücken*—entered a new metamorphosis: his world was a gigantic stage, and life the drama; men were singers, and little Wolfgang was sitting in the royal box with Papa, Mamma, Nannerl, and his new friend, Johann Christian Bach.

This youngest son of Johann Sebastian Bach had acquired Italian experience as an organist in the Milan Cathedral, when he was producing church music and staging operas at the same time. Called to England as music master to the Queen, he and his father's pupil, Karl Friedrich Abel, were shaping the musical life and tastes of the English capital. A friendship was quickly struck up between the sons of the modest Thomaskantor and of the self-assertive Vice-Kapellmeister of Salzburg. Bach was twenty-nine, and Wolfgang was eight; yet Bach treated the boy like an adult colleague. Between serious shop-talks, they had fun—musical fun, of course.

With Wolfgang on his knees, Johann Christian would start a fugue and ask the boy to continue. Or they would play a sonata together, taking turns at every few bars, and have the listeners guess which was playing. Alone, Wolfgang would sit for hours studying his friend's scores. To him they revealed an entirely new world: the world of Italian music.

But much as he adored Bach, there was no one like Papa. When you were tired of listening or playing, Papa provided the bed. When you were hungry, Papa provided food. And Papa often had a hard time getting a bed that was soft, and food that was plentiful and tasty. Papa, above all, helped you to put your brain in order. Those musical ideas which so suddenly hit and pursued you and kept going round in your head for days, which came so quickly that your fingers could hardly put them down properly—Papa would make a few remarks and at once everything seemed easy. And when you had finished, Papa kissed you and said that you were a genius, and Mamma cried with joy, and Nannerl sat down at the clavier and practiced what you had written, and everybody else clapped and sent you presents. Yes, Papa came right after God. All the joys of the world were due to him and his planning.

The season was almost over, but the Mozarts were popular enough to venture a concert of their own. The date, June 5, 1764, 12 o'clock noon, was shrewdly chosen; for June 4 was the King's birthday, and noblemen, ministers, and envoys flocked into the city to offer their congratulations. In the big hall in Spring Gardens, near St. James Park, the Mozarts appeared before an illustrious audience of two hundred. Leopold had the "shock of taking in 100 guineas in three hours," although he had had only a few days to distribute tickets.

Three weeks later, as the *Public Advertiser* announced, "the most extraordinary prodigy and most amazing genius that has appeared in any age" played the organ in a benefit concert for a new hospital in Surrey.

[3 5]

Tunbridge Wells was a fashionable health resort, thirty-six miles south of London. There the nobility assembled during the summer months. Leopold would not have been himself if he had neglected to think of the opportunity.

A few days, however, before their planned departure, he contracted a serious throat inflammation and was laid up for weeks; and even when he had recovered he was not well enough to stand the strain of a fashionable place. So, for a change, the family had a real vacation. Instead, they went to Chelsea—now a part of the city but in those days a village well outside of London, with green gardens along the river Thames. The doctor had prescribed extreme quiet for Leopold; therefore no instrument was touched. As a pastime—Wolfgang would often write music, and pretty good music, just to while away idle hours—the boy filled many pages of his sketch book with notes and even tried his hand at symphonies. Continually before his eyes and in his ears were Bach's scores. "Remind me," he said one day to Nannerl, who did the copying, "remind me to give the horns a lot to do." For the horn was then a favorite instrument in England, and the skillful use of it is typical of Mozart's early compositions.

Anticipating a lucrative concert season, Leopold decided to spend the winter in England.

Wolfgang's first symphonies (K. 16, 19) were played in an all-Mozart concert. A new set of sonatas (K. 10-15) was engraved and dedicated to the Queen. Yet his father had overestimated the durability of impressions; the children had been but a passing fancy. The nobility were unusually late in coming back to town, and the King was two months late in convoking Parliament—the very Parliament that passed the Stamp Act. No one was making much money except perhaps Manzuoli, the famous Italian singer. Manzuoli was so infatuated with Wolferl that he offered him vocal lesson, which the boy enjoyed with all his new enthusiasm for Italian music. He was now initiated into the mysteries of *bel canto* and the first flowers of this new knowledge were soon to bud.

The children had not appeared at Court since October 25, the fourth anniversary of the King's coronation. George III was kept busy with less pleasant affairs. He was unable to settle the question of the American colonies; also there was growing dissatisfaction among the laboring classes, and revolution was threatening. That spring he fell ill, showing the first symptoms of his unfortunate mental disorder. Leopold was living out of his pocket, and hope of having it refilled had vanished. He redoubled his efforts at publicity, but succeeded only in getting himself suspected of falsifying his son's age—suspected to such a point that the scientist Daines Barrington wrote to Salzburg to verify it. One concert had to be postponed three times, and, when it was finally given, the hall was only half filled.

Every day from twelve to three the Mozarts held open house. Visitors were invited to hear the children perform at home, buy copies of Wolfgang's sonatas and engravings of a portrait that had been painted in Paris and tickets for their "last concert" at reduced prices. This concert took place in May. After that Leopold made the poor youngsters play in some tavern for a nominal entrance fee, and again they had to use all their familiar little tricks to attract the public.

Leopold's enthusiasm for England was gone. Suddenly he was shocked to discover that they were in a non-Catholic country. Indignantly he ordered Mamma to pack. They left London on July 24 and crossed the Channel on a bright, calm day, while back in Salzburg the masses for which Leopold had asked were said for them.

Hardly had the Mozarts left London when the Dutch envoy intercepted them with an urgent invitation from the Princess of Nassau-Weilburg, a sister of the Prince of Orange, who lived in The Hague. Leopold was reluctant, but he finally decided that he could not very well refuse.

In Lille, France, they were detained four weeks by illness. After that, they could proceed only slowly, studying Dutch paintings, trying organs. The children were scheduled to appear in The Hague on September 30. But Wolferl played alone. Nannerl was not feeling well, and shortly thereafter she became so ill that the doctor gave up hope. Leopold resigned himself to the will of God. "I didn't want to go to Holland," he mused. *"She* was the one who urged us to accept the invitation. She was driven by fate. It depends upon God whether He will give her strength to recover. If she dies, she will have a happy death."

Relentlessly he communicated this philosophy to the poor girl in her lucid moments between deliriums. Or he read chapters from the Scriptures to her, while Wolferl, next door, distracted himself with music.

The Princess' physician performed a miracle and Nannerl was saved. But now Wolfgang collapsed, and his illness was even more serious than his sister's. The exciting and irregular life, with no substantial rest periods for three years, had obviously exhausted him. At least during the summer months he should have had plenty of air, sleep, exercise, relaxing games with other children. Music was still his favorite game, but it was no relaxation—not with Papa constantly pointing his finger at duty. Leopold realized none of this during his long night vigils at his son's bedside, while he watched the frail body grow frailer and the chubby pretty face grow thin and sharp. But something must have revealed itself subconsciously to Wolfgang. An inner urge drove him to creation—to hurried creation, as though he somehow knew how short was the time he would be allowed to spend in this world. Too weak to walk unaided and almost unable to hold a pencil, he asked to have sheets of music paper brought to him, and scribbled a little symphony in the Italian style (K. 22).

When the children were able to resume their concerts, there was a succession of triumphs in The Hague and other towns of Holland. Wolferl dedicated his most recent violin sonatas (K. 26-31) to the Princess and played at the festival of the installation of her brother—on which occasion Leopold presented a Dutch translation of his *Violin School* to the Prince.

Back in Paris, their old friend Grimm was delighted with Wolfgang's progress and with his singing in particular. They played at Versailles. But in Paris, as in London, people tired easily of the same dish. So they went on to Switzerland, where they gave nine concerts, and then to Munich. Italy had been right in front of them, but they could not lose more time. Leopold had suddenly begun to worry about his welcome in Salzburg.

In Munich, Wolferl fell ill again. Just as four years ago upon returning from Vienna, his toes and knees were paralyzed and pain kept him sleepless. But Leopold still did not see the handwriting on the wall. His letters from Munich were full of big talk and restlessness. Wolfgang was almost ten! What was to become of him?

Throughout the homeward trip, Leopold gave way to outbursts of pride and of anger. He had seven thousand gulden and many boxes full of trinkets, new music, and fan mail. And now he would again have to take up the comparatively servile duties of assistant conductor.

But Wolferl? What had the trip done to him? The violence of new impressions had urged him powerfully toward composition. He had met romantic Schobert and facile Bach. He had become acquainted with his later favorites, the pianoforte and the clarinet. He had heard French choruses in the Chapel of Versailles, popular French tunes in the Paris theaters and streets, and all kinds of Italian and German music. He had seen on the stage *Idomené, Le Devin du village,* and *Il Rè pastore,* all of which he was to set to music some day. He had come to dislike the French and to adore the English. He returned with the memory of a triumphal tour—broken in health, but with the unbroken spirit of a happy child.

CHAPTER 5

BUDS IN SPRING
[1 7 6 6 - 6 9]

LEOPOLD MOZART stood in front of the mirror and looked at his image—a stately man in the red livery of the Salzburg Court band. His proud smile turned into an apologetic grin. There were new lines in his face and new creases in his waistcoat, for he had put on weight since the three years when last he wore it. He suppressed a sigh, glanced at the gala clothes which Mamma was storing in a trunk. Well, *that* was over.

Mamma looked up at him. "Don't be like that, Leopold, please. Don't you like it here? This is home!"

Leopold shrugged his shoulders and went to the Palace to report. Archbishop Sigismund was very much interested and eager to see Wolfgang. There were no reproaches.

Leopold's friends couldn't get enough of his stories. To them, they sounded like fairy tales. But after a while the Mozarts' life returned to its old channels, and Leopold again resented the smallness of his world. Besides, the question of what should become of Wolferl grew increasingly acute.

Leopold's first step had been to put the boy to work on counterpoint. His notebooks showed a tendency toward unevenness of structure, largely due to the wealth of musical ideas which struck him in too quick succession to be thoroughly worked out. Papa placed Fux' *Gradus ad parnassum* before him and started a notebook with rules and examples. Wolferl obediently buried himself in them. This was not composing; this was work! Salty little remarks between the staves reveal the grim humor with which the boy controlled the flow of his imagination.

Leopold had all but given up composing. Between services and instruction he drilled the children in mathematics and grammar, in history and geography, and in languages. They had been made to keep diaries written in the language of the country through which they were passing. Papa laid great stress on neat handwriting, and as a result Mozart's writing of notes always remained exemplary. But his spelling was poor and his knowledge of literature limited. Words did not seem to mean much to him unless they were sung, but then his ear quickly grasped their intrinsic music and rhythm. Mathematics was his favorite science. As a small child, it had so fascinated him that he had temporarily forgotten his music, and the walls, floors, and furniture of the Mozart apartment had been scribbled all over with figures.

The traces of Wolfgang's severe illnesses never disappeared. He remained small and frail. At ten he almost stopped growing, Later, his head became disproportionately large, with a prominent nose, big eyes, and thick blond hair of which he was very proud.

Annually on December 21, the anniversary of the Archbishop's consecration was celebrated, and this year the Mozart boy was asked to write the *Licenza,* the music of homage which was to follow the ceremony proper. At first the Archbishop could not believe that the boy was doing this all by himself. So Wolfgang was summoned to the Palace and locked in a room with the text for the first part of an oratorio. He remained there for a week. When he delivered the sheets of paper blotted all over with ink, with the text clumsily scrawled under the arias, Sigismund was satisfied. The two remaining parts were assigned to Michael Haydn, younger brother of Joseph, who was musical director and concertmaster, and Anton Adlgasser, Court Composer and organist. It was performed in March, 1767, and printed in the same year.

Two months later, Wolfgang's first music for the stage was played. It was the incidental music for a Latin drama, *Apollo et Hyacinthus*

(K. 38) with which the University students marked the closing of the school year. He also wrote church sonatas, small instrumental pieces, and his first four piano concertos based on sonata material by other composers and indicative of ambitious plans.

A few quiet months in Salzburg had sufficed to make Leopold restless. After all, his children were not to end up as small-town folk. Wolfgang had to hear music, more music, and entirely different music from that performed in Salzburg. Also, it was high time to pay homage to Maria Theresa again, lest she forget the Mozarts.

The celebration of a betrothal in the Imperial family, scheduled for October, 1767, seemed to provide an occasion. The aristocracy, too, should be in a generous frame of mind. But Maria Theresa was in no mood to arrange concerts for prodigies. Two years before, in August, 1765, Emperor Francis had died. Although the Empress' married life had been conspicuously happy, no one suspected the depth of her grief. The crown weighed on her more heavily than ever. She believed herself to be mourning not only the loss of a beloved husband, but also that of a strong support—which Emperor Francis had never really been. She cut off her hair, gave away her jewels and gala dresses, and wore clothes as somber as the drapery of her apartments. She immediately raised her eldest son, Archduke Joseph, to the position of a co-regent.

Joseph II, whom legend has turned into a paragon of democratic virtue because he once doffed his coat and worked a plow, or occasionally talked incognito to his subjects on the street, was in fact the Empress' problem child. Sorrowfully she had observed the development of the son who was to continue her life-work. "I am afraid you will never make any friends," she once wrote him. ". . . Who should be Joseph's friend? . . . Be careful not to play with malice! . . . Your heart is not yet bad, but it may become so. . . . Stop finding pleasure in glib phrases and witticisms. They only serve to torment and ridicule others. . . ."

Play with malice? Joseph was a thoroughly unhappy person, self-conscious like many children of too outstanding a parent. His life became a constant struggle against Maria Theresa the Empress, although he was a devoted son to Maria Theresa the mother. To her, rigid conservatism seemed the only way of keeping the complicated workings of Austria under control. Joseph, however, wanted to be a progressive Emperor. He later made well-meant attempts at what we would term democracy; but he was prevented from being a really democratic ruler not only by etiquette but also by shyness which his mother had deplored when he was a boy, and which made him clumsy in his intercourse with people. His inhibitions would often make him appear proud and vain where he had meant to be jovial. Full of inner conflicts, he was trying desperately to make himself loved as a person—without having to give up the prerogatives of the Emperor.

His domestic life was dogged by bad luck, too. He had married when he was nineteen. His beloved Isabella died after a honeymoon that had lasted for three years. After the due interval of mourning, his mother made him marry a Bavarian princess, politically important, respectable, and unattractive. She died of smallpox in May, 1767.

On her deathbed she gave the disease to Maria Theresa. The Empress became dangerously ill, and her eventual recovery evoked public demonstrations of loyalty. But smallpox, unchecked as yet by inoculation, continued to wreak havoc in the Imperial Palace. The next victim was the Princess Maria Josepha, for whose engagement ceremony the Mozarts had come. She died in October.

With the disease spreading all over town, the Mozarts fled. They had arrived on September 15 and waited vainly for an audience, spending their evenings at the theater or opera. When they finally left for Moravia and safety, it was too late; both children came down with smallpox, Wolferl so violently that he was blind for nine days.

Recovered and back in Vienna, they were summoned to Court; the Empress wanted to show her sympathy. The Mozarts were received in private, with no one present but the Imperial family. Maria Theresa could hardly control her emotion. Ceaselessly she talked to Anna Maria, stroked her cheeks, pressed her hands. Maternal anguish created a sort of intimacy. The Mozarts received a medal—beautiful but quite worthless, as Leopold recorded. He didn't know his world any more. The Viennese Court stingy? Joseph's one mania was the saving of expenses. To please him, thrift had been made the fashion among the aristocracy.

The general curtailment of entertainment budgets was a catastrophe not only for the Mozarts but also for the resident musicians. Many of them virtually starved. They ran after what little business there was, fought each other, and intrigued. Most of them put up a more or less silent barrier against Wolfgang. He was no longer young enough to be hugged, kissed and patronized, then dismissed with a few compliments to his father. The best thing, they decided, was not to hear the boy at all, and to spread word that he was a fake. Leopold fought the intriguers with skill and cunning. He raged at the preference shown for the Italians. His son, too, would study in Italy, if it were to cost him his last shirt.

Leopold believed, however, that he might still count on the Court. As a matter of fact, Joseph always liked Wolfgang, although he never fully recognized or rewarded him. Now he decided to help; probably, also, he wanted to put Wolfgang to a severer test than had as yet been given. He asked him whether he would not like to write an opera, and conduct it himself.

But asking Wolfgang and suggesting the matter to the theater management were about all that Joseph was able to do. The Court theater had been leased to one Giuseppe Afflisio for one thousand gulden a year and the Imperial family's free use of their boxes. Afflisio was an adventurer and swindler, who was later convicted of forgery and sent to the galleys. This illiterate man, who freely admitted that he preferred animal-baiting to any other form of entertainment, was now to decide Wolfgang's fate.

At first, Afflisio welcomed the suggestion. In spite of Imperial warning, he had spent seventy thousand gulden on a group of French players, lost most of his investment, and was now on the verge of ruin. To have a boy of twelve in the pit, where he usually had a Gluck, was a hopeful prospect. Anticipating fabulous box-office receipts, he contracted to pay Wolfgang one hundred ducats for an opera. It was decided that it should be an *opera buffa*. The Viennese just then were in no mood for highbrow topics. They were flocking to tents on public squares where famous comedians played the clown under various names such as Lipperl, Bernardon, and the like, in self-written farces filled with a confusing variety of devils and fairies, witches, ghosts and apparitions. Leopold hated "that nonsense"; Wolferl was delighted. What was the matter with Papa anyway? It was different from Gluck's *Alceste* (which Papa didn't like either) and Haydn's symphonies—but life couldn't always be exalted or sentimental. You had to laugh. . . .

In accordance with prevailing Viennese taste, the cast for comic opera was excellent. In the ranks of outstanding *buffa* composers, Italian or Italian-trained, a new name was now to appear: Wolfgang Mozart, aged twelve.

La Finta semplice (K. 51) is a typical specimen of *opera buffa.* Two bachelors, opposing their sister's marriage to a young officer, are outwitted by the officer's own sister, disguised as "Simplicity." It was up to the twelve-year-old to portray convincingly an embittered woman-hater, an elderly philanderer, and two young people in love, while Leopold was canvassing the singers because the music was written for them and they had to like it. Wolfgang, with his love for the theater and his gift for the comic, was composing at amazing speed. That he only half succeeded in the musical characterization of subjects so foreign to his own experience, is not surprising.

Intrigues, gradually involving everyone concerned, put the performance on and off for many months.

Rival composers began: "The boy doesn't know Italian. The music is entirely against the meter."

"We cannot sing the arias," complained the singers, who shortly before had liked them well enough.

"We do not want to be conducted by a baby," said the members of the orchestra.

Afflisio became evasive: "I cannot help it, if they don't want to sing and play in it."

"But *he* was the one who told us that he didn't want to produce it!" retorted the singers.

Leopold took Wolfgang by the hand and led him around the salons. There, in the presence of respected musical authorities, including Gluck, the boy was made to show that he did know Italian as well as music. Papa moved heaven and earth to save the honor of his boy, the honor of the Salzburg Court, his own honor and, last but not least, what he called the honor of Heavenly grace, which had performed the miracle that people refused to recognize. But Afflisio had no great sense of honor—least of all, Leopold's version of honor. He made it plain that he would produce *La Finta* if forced to do so, but would arrange for it to be a failure.

Leopold handed the Emperor an elaborate complaint. An investigation was ordered. *La Finta semplice* was not performed.

During his first experience with the "hell of musicians," Wolfgang had a small compensation. He was asked to write a *Singspiel* for Dr. Anton Mesmer, the interesting physician who later became famous through his advocacy of magnetic therapy—mesmerism. Mesmer had married into a wealthy family and owned a splendid house in the suburb of Landstrasse, where he had a large garden with an open-air theater framed by box-hedges. An adaptation of Rousseau's *Le Devin du village,* the original French version of which Wolfgang had seen in Paris, seemed most suitable. There were only three characters—a shepherd, a shepherdess, and a good-natured wizard—in a pastoral setting, and Wolfgang wrote little songs for them in the French and Austrian manner. *Bastien und Bastienne* (K. 50) has remained a piece *par excellence* for intimate occasions.

Another compensation came from the Emperor himself. In the presence of the Court, Wolfgang conducted a solemn mass, with an offertorium, and a trumpet concerto which he had composed for the ceremonial blessing of an orphanage church. The tremendous acclaim that resulted put his critics to rout.

The Mozarts' honor was restored, but their purse was not. When they returned to Salzburg, early in 1769, Leopold realized that the trip had been financially disastrous. They had been living almost entirely on their savings and on money obtained by the sale of trinkets. In addition, Leopold's Salzburg salary had been stopped. The courtiers at home had pointed out to His Grace the folly of

paying two Vice-Kapellmeisters: Herrn Mozart en route and his substitute on the job. Leopold was graciously granted any leave of absence he might wish, but he was to draw no salary unless actually working.

Leopold had enough sense of justice not to object, and too much pride to beg for something he did not deserve. When the news of his salary loss reached him, he was still dreaming of great success for *La Finta,* which would have opened every door in Italy to the boy. For the trip south had long since been decided on. The Emperor himself had given them introductions. There would be time to return to his desk in Salzburg later.

Should I perhaps sit down in Salzburg with the empty hope of some better fortune, let Wolfgang grow up and allow myself and my children to be made fools of, until I reach the age which prevents me from traveling and until he attains the age and physical appearance which no longer attract admiration for his merits (sic!)? . . .

Leopold had obviously grown fond of the earthly pleasures which the wonders of God provided. Yet he was not really insincere towards anyone except himself.

However unsuccessful the Vienna trip appeared, it had been tremendously valuable for Wolfgang. It was his first step towards becoming a true Austrian master. The symphonies which he wrote during this period prove it, as do the orchestration of *La Finta* and the treatment of the ariettas in *Bastien*.

Still strongly under the spell of Johann Christian Bach and his Italian manifestations of gaiety, Wolfgang was deeply stirred by his native music. The two Haydns, Joseph and Michael, became his guides for the immediate future. He was soon to reach a stage at which musical elements acquired by imitation would drop from him, leaving those that were part of his natural disposition to blossom and thrive. At thirteen, he had found his own musical language, although he still had to look for models, so to speak, in grammar and spelling.

CHAPTER 6

FAME IN ITALY

[1 7 6 9 - 7 0]

WITH THE VIENNA TRIP, Nannerl's musical career came to a close. She was now eighteen and a very good pianist, but there was nothing unusual about her any more. She remained in Salzburg, pretty and popular, gave a few music lessons and, without a shadow of envy, let Wolfgang supply the family fame.

Wolfgang had not yet come to dislike Salzburg. It was home. There were the cat, the dog, and the birds, and there were a comfortable bed and Theresa's cooking. Everybody spoiled him. Archbishop Sigismund ordered a performance of the unfortunate *La Finta semplice* in his own theater; most of Papa's friends were in the cast or the orchestra, and the pretty Mme. Haydn, Michael's wife, sang the title part.

Court and University wanted Wolfgang's music, and all Salzburg seemed to want minuets for the Carnival. Young Hagenauer, who had turned priest and was now Father Dominicus, asked him to write a mass for his first celebration at St. Peter's. It was in C major and retained the surname of *Dominicus* Mass (K. 66).

In the dead of winter, father and son left for the sunny skies of Italy. The Archbishop granted the leave willingly and as a farewell present bestowed upon young Mozart the imposing title of "Concertmaster to the Archiepiscopal Court of Salzburg." To distinguish him from other concertmasters, the title was adorned with the modest qualification "unsalaried." Mamma stayed behind with Nannerl. All Leopold could do, to give them a proper share in the trip, was to leave them *Keyssler's Reisebeschreibung,* an atrocious eighteenth-century guidebook, which helped them to follow Leopold and Wolfgang in their imaginations. Letters reached them on every post-day. Wolfgang's resounded with gaiety and good humor:

My heart is completely enchanted with all these pleasures, because it is so jolly on this journey, because it is so warm in the carriage, and because our coachman is a fine fellow who, when the road gives him the slightest chance, drives very fast.

Italy was the promised land of music. From there church music had come in olden times; from there also opera had come, the strongest formative element of the young symphonic art. Just as the Roman legions had brought culture and Roman missionaries the message of Christ, Italian music had brought cheerful edification to the shores of the Danube, the Rhine, and the Thames. And for nearly two hundred years, Northern musicians had been studying in Italy. Joseph Haydn was the first to rise to widespread fame without the prestige of the training, while even Johann Sebastian Bach, who could not afford the trip, had remained merely a local celebrity during his lifetime.

Now Wolfgang Mozart was going to Italy. The trip was meant to be an apprenticeship in composition, and his appearances as a virtuoso were only a means to that end.

After climbing over the Brenner Pass through drifts of snow and stopping at many places, Leopold and Wolfgang reached Milan on January 23, 1770.

Wolfgang's first experiences in Italy did not much differ from his previous tours elsewhere. He was wildly acclaimed, and heard a lot of music. He wrote little about the beauties of the country, even less about sight-seeing, although Papa dragged the dreaming boy through the museums and churches, quoting the unavoidable *Keyssler*. It is one of the most striking features of Mozart's personality that he did not care for the beauties of nature. In addition he, as well as his father, thoroughly disliked high mountains. They found them oppressive, as did most eighteenth-century people who were not yet fascinated by skiing and hiking.

In Milan, they were comfortably lodged in three rooms at the Augustinian monastery of San Marco. Pleasant contacts were established for them with leading nobles and musicians of Milan, among them Sammartini, the important pre-classical symphonist, and Piccini whose operas, frequently performed in Vienna, had been Wolfgang's principal models for *La Finta*.

Back home, Mamma was worried. Italy was a dangerous country, she had been told. Italians had no stoves, and they made you eat the queerest things. Don't worry, Papa wrote back; Wolfgang was exceptionally reasonable for his age, he reported; "he often eats very little, yet none-the-less he is fat and cheerful and jolly all day long."

Actually, Wolfgang's portrait made at Verona does not show him to be fat; but gay and jolly he certainly was, for this was Carnival. They had to dress in Carnival fashion, cloak and hood falling down over the shoulders and almost entirely covering the head. Father and son stood in front of the mirror to try on the costumes. Wolfgang's eyes shone in anticipation. He looked very handsome and this comforted Papa, who scorned such "tomfoolery" and cursed the ridiculous expense.

For an entire week, Milan seemed inhabited by nothing but masks. They strode through the streets, singly, in groups, or parading. They barricaded doorways and crowded eating places. One day, they all dressed up as valets and were accompanied by fiddlers, bands, and drummers. The next day crowds would ride on horseback, followed by singing and shouting masses. Cavaliers drove in carriages. Anyone who grew tired could watch the show from a window. Waiters and musicians were the only people who did any sort of work.

Count Firmian, Austrian Governor General of Lombardy and one of the most highly educated men of his generation, decided to give Wolfgang a chance. He arranged a musicale where the boy was to prove his ability to write opera. Out of Metastasio's works, which the Governor had given him, Wolfgang composed four arias; and their performance at the soirée brought him a regular *scrittura* —a contract—for the first opera to be given in Milan next Carnival.

Their goal had been reached. Wolfgang on a first-class stage of Italy, with a serious opera! Their journey could be continued un-hampered, since the libretto would be sent after them. Wolfgang was to forward the recitatives to Milan by October. In November, he was scheduled to return there to write the arias in personal con-ference with the leading singers, as was the custom.

In Bologna, Count Pallavicini received them as generously as Count Firmian in Milan. He, too, arranged an evening of music at his home and managed even to interest Padre Martini, although the 64-year-old monk no longer attended concerts. Padre Martini was the musical oracle of the eighteenth century. His library was mar-velous; an elaborate correspondence connected him with European princes, musicians, scientists; crowds of disciples gathered around him. A recommendation from Padre Martini was worth more than ten times its weight in gold.

The learned man twice put Wolfgang to severe tests in fugue writing and was very pleased with the results. He talked freely to everybody about his enthusiasm for young Mozart and the news about the wonder-boy spread like wildfire.

Easter was to be spent in Rome, after a brief stop in Florence. A five-day ride in a small carriage that shook and bounced, punctuated by stops at inns, which were dirty and had little food, brought the Mozarts to Rome on Wednesday of Holy Week. A heavy thunder-storm raged in the outskirts of the Eternal City. Heaven is greeting its elect with rockets and cannons, Leopold thought, shivering with cold. Wolfgang's fingers drummed on an invisible piano and his eyes, red with fatigue, seemed to penetrate the thick rain-clouds and see the dark blue sky and the golden sun behind them.

"Aren't we like the bells?" he murmured.

"What bells?"

"Why, Papa, the Easter bells. Don't you remember? At Easter the bells fly to Rome from every church in the world, and they come back, blessed, to ring in the Resurrection."

Leopold certainly remembered the old legend of the flying bells. Wolferl's reminder took his thoughts off the tiring journey. For him, the dream of every devout Catholic—Easter in Rome—was coming true.

Leopold was deeply moved when they entered the Sistine Chapel of the Vatican. Wolfgang, blind as usual to its wonders of structure and painting, was entranced by the music that was being sung—the famous *Miserere* by Allegri. The highlight of Easter music in Rome, the most cherished work of its kind, all copies of it were jealously guarded, and excommunication was the penalty for "taking the music out of the Chapel." Only members of certain royal families and Padre Martini were said to possess copies, which had been given to them by the Pope himself.

When the Mozarts left the Chapel, Wolfgang hardly spoke. Back in their rooms, he seized music paper and a pen and wrote with flying hands for hours.

"What are you writing, Wolferl? Something new?" Leopold asked him finally. Maybe inspiration had come during the divine service.

"No, Papa, something old. I'm writing down the *Miserere*."

"For Heaven's sake!" Leopold exclaimed. "Don't you know it is forbidden to take it out? Whether you steal it with your hands or with your ears. . . ." But he was very proud. On Good Friday—two days later—the *Miserere* was performed again, and the Mozarts heard it for the second time. Wolfgang took his music sheets with him, and, hiding them under his hat, made a few secret corrections.

Somehow word got around. At some party, in the presence of a famous chapel singer, Wolferl's manuscript was examined and found authentic. The Pope learned about it. And when an anxious letter from Mamma, to whom Papa had revealed the dangerous secret, reached Leopold, he could report that the achievement had done Wolferl great credit all over Italy—including the Vatican. And he did not forget to add that she must "see to it that the letter is read out everywhere."

Other letters supposed to be given wide publicity in Salzburg told about their meeting with Cardinal Pallavicini, a relative of their host at Bologna. Preceded by a solemn-looking valet and dressed up like noblemen, the Mozarts had managed to penetrate a line of Swiss guards during an official function. As they approached the Cardinals' table, they attracted the attention of Pallavicini who graciously remembered having heard about the "famous boy."

The Cardinal became one of their most active sponsors. Nobility and English visitors became their friends. Before long, they expected to be received in audience by His Holiness, the Pope. Wolfgang was greatly inspired by his experiences, to which he often referred later in life. "How I felt there, oh, how I felt there!" he would exclaim when the conversation turned to his Roman pilgrimage.

Then they were in Naples, and there were happy reunions. The young Queen, one of Maria Theresa's many daughters, greeted Leopold and Wolfgang as old acquaintances. And there was the English ambassador, Sir William Hamilton, with his beautiful young wife Emma, both of whom the Mozarts had met in London. Mejnheer Jonker of Amsterdam, too, was there; and M. Meurikofen of Lyons, that funny man who had amused Wolfgang years ago when he sang an Italian song with his eyeglasses on the tip of his nose; and there was, above all, the famous Italian composer, old Jommelli. They had met him on their grand tour, in Ludwigsburg, where he had annoyed Leopold with the well-meant statement that Wolfgang's achievements were quite unusual for a non-Italian child. Now he proved that his admiration had been genuine. He had Wolfgang meet the impresario of the San Carlo Theater, who offered him a contract. Wolfgang had to decline the offer on account of his Milan assignment, just as he had declined others in Rome and Bologna.

They were introduced to the society of Naples, and on May 28 they gave a highly successful recital. Wolfgang was admired for his good looks and fine manners as much as for his playing. He looked very handsome in his new gala costumes, one in apple-green with pink lining, the other rose moiré with sky-blue lining, and both adorned with silver lace and silver buttons. Italian sun and winds had given him a nice tan which was becoming with his blond hair.

Leopold was gratified that they could afford little luxuries and travel in what he called an honorable fashion. They were now living as did the most elegant folk. They had invitations to the opera and to every conceivable kind of entertainment, the most glamorous being the ball at the French Embassy given to celebrate the betrothal of the young Dauphin of France to the Archduchess Marie Antoinette of Austria.

Every afternoon there was the *passeggio:* a parade of hundreds of private carriages on a splendid road along the seashore. At twilight, flambeaux were lighted on all of them. Growing brighter as daylight faded, they looked like a moving column of huge glow-worms. On Sundays and holidays the Queen would participate in the *passeggio.* Guns were fired on the ships at anchor when she passed by, and upon her approach the other carriages stopped with the occupants saluting her. More than once the Queen saw among the crowds the boy from her own country with his father, driving in the carriage of some noble, with two servants, their own and their patron's, carrying the lights.

But Wolfgang was not invited to play at Naples' Court; the King was not interested. Leopold became critical. His well-organized mind had no use for the strange mixture of beauty and filth, abundance and poverty, which is so characteristic of many Southern Italian towns. To him, all this was not romantic but shocking. And shocking, too, were the people: godless, superstitious, bringing up children the wrong way. Superstitious the Neapolitans were indeed; once they even made Wolfgang remove his ring because they thought it was tainted with witchcraft.

Ruins, old temples, underground chambers and old baths interested Wolfgang to a certain extent. But he was near-sighted—though he never wore glasses—and near-sighted people usually tire rapidly of details. So he went around dreaming or joking (joking would always be the reverse side of his emotions), while Papa read to him dates, inscriptions, and descriptions of the minerals contained in the lava of Vesuvius.

The unaccustomed climate, the long drives, the strong impressions, and the strenuous life wore Wolfgang out. He was always tired. So Leopold decided to spend a restful summer in Bologna, going there via Rome before the heat set in.

CHAPTER 7

"CAVALIERE FILARMONICO"

[1 7 7 0 - 7 1]

NO VEHICLE was available but a two-wheeled carriage, and Leopold grumbled over the poor transportation, the dirty roads full of holes, and the unreliable postmasters and inn-keepers. To impress these lax Southerners, he posed as the Imperial Ambassador's steward—a device that gained some deference from the people who waited on him, but was utterly wasted on one of the horses which dragged the two-wheeler over the last part of the twenty-seven-hour journey. The disrespectful animal reacted to the coachman's fast driving with a sudden jerk that upset the carriage. In the resulting spill, Leopold's leg was painfully injured, though Wolfgang fortunately was unhurt. Limping, Papa dragged the dazed boy to their quarters.

Here the two quickly swallowed some rice and eggs, and Papa got out some ointment he had brought from home.

"Wolfgang," he called, "please help me put this bandage on my foot."

No answer.

"Wolfgang!" Papa was growing impatient.

From the chair at the table came a snore. Wolfgang had fallen fast asleep. Poor child, Leopold thought. In spite of his pain he undressed his son and put him to bed—and Wolfgang slept soundly in the same spot until nine o'clock the next morning.

Papa had to stay in bed for two days, and even after that he limped badly. The accident prevented the immediate continuation of their journey, but there was something else awaiting them which they had not foreseen.

At a dinner with Cardinal Pallavicini, His Eminence suddenly addressed Wolfgang as *Signor Cavaliere*. Leopold looked at him, startled. The Cardinal's kind eyes smiled; then, when he noticed Leopold's puzzled stare, his lips smiled, too.

"Signor Cavaliere, some more cake?" This time he was quite serious. Leopold was thoroughly embarrassed to hear his son addressed as a knight.

On his way home, Papa decided that Wolfgang was too big a boy for that sort of foolish petting. He had noticed with satisfaction that Wolfgang was growing. He would never be very tall, but his limbs were getting stronger, and he was outgrowing his shirts. The other day, Leopold had watched him remove the silk thread from his ring, which until now had been too big for him. And Papa's musical ear had discovered slight changes in Wolfgang's voice when he sang or hummed. Soon he would have to bid good-by to the child prodigy. But this did not matter. Since he had been so far ahead of boys his age when he was a baby, why should he not be ahead of grown-ups now? Why *shouldn't* he become *Cavaliere* after all?

"Ridiculous," he said to himself an hour later when he observed the boy pirouetting around the room making funny gestures to chairs and tables. *"Cavaliere* Jack Pudding!"

But Jack Pudding shortly thereafter was summoned to the Pope. With all the signs of highest grace, His Holiness bestowed upon Wolfgang the Order of the Golden Spur. The Cardinal had known about it long before.

"The same order as Gluck's!" Leopold exulted, not realizing how freely the honor was being distributed lately, thus losing much of its importance. But, whereas *Cavaliere* Gluck was clever enough to take every possible advantage of the golden cross and the patent of nobility, Papa's strong advice was needed to make Wolfgang sensibly aware of his distinction. The nice musical word *Cavaliere* adorned young Mozart's signature for a little while; he painted its letters just as he had painted notes as a child. But he soon grew tired of it as of a new toy—and forgot all about it.

Wolfgang, for the time being, had become an Italian composer. The operatic spirit of Italian music had led him away gradually from the Salzburg and Vienna instrumental idiom. A few months before, at an inn at Lodi where they had stopped for the night, he had written his first string quartet (K. 80), filled with echoes of North Italian chamber music style. This had been a period of transition. Now his instruments were treated almost as if they were voices. Only later was he gradually to develop his unequaled balance of singing melody and instrumental characterization.

The Mozarts spent the summer at the country place of Count Pallavicini near Bologna. They had the best rooms in the house, where Leopold could nurse both his feet—one with the wound, the other with gout. Two servants were at their beck and call. The Count's young son was congenial and well educated; the Countess loved to hear Wolfgang play and during the daytime she took him driving around the country.

After returning to town, they saw a great deal of Padre Martini, who liked to talk music with Leopold and grew ever fonder of Wolfgang. He admired the boy's perseverance and seriousness, his eagerness to learn. This youth, Padre Martini recognized, was looking for the highest and purest in art.

In Bologna, nobody gave a thought to opera. Musicians there were serious, dignified, conservative. They wrote masses and fugues instead of arias of love and vengeance. Bologna was full of churches, and the churches were full of music which had been preserved unchanged. It was like an island of tradition in the changing tides of musical taste.

Padre Martini made the most affectionate effort to convey to Wolfgang as much knowledge as possible, and the boy drank it in eagerly. No one could suspect a future master of comic opera in his

Miserere (K. 85) for three voices. During these few weeks with Padre Martini, Wolfgang learned to write cleanly and clearly. It was purifying, like his contrapuntal studies with Papa, three years ago. Now Papa had little more to teach him, but Padre Martini's instruction remained invaluable to Wolfgang's works through life.

One day, Padre Martini made the surprise announcement that he had taken steps to have Wolfgang admitted as a member of the Accademia Filarmonica, that century-old institution which controlled church music all over Italy, the most dignified of its kind. The terms of admission were very strict. Many tried it, and many failed. In Wolfgang's case the authorities waived the rule requiring an age limit of twenty and a two-year attendance in lower classes at the Academy itself, but he would have to pass the customary test to prove his mastery of counterpoint.

"Don't worry, child," comforted Padre Martini. "It is difficult, but you will succeed. Don't write in a hurry. You have three hours, and almost everybody takes that long."

On October 9, at 4 P.M., Wolfgang and Leopold entered the big hall of the Academy. Around a long table sat the Principal and the censors, together with the rest of the judges. Padre Martini introduced Wolfgang formally. Then came a few instructions, and there was handed to him the theme that he was required to write out for four voices. He was escorted to an adjoining room. At the door he turned around and caught Padre Martini's eyes. The old monk nodded encouragement. Then the door closed behind Wolfgang.

"Come, Signor Mozart," said Padre Martini. "We have plenty of time."

As they walked around in the big hallway of the Academy, they talked but little. Padre Martini had taken on an enormous responsibility. This boy was his fledgling. He had asked for an exception on his behalf. As to Papa, he was free from responsibility, for once, though not from ambition.

"What if he fails?" Leopold asked suddenly.

"He won't," replied Padre Martini.

"No, he won't. God will help."

An attendant rushed up to them. They looked at the clock. Hardly thirty minutes had gone by.

"It's *Cavaliere* Mozart," the attendant said uneasily. "He says he should like to see you."

Leopold grew pale and his lips tightened. Had Wolfgang fallen ill or given up? He had never been very good in counterpoint. He looked at Padre Martini. Two pairs of anxious eyes met, then turned toward the door.

"What is the matter, my boy?" asked the monk. His voice was controlled but unsteady.

"Why, nothing is the matter. I am through."

Padre Martini gave a sigh of relief. Leopold wiped his eyes. They both knew that if Wolfgang said he was through, he meant it.

The judges and censors, who had meantime reassembled, looked incredulous. Some of them showed expressions of sincere sympathy. "Such a nice boy!" they seemed to think. "Why didn't Padre Martini spare him this humiliation?"

Then they all set to work examining Wolfgang's manuscript, while the boy was sent again into the other room, sleepy and slightly bored. Leopold, locked up in the library, paced the floor with excitement.

When both were recalled into the hall, the judges rose, applauded, congratulated. Then they sat down again. Only the old Principal remained standing. His eyes glowed mildly like the rays of autumn sun that slanted through the high windows. He announced solemnly that Wolfgang had been accepted as a member by an unanimous vote. "The youngest the Academy was ever privileged to have," he added.

Only now did Wolfgang get excited. This was very different from the applause he received in the salons. The test had not been really hard. At least it had not seemed so—he had often gone over similar exercises with Padre Martini.

"I know," he said, now solemn himself, when he was walking

home with his father and his instructor, "I know how much I owe to you, *Padre mio*."

Leopold wondered for a moment which the boy meant—himself or Padre Martini.

Now Wolfgang had to think seriously of his opera if it was to be ready on time. There were only two months and a half left to write and produce it.

The libretto had arrived during the summer; *Mitridate, Rè di Ponto* (K. 87) was a sugary operatic version of Racine's—the seventeenth-century French dramatist's—tragedy in which a King and his two sons are in love with the same woman. On October 18, Leopold and Wolfgang settled down in Milan, in comfortable quarters near the theater, two large rooms with a fireplace and a balcony. With aching fingers and burning eyes, Wolfgang wrote recitatives all day and part of the night. In November, he started on the arias. Papa kept himself busy trying to win over influential people, fighting real and imaginary enemies, looking after details of food, clothing, exercise and relaxation. "Add a joke to your letters," he wrote to Salzburg. "Wolfgang is now busy with serious matters and is therefore very serious himself. So I am delighted when he occasionally gets hold of something funny."

Leopold, too, was very serious, and no joke could cheer him up. He was past fifty and growing tired. He was plagued with rheumatism and his attack of gout had been a warning. Prices in Salzburg were constantly rising, Mamma had complained. What was to become of those who were living on yearly wages?

Wolfgang labored on the arias. Vainly did he try to penetrate the libretto's family conflict; nor did he have sufficient theatrical experience to take full advantage of its dramatic climaxes. He shrugged his shoulders mentally and wrote what came into his mind. Italian opera had impressed him anew, and Padre Martini's lessons had not been wasted. The singers tried out their arias just as they tried on their costumes. Like a tailor, Wolfgang had to alter, to discard, to replace—a *coloratura* here, a *fioritura* there. . . . The main thing was that the singers were satisfied, that the orchestra liked the music, and that the copyist anticipated good business. For the copyist could sell the arias as often as he wanted. When they were popular, he made more money than the composer.

All the odds were in Wolfgang's favor on this December 26, 1770, the night of the first performance.

"Evviva il Maestro! Evviva il Maestrino!" After almost every aria the crowds would get up, cheer, stamp, clap hands. Leopold beamed in the box above the pit. He had been told that the house was usually half empty on first nights, as people waited to see whether a work was going to be successful. But the controversy over Wolfgang had aroused great public curiosity. When the audience found that the opera was not ridiculous—not an incoherent mixture of everything, not barbarously German, as many had predicted—waves of sympathy flowed toward the winsome young man in the scarlet suit with gilt braid who sat in the conductor's place.

It was Wolfgang's first big success in the theater, one which he often recalled with longing in later years when he was forced to do other things merely to earn a living. Figures from bygone centuries which he had brought to life moved on the stage. What he believed them to be, they expressed with his music. The singers before him on the stage, the men around him in the pit, were living keys of a huge instrument called Opera. And Opera, to him, was the essence of life.

Mitridate was repeated twenty times—a high figure considering the short opera seasons in Italy. Its success earned Wolfgang the nickname of *Cavaliere Filarmonico,* membership in the Accademia Filarmonica in Verona, and a commission to write an oratorio, *La Betulia liberata* (K. 118), for Padua where father and son stopped on their way home. There was more news before they reached Salzburg, assuring two more trips to Milan: by Imperial command, Wolfgang was to do the cantata for Archduke Ferdinand's wedding to the Princess of Modena in the fall, and he also had another opera contract for the Carnival of 1773.

CHAPTER 8

FIRST SHADOWS

[1 7 7 1 - 7 3]

THE WEDDING CANTATA was *Ascanio in Alba* (K. 111), a "festive serenade for the theater," with words by a professor at the University of Milan. With two violinists, a singing teacher and a oboe player living in the same house where the Mozarts then lodged, Wolfgang groped his way through the allegorical libretto overstuffed with goddesses, graces, genii, and shepherds, who in the baroque fashion paid homage to the princely pair. Any other musician having to work under such conditions against a close deadline would have become insane or committed wholesale murder. Wolfgang thought it merely funny; he said it gave him good ideas.

For the production of the opera, Signor Hasse, the celebrated dean of opera composers, arrived on the scene. He and Wolfgang had already met in Vienna. Far from envy or pettiness, Hasse was unsparing in his praise of his youthful competitor. With solemn enthusiasm he prophesied that this boy was likely to send them all to oblivion. As far as he personally was concerned, this forecast came true sooner than he had expected. The cheerful holiday crowd relegated their *caro Sassone* ("Dear Saxon"—Hasse was from Saxony where he had lived before) to the scrap-heap, and the youthful *Cavaliere Filarmonico* carried off the palm.

The newly married Archduke was delighted. He was barely two years Wolfgang's senior and remembered well having heard him in

Schönbrunn. When he was told that father Mozart was trying to find a position for his son at a respectable court, the young Prince was more than half inclined to appoint Wolfgang right away. Never before, and hardly ever after, had Wolfgang been so near to a secure future and Papa so near to his ultimate goal.

As an Archduke in Vienna, the young Prince had been entitled to all sorts of honors and distinctions; but, when he wanted anything beyond the ordinary, he had to ask Mother for it like any other child, and Mother preached modesty more often than many other mothers. Never would he have been allowed to add a boy of his own age to his escort just to satisfy a personal fancy. Now, as a Governor General, he might get away with it—but better ask first.

Maria Theresa was not pleased at all. The puppy had hardly learned to run before he wanted a Court Composer—and young Mozart at that! The Empress was taken with sudden anger when she remembered Leopold: bowing, grinning, rubbing hands, and noisily promoting himself as the caretaker of a heavenly miracle. These Mozarts were a beggarly crew. Gypsies, that's what they were. The boy was talented and very charming—but this pompous bore of a father? Would *he* hang around, too?

Back came her advice: Don't employ people you don't need, particularly people with large families; by no means give a title to anyone whose deportment might discredit the service . . . but, of course, if it gives you great pleasure, do as you please.

The Archduke knew what this meant. It *would* have given him great pleasure, but he preferred to save his mother's good will for something more important. He sighed—and forgot all about it.

Meantime, the Mozarts were already struggling homeward over the poor mountain roads of the Tyrol. More than once, Wolfgang looked proudly at the beautiful gold watch set with diamonds which he had received after the performance of *Ascanio*—a token of the Empress' appreciation of his work.

On December 15, 1771, their carriage rumbled into the Salzburg streets. Life would be less glamorous again, less colorful; but there were Mamma, and Nannerl, and all their friends—and maybe Archbishop Sigismund would add a salary to Wolfgang's empty title.

But the Mozarts were never to see their kind overlord again. On December 16, Archbishop Sigismund breathed his last. The Salzburgers mourned him sincerely. Life had been somewhat dreary at times, but there was almost nobody who had not in one way or another benefited by the kindness of the pious old man. For this kindness they might now have to pay. The Archbishop had been no financial genius, and the budget was not in a happy state. Salzburg wondered, worried, and finally cheered up.

The Bishop of Chiemsee, Count Zeill, seemed to have the best chances for the Archbishop's post. He was said to be both efficient and generous. Leopold beamed. On a state visit in Vienna, the Bishop of Chiemsee had witnessed the *La Finta* affair and had been one of Wolfgang's most emphatic supporters.

Painters had already started portraits of Count Zeill; a nice, pleasant face, indeed. But suddenly and in a hurry they had to cover it with a new layer of colors. Pale and sharp features appeared, topped by a blond wig, dominated by piercing, grayish green eyes. Salzburg's new Archbishop was Hieronymus Count Colloredo, Bishop of Gurk.

Colloredo's reputation was anything but encouraging. Obedient but highly uneasy, the Salzburgers paid homage to their new Prince, who took office in April, 1772. The youngest member of his orchestra, Concertmaster Mozart, had composed the festival cantata. *Il Sogno di Scipione* (K. 126) sounded forced, stiff, uncomfortable. To Wolfgang's tunes the Salzburgers buried their favorite maxim, "Live and let live."

Hieronymus was not fooled by the loud acclaim of his new subjects. Like every tyrant, he had a good ear for opposition lurking beneath dutiful cheers. So these Salzburgers did not like him? These lazy, indolent creatures? He would teach them how to behave!

The teaching began at home, and promptly. Archbishop Hieronymus, thrifty son of an extravagant father, was a wizard at collecting and saving money, and a master of the art of making things unpleasant for everybody. He had his cook report daily on household expenditures, and directed that the salaries of Court employees were not to exceed "reasonable limits"—and "reasonable" meant stingy. Nobody ever remembered hearing a kind word from him—except, of course, members of the high nobility. Fundamentally well-meant reforms were imposed like penalties; when a new dance hall was opened for public entertainment, it was like an order to amuse oneself. The Archbishop thought he knew a good deal about music; and indeed, he was a fair violinist. But he considered himself an expert, and therefore—since it was his pleasure to join his orchestra for the evening concerts—the programs had to be shaped according to his taste which ran to gallant, noisy trifles.

For his new subjects and their traditions, Hieronymus did not even try to conceal his contempt. Passion plays and processions were gradually banned as blasphemous mixtures of religion and buffoonery. The University was advised to teach useful things instead of wasting time and money on plays. Holidays were restricted and more rigid Sunday observance was enforced. Everything that the centuries had developed from the desires of the Salzburg heart and soul was sacrificed to "reason" or to the archiepiscopal treasury.

The Mozarts in particular had a bad time. This man Leopold Mozart was too conceited. And his dwarf of a son—Hieronymus, to his utter annoyance, was small, and therefore disliked small people thoroughly—had been taught to pose as a genius. True, the boy had an amazing amount of talent for a Salzburger—the more reason for him to devote it to his sovereign. And he added the pittance of 150 gulden a year to Wolfgang's title.

Wolfgang's obligations were much greater than the salary warranted. A great deal of music was needed for the Cathedral and for the Court. The orchestra had to play daily after supper, and, on festive occasions, during the meal also. Compositions must not be repeated. During the summer months, candlelight concerts were held in the open air in the courtyard of the Residence.

Candles, glow-worms, stars; the scent of blossoms and of the

humid soil; the murmur of the fountains and the rustle of skirts—all these gave a new direction to Wolfgang's mind. His voice had long since grown steady. Now a new tone appeared in it when he spoke to ladies; a new tone also appeared in his music. He had already known the charms of secret flirtations, and the infinite pleasure of graceful rewards for a fine piece of music. He knew, too, romantic reverie and disappointment when the girl of his first dreams had married while he was away.

Now the changes and upheavals of adolescence made themselves felt. His music, now again largely instrumental, had slow movements full of hidden passion, often in minor keys. For those who knew how to listen, Wolfgang wore his heart on his sleeve.

Treasures of wonderful music were born. The Archbishop had every reason to be satisfied, though he could not be made to utter a word of appreciation. His unpleasant eyes—the left was usually half closed—stared at his youthful concertmaster in suspicion. He never knew where he stood with the two Mozarts. And when the position of the head conductor became vacant, a position which Leopold had long felt he had a right to expect, His Grace appointed an Italian. He would not dream of placing this disorganized lot of musicians under a man who regarded his work at home as a stop-gap between pleasure trips.

But when the time came for the Mozarts to go to Milan according to Wolfgang's contract for a new opera, Hieronymus did not dare refuse the leave of absence. Greatly relieved, father and son left the cold atmosphere of Salzburg in October, craving more than ever the warmth of Italy.

It was for the last time. *Lucio Silla* (K. 135) was only half a success. No more was Wolfgang the *Cavaliere Filarmonico* who had showered melodies over his audiences. This was a highly personal, complicated young man, whose instrumental idiom weighed on his music and on the public's mind.

Having flouted Italian convention, Wolfgang now became a stranger in Italy. His fate pointed him home to the Austrian hills and his mother's comforting laughter, to the gloomy mountains in the distance and his master's arrogance. But grace, tenderness, beauty *per se*—everything his beloved Italy stood for—now penetrated his sensitive being. The beauty and liveliness of the South became the melodic language in which he thereafter expressed himself. As long as he lived he would yearn for the Italy to which his eyes, as well as his ears, had been opened on the doorstep of farewell.

CHAPTER 9

ONE DARK SPOT

[1773-77]

ALL THE WAY HOME to Salzburg, Leopold was a prey to somber thoughts. Back in the days of Archbishop Sigismund it had not always been easy to obtain extended leaves; but Hieronymus' urgent and frequent inquiries about their return made the old régime now seem like Heaven. Leopold had been obliged to resort to lies. In ciphered letters, he had told Mamma about his desperate attempts to establish Wolfgang in Florence at the Court of Grand Duke Leopold, second son of Maria Theresa, while officially playing sick.

This hypocrisy wore heavily on Leopold and so did the lack of recognition for him at home as the father and tutor of an outstanding son. He started to plan another grand tour, regardless of difficulties. Mamma and Nannerl were constantly urged to save money. Every penny spent in Salzburg meant one minute lost abroad. For once, however, Leopold was too optimistic. Leave was not granted.

Wolfgang was so much absorbed in his own small affairs and big emotions that at first he could not be seriously disturbed by the situation. He merely laughed over his sovereign and the pettiness of his Court. He was used to Papa's fretting, accustomed also to writing music to order, and it had never occurred to him that anyone could dislike him. Since his early years he had known only sudden friendships, followed by hasty, painful farewells, and changing impressions that had followed one another too swiftly to be fully grasped. Now

[71]

he rejoiced in planning his life for longer than a week or a month ahead. His drudgery at the Palace still seemed unreal. When he lifted his eyes from the music stand in front of him, he saw Life, painted in the brightest colors and usually reflected by a pair of eyes —blue, brown, or gray. He liked women and they liked him. He liked them all, whatever their name or social rank. Wolfgang was in love with love, with beauty, and with the charm of life.

1774, 1775, 1776. His features grew sharper, his nose and eyes more prominent. His rich crop of flaxen hair and his fine hands were the only beautiful things left of his once handsome appearance. When these hands, sparkling with valuable rings that were the gifts of princes, framed in lace cuffs which Mamma washed and pressed and ruffled untiringly, moved over the clavier keys, they evoked a wonderland of sounds. When they finally stopped and lay still on the keyboard while the dreamy eyes came back to earth and looked around, smiling, there was hardly a woman who could resist the charm of such hands and eyes.

Wolfgang loved fine clothes and wore them with taste and distinction. He felt at home in the private palaces of the Salzburg nobles and the comfortable drawing rooms of the rich bourgeoisie. He was amusing, witty, and extremely interesting when he told of countries and people they knew only by hearsay. This amiable young man, who had kissed the cheeks of the Empress and the ring of the Pope, under whose direction the most famous singers had sung to the cheers of the most illustrious audiences in the world, appeared to the mothers of Salzburg—and their daughters!—a most eligible youth. There were masked balls in the city hall, sleigh rides in fancy dress, private parties which kept Wolfgang dancing throughout the night to the sounds of his own music. He danced with incomparable grace.

The Mozarts, whose joint salaries were supplemented by earnings from teaching and compositions, were fairly comfortably off. They had moved from the Getreidegasse to larger quarters at the Hannibalplatz on the right hand side of the river. Family life revolved around Bimperl, their new dog. Wolfgang was very much in demand for lessons, and some Salzburgers have been immortalized through music he wrote for them and which carries their names. For the Countess Lodron and her two daughters he composed a concerto for three pianos (K. 242); for the Countess Lützow, wife of the fortress commander, a piano concerto (K. 246); for a wedding in Mayor Haffner's family, the famous *Haffner* Serenade (K. 250). (The no less famous *Haffner* Symphony [K. 385] was written in 1782, in Vienna, when Leopold urged his son to contribute to the celebration of Haffner's being raised to noble rank.) There were compositions for visiting artists and for his own use, such as his first five violin concertos.

On Sundays, the Mozarts saw the family friends; they had chamber music and games. *Bölzelschiessen* (shooting at targets from an air gun) was the favorite; the target was provided by some member of the small circle and decorated with a painted and rhymed allusion to someone's weakness or mishaps. Wolfgang seemed to enjoy himself thoroughly. But sometimes, when he had laughed until the tears came, played the fool in some disguise or danced until he lost his breath, he would stop for a moment, his chin would drop and a sudden painful sadness creep over him. It was like the transient sounds of melancholy in his music. What was he doing here? Why was he wasting his time? The master was rude and unappreciative, his colleagues were an inartistic, dissolute bunch of music-makers. "In Salzburg I always felt that I was writing for chairs and tables," he used to say later.

Since his return from Italy, there had been but two brief vacations: one to Vienna to seek an appointment, the other to Munich, which had commissioned an *opera buffa, La Finta giardiniera* (K. 196). Papa corresponded indefatigably with all sorts of people on his behalf. No luck.

If His Grace had tried to understand his subjects, Mozart's life might have taken a different turn. Accustomed to and craving affection, Wolfgang was ready to go all out for anyone who offered him a kind word. But in Hieronymus' opinion, young Mozart was too nonchalant in his manners, too sure of himself, too free in his speech, too independent artistically. As a lone token of appreciation, he ordered from him the music for *Il Rè pastore* (K. 208), a festival play to be given before visiting royalty; but mostly he was volubly abusive, and Wolfgang, who had grown up an obedient child unacquainted with harsh words, flinched under the undeserved rebukes. As a climax, the Archbishop told him that he ought to study composition at the Naples Conservatory!

Wolfgang's amiable soul then learned to hate. He hated "the Mufti," as he called Hieronymus. He hated his coarse colleagues in the orchestra. He even grew annoyed with his friends and their simple pleasures, and with himself for sharing them. Once, life had been easy and hard work rewarding; now work was easy, but life was difficult to bear and not rewarding at all.

"But, Wolfgang, open your eyes and look around," said his friend Father Dominicus, Hagenauer's son, one day in spring. "Salzburg is so beautiful!"

They had gone for a walk on the Mönchsberg, where they had met Abbé Bullinger, Papa's very best friend. Now the three of them were sitting on a bench with the city spread out below them, the pale young man between the old Abbé and the young priest. Wolfgang sighed and thought of Italy. His sad glance roamed the blooming landscape; stopped on a wide square surrounded by pompous buildings glowing in the sunlight.

"Maybe," he said. "But there is one dark spot in it." He pointed at the Archbishop's Residence.

"But it makes you write very good music."

"Good music? Well—*music,* I guess. I know it isn't bad; but if I were somewhere else . . . what music I could write. . . ."

Bullinger and Hagenauer exchanged a glance. There was nothing they could say.

Wolfgang went on. "You know, when I was away I missed you all terribly. Particularly in Italy, when Mamma and Nannerl had to stay here. Then I thought that home was where people loved you. But I find that this is not enough. My home is where I can make music. I mean MUSIC. Not forty-five-minute masses, and small pieces for salons, noisy—so that when His Grace takes part you don't hear his mistakes. No . . . this Salzburg is not my home. So I must go out and find it, for it must be somewhere."

Bullinger pressed his hand. Wolfgang murmured between his teeth: "I don't want to become another Michael Haydn."

"Don't you like Michael Haydn?" asked Hagenauer.

"He is a genius!" Wolfgang exclaimed. "Even Papa, who does not care for him because of his drinking, likes his music. If this man only had the kind of audience his brother has. . . . But look at him! Buried alive. What can he do *but* drink?"

"Have you made any plans?"

"We have a new plan every day," Wolfgang replied grimly. "But it's no use. You know that, Abbé, don't you? He wouldn't let us go. He says that he does not want his men to go 'begging.' And that's that."

They sat silent for a long time. The sun was setting behind the fortress, now dipped into pinkish gray light and fantastically near. Finally they rose and walked down the hill. They passed through the narrow streets, now full of people hurrying home from work. On the bridge that crossed the Salzach, Wolfgang stopped for a moment and looked down at the waves.

"They have a long way to go to get to Vienna," he said in a low voice. "But they will get there eventually."

Leopold knew that Wolfgang dreamed of going to Vienna. But no important posts were open there, and the Mozarts could no longer count on the Court. In 1773 the Empress had received them graciously, but by this time she had lost all her former interest in music, while the Emperor was mostly away on unpleasant political missions. Offering more promise of success was a tour of the numerous courts of southern Germany; any one of them was livelier and less stingy than Salzburg. But how to get away?

Wolfgang eagerly advocated breaking up their home in Salzburg and traveling around *en famille* as they had done in the good old days. But Papa objected strongly. Nannerl had been an attraction only as a child prodigy, and even Wolfgang had just started to establish himself beyond that.

Leopold again tried the impossible. He applied for a leave of absence for them both. The answer was a blunt refusal. Although a favorable decision would have been a tremendous surprise, the order to stay was most offensive. Finally, and unwillingly, His Grace hinted that he might permit Wolfgang to go alone.

"Impossible," Leopold cried out. "You will get stranded . . . the worst things can happen. . . ." Wolfgang was so easy to handle. Some bad woman might get hold of him . . . new friends exploit him . . . he might lose his luggage . . . he would visit the wrong people and say the wrong things . . . be cheated by innkeepers. . . . No, Wolfgang had never been away from his father, and Leopold did not feel like risking the experiment.

"Is it really so bad?" asked Mamma when they were alone. "Why not stay at home like everybody else? Why split up if God doesn't want it?"

There was a timid reproach in her words. She had a strong aversion to traveling. She had suffered a good deal from Leopold's restlessness and had borne it without complaint.

"Do try to understand me," Leopold replied gloomily. "Wolferl cannot be happy here. Look at the orchestra people. There is much talent among them, but it has been drowned in routine and alcohol. Do you want Wolferl to go on forever playing the fiddle in this atmosphere of bad moods and low company? Luck may be around the corner—but he must go and meet it."

Anna Maria nodded. Her darling, her Wolferl, an aging fiddler given to drinking? No. Even if it meant painful separation, he had to meet luck, and be happy, famous, rich. . . .

She bravely swallowed her tears. Something in her spoke, and she listened with surprise to her own voice: "If you have to stay here, Leopold, then I shall go with him." Yes, she would go with him, be it even to Germany with its bad religious habits or to France with its bad morals.

"You?" said Leopold. "You, Anna? But he twists you around

his little finger? You can't deny him anything! And how will you be able to manage all the details?"

"He must meet luck, mustn't he? And he can't go alone. And you can't go. So it's my turn. I shall keep his clothes in order, and shall talk him out of nonsense. It won't be for long. He'll find a position soon, I'm sure."

For the first time in many weeks, Leopold slept through the night.

When Wolfgang applied for his leave of absence that was already half granted, His Grace again made "some most gracious objections." The preparations for the voyage were interrupted. Leopold paced the room again in helpless rage. Wolfgang said nothing and retired. When he was sure that everybody was asleep, he slipped out of his bed, lit a candle, took a pen, paper and ink, and wrote for the better part of the night. He folded the sheet carefully, sealed it, and hid it in the pocket of his livery.

The next day he announced to his family that he had just handed in his resignation.

"For Heaven's sake!" Papa exclaimed. "Now we can all go begging."

"You don't mean that you are going to adopt the Mufti's way of expressing himself?" Wolfgang joked. Leopold continued to breathe heavily, growing pale and red by turns. "Seriously Papa, would you mind if you lost your job? Can't I support us all? But I don't think that he'll let you go. He needs you too badly."

Wolfgang was right. The Archbishop, furious that this boy had dared to defy him, first dismissed both the Mozarts. Then he changed his mind. That boy was a trouble-maker. Let him go to the dogs! But the father, though he, too, was difficult, at least tried to appear submissive. He was a useful man. Leopold was ordered to stay.

With his service nearly ended for good—so Wolfgang thought—his high spirits returned. He sang and joked all day. He danced around the room with Nannerl. In vain Leopold tried to impress upon him the seriousness of his responsibilities and the possibility of complications. "Papa comes right after God," Wolfgang would exclaim, and burst into laughter.

Sometimes Wolfgang would find Mamma crying over the pieces of luggage, clothes, music, and a million little things. Then he grew tender, kissed her, and promised that it would be Heaven.

He liked the idea of traveling with Mamma. She understood him well and accepted his little whims. They would have good fun. She was easily pleased and amused. They were so much alike. He knew a lot about traveling by now, and for the first time he could show himself as a cavalier who took care of a lady.

Leopold, in his turn, could not imagine home without his wife. And how would she stand the strain? How would Wolfgang, so inexperienced and light-headed, look after her health and comfort? More than once he thought of calling everything off until he himself could get away. But then he looked into the boy's happy face, heard his chatter, watched him select his music to take with him, heard him practice the piano and the violin—and knew that to hold him back would be a crime which God would never forgive.

With an aching heart and in spite of an attack of illness, Leopold supervised the packing, bought a good carriage, sat down to write lists of the people whom Wolfgang was to see, and procured letters of credit and letters of introduction. He made no speech. He patted Wolferl's cheeks with a forced smile and kissed Mamma good-by with red eyes. He would never see her again.

CHAPTER 10

PRELUDE

[1777]

WHEN THE LAST CLOUD of dust behind the departing carriage had disappeared, Nannerl burst into hysterical sobs. Leopold put his arm around her, and together they went slowly upstairs.

Nannerl flung herself on the sofa and wept bitterly. Papa sat down beside her, took her hand and began to talk, reassuring her, and himself, that this had been the only solution and that they must try to make the best of it.

Nannerl finally stopped crying. She had a headache, she said, and would try to sleep. She closed the shutters and went to bed. Papa was sweet to comfort her with his own heart so heavy. But she had hardly ever been without her mother, and if she had ever needed Mamma, she needed her now. She was already twenty-six! Whom could she talk to about how she felt when it crept up in her—that deadly fear of remaining alone? Papa, in his room, said fervent prayers before falling asleep.

This was on September 23, 1777. Two days later they had Wolfgang's first letter. He was proud and happy. He felt even more important than on their earlier travels when he had been the star. For now he was the boss. It was he who dealt with the postillions and porters, and he tried to talk and look as dignified as possible —a distinguished and experienced gentleman en route. "I am just a second Papa," he wrote, and added, merry as a schoolboy who has escaped classes: ". . . and, please, always remember as we do that our Mufti H.C. is an idiot, but God is compassionate, merciful and loving. . . ."

"My dear Wolfgang, I beg you to write no more jokes about our Mufti," was Papa's first reaction. "Remember that *I* am in Salzburg. . . ." He had just received a silly and offensive reminder "to conduct himself calmly and peaceably with the Kapellmeister and other persons appointed to the court orchestra . . . and render good service both to the Church and to His Grace's person." Thank God Wolfgang had escaped! Leopold had a good laugh over his son's letter. But he was afraid the boy would never be "a second Papa."

For many years his son had filled his life. When Leopold came home, he still expected to hear the sound of his music. Would Wolferl miss him as much as he missed Wolferl? Somehow he had a strange premonition that their happy family life had gone to pieces with the carriage turning around the corner.

The spare time that had hitherto been devoted to Wolfgang was to be given to music lessons, resumed now to meet the heavy expenses. In long night vigils he wrote his travelers elaborate letters of directions that covered everything: how to dress, what to eat, how to behave, whom to see and what to say. Don't you need the gray trousers? And, by the way, remember to have the stretchers put into your boots at night. . . .

Wolfgang's questions, marked with a red pencil, and a list of the things he wanted to mention were spread out before Leopold as he wrote. He expected Wolfgang to do the same, but the boy was sometimes too careless. And he hardly ever wrote about money matters—the most vital problem; neither did Mamma.

But even if Wolfgang did not reply to all of the million-and-one questions, he did not dream of doing anything contrary to Papa's instructions. Not yet. He wore the garments Papa had selected; saw the people Papa wanted him to see; played what Papa had suggested he should play; he had his music re-copied for possible sponsors, as Papa had advised, and on the very path that Papa had prescribed, ran into the trap which Papa dreaded most.

Leopold and Wolfgang had expected that the Elector of Munich, who had heard the young man as a child and had later commissioned *La Finta giardiniera,* would offer him some sort of assignment. But Maximilian III gave all kinds of excuses. Wolfgang was too young for a permanent position at his Court. Too old for a child prodigy, too young for a Court Conductor. The first cloud appeared on the serene sky of Wolfgang's hopes. And together with the cloud came the first fantastic schemes which would remain typical of Wolfgang and would drive Papa into frenzy while he sat helplessly at home, writing his fingers off in order to teach the boy method and system, and, above all, a sense of business.

From Northern Germany a new fashion had come: opera in German. Many theaters made a point of employing German singers and conductors, and giving Italian opera in translation until there should be a sufficient production of native works. Wolfgang had heard a German version of an opus by Piccini, and the Munich opera manager knew about his enthusiasm. This young Mozart might be the right person to grow up together with the young art. If he pledged himself to write four operas a year—two comic and two serious—he would give him a nominal guarantee. Did he have any other source of income? Would his father take care of the rest?

Wolfgang knew there was little sense even in trying. But Herr Albert, their innkeeper, who was known for his interest in music and had good connections, declared himself ready to set up a committee of private sponsors to cover the deficit, and a substantial addition would come from the customary performances for the composer's benefit.

At this point Wolfgang wrote to Papa. He would eat very little, drink nothing, and be mostly invited out anyway. In a year or two he would be the most prominent promoter of national opera in Southern Germany, and Papa and Nannerl could move to

Munich out of the Mufti's reach. He was already so popular in Munich! The Elector would soon ask for him instead of having to be approached hat-in-hand, and since he had heard young Mlle. Keiser sing in the Piccini opera, he was "simply itching" to write an original. So what did Papa think of this idea? Wasn't Herr Albert a nice man? Wasn't it simply splendid?

Papa pounded the table with his fist. People were gossiping about Wolfgang's tremendous success with the Elector, about a present that would take care of his entire journey, after which both he and Leopold would receive an appointment for an astronomical fee. Now the fabulous sponsor turned out to be an innkeeper who knew some people! The Archbishop would have a good laugh. Herr Albert certainly meant well, and if he really found these generous one-ducat-a-month friends, plus a guarantee that they would keep their promises, Wolfgang could always return to Munich later. But now, for Heaven's sake, let him keep going!

It was probably mere vanity that caused Leopold to suggest that Wolfgang visit Augsburg, his native town. Nothing could be expected from the narrow-minded, conceited burghers and their stuffy magistrates. But Leopold's brother lived in Augsburg, a humble bookbinder as their father had been, and Leopold wanted his family to see how much better he had fared. Franz Aloys Mozart was good-natured and without envy. He asked his nephew and sister-in-law to stay with them, and assigned his eighteen-year-old daughter to show her cousin around town.

Anna Maria Thekla Mozart, whom Wolfgang called *Bäsle,* was plump and plain, and entirely lacking in talent of any sort. But she had other qualities which made her appear to him glamorous and brilliant. What attracted him in particular was her sense of humor. Coarse jokes were customary in eighteenth-century middle-class families. Mamma loved them and so did Wolfgang, and Papa was so used to them that he did not mind.

For two weeks Bäsle was Wolfgang's untiring companion. Later he sent her a number of letters that are mostly eliminated from the collections for reasons of delicacy.

Wolfgang always loved nonsensical letters. Puns and distorted words, impossible dates, non-existent places, senseless rhymes, endless repetitions. There is a certain rhythm in these letters, perceptible to the reader who merely listens to the intrinsic sound of the words. Forms of musical structure appear in them—variations, rondos, canons, dances. The letters to Bäsle to whom Wolfgang had nothing serious to say, were mere buffoonery, and often impossible.

If it had not been for Bäsle, Wolfgang would probably have turned on his heel and cleared out of his father's native town as soon as he poked his nose into it. Consideration for his father's home town, however, made him put on his most charming smile and play at the home of the Magistrate and at a "beggarly" academy. At least it gave him satisfaction that a notice about this concert appeared in an Augsburg paper, one of the papers the Mufti used to read.

But even dreary Augsburg had a musical attraction ready for Wolfgang. Since his early Paris days, he had preferred the sound of the piano to that of the harpsichord. And here was that man Stein, organ builder by profession, piano builder by hobby. His instruments had an even, long-lasting tone. They were by far the best that Wolfgang had ever played. More artist than artisan, Stein loved his instruments as though they were human beings. When he had finished one, he sat down patiently and tried it out, modeled and remodeled it until it was perfect. A new method of gluing made it durable, unaffected by atmospheric changes, and well worth its three hundred gulden.

Stein had seen Wolfgang fifteen years ago when Leopold had bought a portable clavier from him on their grand tour. Wolfgang was sure he would not be recognized.

"My name is Trazom," he introduced himself, "and I am a music student from Munich." He loved to use the reverse of his name as a jest. Stein wondered but was not sure. Then Wolfgang started to play. And Stein knew.

Wolfgang's piano playing was indeed exceptional. Both his dexterity and expression were unique. The singing quality of *bel canto* had entered into his execution; the right hand was like the human voice and could enjoy some freedom of interpretation, while the left hand kept the piece going. Wolfgang could not understand why people were surprised that he kept strict time. It was so simple! Just a trick. Don't permit the left hand to yield to the right in *espressivo* passages . . . but *rubato?* Of course, you must play *rubato!* Many pianists still believe that *rubato* playing in eighteenth-century music should be taboo; this, however, is not true in the case of Mozart. As a virtuoso also he was ahead of his time.

Wolfgang gave Stein another surprise when he insisted on trying his organs. To the piano fan, the organ was void of expression. Perfect pianists were bound to be bad organists, and vice versa, Stein thought. Wolfgang gave most generous proofs to the contrary in the very churches and monasteries where his father had bustled about as a choir boy. Bäsle sat admiring in the nave and was very much in love.

Wolfgang still wrote Papa everything. Leopold was clever enough not to object to his son's small affairs—as long as they remained small. By the time Wolfgang left Augsburg, all Salzburg knew about his weakness for his cousin. In one of the next shooting games of the Mozart clique, the target showed a young man in a traveler's outfit and an Augsburg girl weeping bitter tears into an oversized sheet.

By this time Wolfgang was already in Mannheim, in the hands of destiny.

CHAPTER II

MANNHEIM, FRIENDSHIP AND LOVE

[1777-78]

PAPA didn't think it funny at all. He was sitting with Wolfgang's latest letter in his hand, dated November 14-16, 1777, from Mannheim. Doubtless Wolfgang had enjoyed himself hugely while writing it.

I, Johannes, Chrysostomus, Amadeus, Wolfgangus, Sigismundus Mozart, plead guilty to having both yesterday and the day before (and very often besides) stayed away from home till twelve o'clock at night . . . making doggerel rhymes with the utmost facility. . . . I should not, however, have conducted myself in so reckless a manner if our ringleader, the so-called Liesl [Elisabeth Cannabich] had not inveigled me to mischief, and I am bound to admit that I took great pleasure in it myself. I confess all these my sins and shortcomings from the depths of my heart; and in the hope of often having similar ones to confess, I am firmly resolved to amend my present sinful life. I therefore beg for a dispensation if it can be granted; but, if not, it is a matter of indifference to me, for the game will go on all the same. . . .

No—Papa didn't think it funny at all. Here they were at home, he and Nannerl, slaving from morning to night and saving pennies, so that Wolfgang might have this fine opportunity. Leopold's dressing-gown was so worn that he had to deny himself to chance callers, and in winter he would have to use Wolfgang's old felt shoes to protect himself from the cold. He liked teaching as little as did Wolfgang, and yet every spare hour was taken up with instruction. At night he was coaching Nannerl so that she might take care of herself in an emergency. And the boy on whose account all this was done had the nerve to write rigmaroles! It seemed as if all advice and orders were wasted.

As a matter of fact, Wolfgang did follow instructions, circumstances permitting. But his heart was no longer in it. The boy had never before been faced with practical things. Moreover, he had never known the proper balance of music and fun; there had always been too much of the one and too little of the other. Like many a youth whose education has been overdone by a dominating father, he had grown tired of obeying minute orders and now longed to decide at least small details for himself. And in this frame of mind, he had to come to Mannheim, of all places.

Mannheim, capital of the Palatinate, had the liveliest Court in Germany and in Karl Theodor the most popular Elector. His figure was majestic, his smile irresistible. Infatuated with France, he had succeeded in making his Court a miniature Versailles and his capital a miniature Paris. Nature, indeed, had bestowed upon him all the weaknesses of the French kings, but his good heart saved him from their despotism. The liberal atmosphere of his Court and its epicurean pleasures were enthusiastically copied by his subjects.

Love of splendor had made Mannheim an undisputed cultural center of Germany. Libraries, art collections, and academies mushroomed. The dominant influence of Italy in art was overcome for good. Wolfgang had the chance to watch the poet Wieland and the composer Schweitzer experiment on German opera.

The reputation of its Court orchestra, dating back to the 1740's and the leadership of the fascinating Bohemian, Johann Wenzel Anton Stamitz, had raised the city to musical prominence. Gradually, there developed an entirely new idiom of expression which consisted chiefly in the art of building up climaxes. A new balance of instrumental groups created colors undreamed of before. This, and experiments with structural and thematic work, reflected strongly upon the growth of classical symphony which was taking place just then. Many novel developments had originated elsewhere, but so impressive must have been the exploits of the Mannheimers that they were credited with them all for a long time. In the history of music the group has become known as the Mannheim School, and Mozart's early models, Johann Schobert and Johann Christian Bach, were among its disciples.

When Mozart came to Mannheim, the orchestra was headed by the Viennese Ignaz Holzbauer and the Mannheimer Christian Cannabich. The players were inspiring artists, each unexcelled on his instrument. Twelve years earlier, Mozart had played with the orchestra in Schwetzingen, and in Paris he had met Cannabich. Some musicians remembered him, or his name. The others first sneered at the small young man when Cannabich brought him to a rehearsal. Wolfgang noted this with some resentment. He was firmly determined to show them how far his artistic capacities went beyond his physique.

Cannabich and Wendling, the first flutist, opened their gay houses to Mamma and Wolfgang. Here they met everyone: Ramm, the oboist; Ritter, the bassoonist; Lang, the horn player; Fränzl, Cannabich's favorite violin pupil; and Raaff, the famous aging tenor. Wendling's brother was a violinist; his wife and sister-in-law were opera singers. His daughter Augusta, or Mlle. Gustl as friends called her, was frail and ailing, but of rare beauty. In this atmosphere of talent and gaiety, Wolfgang felt perfectly at ease. He was pleasantly surprised to see how these people belied what Papa had always said about musicians. Since early youth, Wolfgang had been led to consider every musician a potential enemy. But here they were agreeable and helpful; they were the aristocrats of their profession. What amount of discipline in their work, of artistic devotion, and of honesty, compared with the Mufti's band! Gradually, he presented them all with gems from his musical treasury; he also helped Cannabich with piano scores of his ballets, and for charming Rosl, Cannabich's young daughter who had become his pupil, he wrote a sonata with an adagio "just like her."

Shortly after he arrived, Wolfgang's new friends managed that he give a concert at Court. It was a big success and Karl Theodor's natural amiability led to exaggerated hopes. He had even hinted that it would not be impossible to have Wolfgang write German opera. So the Mozarts prepared to stay, perhaps all winter. His friends tried to secure a position for him as a chamber-music composer at Court. Also, he hoped to be appointed music teacher to the Elector's children. But Karl Theodor did not want to be rushed in his decisions. Gala days, hunting parties, and other pleasures prevented the matter from being clinched.

It was almost December. Wolfgang and Mamma shared a tiny hotel room. It was no use looking for private lodgings until they should be sure of their plans. Though they spent as little as they could, the lengthening visit was a heavy drain on their purse. Wolfgang had to be well dressed and soon he would need a barber. They were mostly invited out for meals, but the few they had to pay for were expensive. The only saving Mamma could think of was on heat. She had small fires lit in the morning and at night. During the day it was bitter cold in the room, and Mamma got the worst of it. Since she had no umbrella and did not want to buy one, bad weather always kept her at home, where she sat with her fur coat and felt shoes on, her stiff blue fingers turning the pages of the Bible or writing pathetic little notes to Salzburg. However confident she was of ultimate success, this hotel life was a nightmare.

On December 8, the answer finally came. There was a gala concert at Court, and Wolfgang sat in the audience. The manager, Count Savioli, who had promised to act on his behalf, conspicuously evaded his eyes. With desperate determination Wolfgang addressed him:

"Still no reply?"

"Sorry. Very sorry, indeed. There is nothing to be done at present."

Intrigues? Probably. But there were still his friends.

Wolfgang stormed to the Cannabichs'. Christian was away on a hunting trip. His wife and daughter were thunderstruck. Everybody wept. But tears would not help; something more substantial had to be done.

Next day, the flutist Wendling presented a perfect plan. He had rounded up a sponsor. M. de Jean, a wealthy Dutch amateur, was ready to pay two hundred gulden for a few concertos and quartets for flute—the instrument Wolfgang disliked above all others. But two hundred gulden would be a foundation to build on. In addition there would be lessons; and duos for violin and piano to be engraved by subscription; and a mass to be dedicated to the Elector. Wolfgang could give instruction in exchange for board and room for himself and Mamma. Then, on March 6, together with Wendling, Ramm, and Lang, he would leave for Paris, and all four would give concerts. Mamma could travel home by way of Augsburg.

At last Papa agreed; anything was acceptable to him, as long as Wolfgang made some money and got to Paris eventually. Mamma had assured him that Wendling would care for Wolfgang as if he were his son. She could be spared the tiresome trip and Leopold the expense.

Then, on December 30, the Elector of Bavaria died of smallpox, and with him his line died out. Karl Theodor, proclaimed his successor, hurried to Munich in order to protect his new domain against possible Austrian claims or Prussian invasion. Soon it became known that he would stay there for good with all his retinue. Overnight, gay Mannheim had become a minor provincial town.

The official mourning canceled all performances and the usual Carnival activities. Everybody's plans were changed and Wolfgang, too, had to reconsider his own. He felt that Karl Theodor, despite his reluctance to appoint him in Mannheim, liked him well enough to call him to Munich eventually. In Vienna, a new opera group was being formed to try out national *Singspiel,* in German; the

Emperor might need a young Kapellmeister who knew the language. But the trip to Paris with Wendling and his party, now to be started already in mid-February, was still uppermost in Wolfgang's mind.

Wolfgang could never have known that his fortune, career, and lifelong happiness were taking a decisive turn when, upon inquiring for someone to copy his music, he was referred to one Fridolin Weber, singer, copyist, and prompter at the theater.

"Won't he charge me very much?" he asked.

"Not *you*. He is sort of crazy. They say he was a lawyer or something of that sort, but gave it all up for the sake of music. Now they are giving him some odd jobs to keep his family from starving. It is pathetic."

Pathetic, indeed, was the street where the Webers lived. The snow that had fallen a week before had not been removed. Large puddles of slush made the sidewalk almost impassable. A blast of unseasonably warm wind caught Wolfgang's coat. He drew it tight around him until he finally reached the shabby house. The hallway smelled of cabbage and rancid fat. The steps were rickety and dark. Wolfgang groped his way upstairs trying not to fall or get entangled with his sword.

A soprano voice of unusual quality reached his ear from above. He stopped. The voice was young, elastic and crystal clear—a soul singing itself out in complete darkness, Wolfgang thought, and wondered whether he had heard those words somewhere or whether his lips had shaped them by themselves.

He stood there for a long time.

"Excuse me."

Wolfgang turned around to find a very young girl standing behind him and waiting politely for him to step aside. He could not see her face distinctly, but he did see black curls and small black eyes. He pulled himself together.

"Can you tell me where Herr Weber lives?" he asked.

"There, upstairs," said the girl. "Don't you hear the singing?

That's my sister Aloysia. We call her Luise. Herr Weber is my Papa. I am Constanze. Wait, I'll show you."

The two mounted the stairs together. "So that's your sister," Wolfgang said thoughtfully. He had to talk to someone about it, even to this little creature whose face he had hardly seen.

"Yes, haven't you heard her at the opera? Or maybe you don't go to the opera? Papa works there too, you know."

Wolfgang could hardly restrain his impatience to get upstairs. Aloysia Weber—he remembered the name vaguely. Constanze opened the door and left him standing on the threshold. "A gentleman who wants to talk to Papa!" she screamed at the top of her lungs and ran into the other room. The singing stopped.

Four pairs of feet sprang up. Four pairs of black eyes stared at him. Mme. Weber struggled with the strings of a dirty apron, which she tried to remove unobserved. A girl who had been sitting with her at the window put something quickly into a drawer. Another child, still younger than Constanze, hastily rose from the floor and withdrew into a corner, clutching a rag doll in her arms.

Wolfgang did not notice the disorder and embarrassment that his sudden appearance caused. His eyes sought the piano. During the few moments on the staircase behind Constanze it had suddenly given him a shock to think: What if she is ugly?

She stood in front of the piano with her hands resting behind her on the lid that she had closed automatically. She had lively black eyes, soft dark curls, and the most perfect figure Wolfgang had ever seen. She looked older than her sixteen years, and her occasional public appearances had given her some poise. When Wolfgang's eager eyes met hers, she ventured a smile.

"Oh, Kapellmeister Mozart!" Fridolin Weber bustled in and greeted Wolfgang noisily. "Do you want me to copy something for you?"

"The French ariette for Mlle. Wendling—not very long."

"You'll have it shortly. Know who this is?" he said to his family. "This is Kapellmeister Mozart, Knight of the Golden Spur, member of—"

"Oh, please. . . ." Wolfgang protested.

"All right. This is my wife [Cäcilia Weber extended her hand], and these are my daughters: Josefa who helps my wife to keep house, and Aloysia [Wolfgang turned scarlet] who helps me to make some money with her singing; you know Constanze, and the little shrimp over there is Sophie. You see, Herr Kapellmeister," he added jovially, "we don't have a very comfortable home, but we all love music."

"I hope it will be comfortable enough for Kapellmeister Mozart to have some coffee and cake with us," Cäcilia Weber broke in. She was always slightly irritated when her husband became talkative.

"No, thank you, no indeed." Wolfgang was confused. "I couldn't stay. . . . Maybe some other day . . . ," he added quickly. He was expected at Cannabich's and was pressed for time. He had not anticipated that he would fall in love. The few moments he had should not be wasted on banalities. Something had to be done, something had to be said . . . but what?

"I heard your daughter singing as I came upstairs." He wanted to be casual but his voice was just a shade too high with excitement. "There must indeed be musical talent in the family!"

Now it was Aloysia's turn to blush. Mozart . . . she had heard about him. She had not imagined him so small and shy. He had written opera for Italy . . . wanted to write one in German . . . powerful Herr Cannabich was his friend . . . he was writing arias for Mlle. Gustl, that dilettante . . . an angry determination rose in her while her lips smiled and her little brain wondered how to go about it.

Mother Cäcilia knew how to go about it. She had observed Wolfgang shrewdly. She was, in fact, the one who ran the family—calculating and persistent, boastful in success, hysterical in failure. She loved intriguing and always knew how to cover it up with convincing exhibitions of honesty. This young Mozart was no problem for her.

"Maybe Kapellmeister Mozart would like to hear you sing some more?" she asked sweetly.

Aloysia was not prepared . . . she did not know what . . . But Wolfgang was eager.

"Anything, Mademoiselle, anything you like. Maybe you would like to try this." He pointed to the manuscript he had brought.

Aloysia looked at it furtively. "I am afraid this is too light for my voice."

"Don't be fussy," her mother interrupted. "Do it as well as you can." What possessed Aloysia to act so coy?

"All right." Aloysia gave in and tried to act the perfect prima donna. "If you will forgive occasional slips . . ."

Wolfgang was already seated at the piano. Aloysia stood next to him. He saw her black curls, her white forehead, her shining eyes. He listened with admiration. A perfect musician, he thought. Her voice lent itself to anything. She could do with it whatever she wanted, without effort.

The light mood of the French song entered into their hearts. When they had finished, they looked at each other and smiled. Wolfgang bowed lightly, Aloysia made a mock curtsy. Their initial shyness had gone.

"We must do this again, Mlle. Aloysia . . . Luise—do you realize how well you sing?"

His voice quivered when he took his leave.

As the outside door closed, Aloysia burst out passionately: "That was no song for me! Why did you make me do it? He won't come back!"

"You sang well, Luise," said Fridolin.

"He *will* come back," said Cäcilia with a cynical laugh.

Constanze said nothing. She was only fourteen.

CHAPTER 12

ARDENT INTERLUDE
[1778]

O N HIS WAY to the Cannabichs', the mud and the darkness forced Wolfgang to watch his step and distracted
him from thinking. When he reached broader streets
that were better lighted, he looked around. How had it ever escaped
him that Mannheim was such a wonderful place? Mannheim, wonderful city! Aloysia, beautiful name! Aloysia . . . Luise . . . these
two versions of her name were just like her. "Aloysia" it had been
when he had heard her on the stairway, remote, full of pathos and
mystery. But when she had looked down on him with a mischiev-
ous smile while she sang the tittering French words—she had been
"Luise," agreeable, light-hearted. She was the girl for whom he
wanted to write, perhaps to live. He would compose and she would
sing. Wherever he might be, he would write opera, and she would
be the prima donna.

It was getting cold again. Thrusting his hands into his pockets,
Wolfgang felt something bulky. Oh, Papa's last letter. That reminded him. He and Mamma had brooded over it all morning.
These complicated money matters and traveling arrangements . . .
Wolfgang was handling them as best he could, but Papa was never
satisfied. Papa really ought to have more confidence in him. He
was grown up! He was in love!

Wolfgang was not the person to hide whatever occupied his
mind. Hardly arrived at the Cannabichs', he reported on his

[94]

visit to Weber. "And then his daughter sang for me . . . marvelous. . . ."

"She has remarkable talent and a good voice," Raaff responded, "but still untrained."

"Untrained . . . ?" Wolfgang echoed abstractedly.

The others were startled. Was this Wolfgang, usually so cynical about the slightest flaws of celebrities?

Most of Wolfgang's spare time was now spent coaching Aloysia. Gossip spread. Wolfgang, however, was so naïve as to believe that people suspected nothing beyond a sympathetic interest in a poor but gifted girl.

Actually, their impoverished circumstances were a strong factor in his attachment to the Webers, from which he was unable to free himself for the rest of his life. The Mozarts, too, had often had to be thrifty. But their apartment was fastidiously clean; they all wore decent clothes and had their hair nicely dressed. They always had a servant and sometimes two. In their darkest times they never had come to consider themselves poor people; they were honorable bourgeois, temporarily short of funds.

But the Webers were really *poor*. They did not bother to keep up appearances. Their chairs were shaky, their dishes chipped or broken, their attire untidy. When Wolfgang sat at the piano and listened to Aloysia's heavenly voice filling the shabby room, while Papa Weber copied his music and Josefa prepared her thin coffee, his eyes would moisten with love and pity. He was determined to provide a settled life for his beloved and her entire family, of whom he grew ever fonder.

Was Aloysia in love with him? He did not question it. Her enthusiasm for music swept him off his feet, and her curious mixture of light-headedness and shrewdness—heritage from both parents—easily gave her the upper hand over the hopelessly frank Wolfgang, who was so much in love.

Mamma Mozart was no psychologist, but she had sound instincts. Once she ventured a timid remonstrance: Would Papa like it that Wolfgang spent so much time with these Webers? Wolfgang was hurt and showed it. He had become very touchy recently. Papa's well-meant instructions had already upset him, and now Mamma had started too—Mamma, of all people, who had always sided with him.

"You see, darling," she said helplessly, "I am responsible for you. We all want you to be happy."

As long as Wolfgang could remember, someone had been "responsible" for him and "wanted him to be happy." Now 'he was responsible for Aloysia, and this would take care of his happiness too. Affection for his parents and the urgent desire to free himself from their control, struggled in him while he said casually:

"Look, Mamma, Herr Weber is copying all my music for nothing. We have agreed that I should teach his daughter in return. And I couldn't find a better singer for my arias."

Saving a few kreutzer and giving his whole heart, Mamma thought. But she said nothing.

Wolfgang sat down to work on a quartet for M. de Jean. Suddenly he looked up. He could not bear it any longer. "Mamma," he asked with a low voice, "is it so bad when a man is in love?"

Anna Maria went over to him and stroked his hair. Wolfgang took her hand and kissed it.

"Please, Mamma, don't write anything to Papa. Promise, will you?"

Anna Maria promised. Why, after all, should she cause Leopold to worry? There would be small sense in scolding or reasoning. Wolfgang would get over it in Paris. This was perhaps just another of his little affairs. . . .

In the middle of January, the Princess of Nassau-Weilburg—the same Princess whom the Mozarts had visited in The Hague—sent word that she would like to hear Wolfgang again. She now lived only a ten-hour ride from Mannheim. She had her own small orchestra which played every day, and she was especially fond of singing.

There was no permanent assignment to be hoped for, but Wolfgang anticipated a nice present. He would take her copies of the *Lucio Silla* arias and a little symphony.

He announced to Mamma that he was leaving for a few days on a concert tour. She could safely stay at Mannheim meanwhile. And, by the way, Aloysia Weber would be coming along to introduce the arias, and her father too, of course, as a chaperon.

There was no time left to consult Leopold and early one morning Wolfgang, Fridolin, and Aloysia left in a hired carriage. Wolfgang took care of all the traveling arrangements. For days he would be in the company of his beloved. They would share applause and presents, and on Sunday they would hear Mass together. He was deliriously happy. He wished the ten-day trip could last for ten years—no, for a lifetime! All day long he could watch her slightest movements—the way she ate, how she put on her cape, how she turned the pages of a book, how she greeted people—all delightful revelations.

Aloysia showed enthusiasm for everything. This made him even happier. He had seen her only in the impoverished Weber home, but not even the Princess' castle was really good enough. He would build her castles. They would travel together and have the world at their feet.

She was grateful for the little he had to offer now, mended some of his clothes in return—and smiled. He was madly in love and felt tremendously important as someone's sponsor. (So important did he feel that he paid for part of Fridolin's and Aloysia's expenses along with his own, and he was so much in love that he did not notice how easily they gave in to his generosity.)

The concerts at the Princess' were a great success, but the money return was just average. Wolfgang's share was not more than seven ducats, and now hardly forty-four gulden remained. Papa was not likely to be pleased.

Back in Mannheim he found a letter from Leopold: The Emperor in Vienna did not intend to appoint another composer. The first *Singspiel* was being written by one Umlauff, a member of the opera orchestra, and the future of the undertaking was still uncertain. Friends had suggested that Wolfgang ought to try a work of this kind and submit it to Joseph II in person. The Mesmers would be glad to have him stay with them whenever he came to Vienna.

At this Wolfgang sneered. Take a chance? When he felt surer of himself than ever? And a comic opera in German? His girl's voice was created to sing Italian *opera seria*. He would write for her so she could sing—and in Italy! How remote all were—Salzburg and Paris—even Vienna . . .

He hinted to his Mannheim friends that he might not accompany them to Paris for that series of concerts after all. Some very important letters had come in . . . perhaps he would join them later. Eventually they left without him.

To Mamma he did not say much, but it was enough to make the poor woman cross herself and fall back into a chair, too disturbed to start an argument.

But there was still Papa. . . .

Energetically, Wolfgang sat down to write. He gave a lengthy description of his recent journey with this "thoroughly honest, good, Catholic Christian family." He chose the words of praise Papa might have chosen.

And for the friends with whom he had planned the Paris trip, he chose the words of blame Papa used for people who had disappointed him: Wendling had no religion whatsoever. Ramm, too, was a libertine. He could not travel with such people. Why, he wouldn't know what to talk about! So he had another idea.

Up to this point it had gone well. But this idea—how to put it? His hand trembled. He turned around.

"Mamma," he asked meekly, "do you think Papa will say yes?"

"I don't know, Wolferl," came the faint voice out of the armchair. "You just ask him. . . ."

Wolfgang continued his letter:

I propose to remain here and finish entirely at my leisure that music for de Jean. . . . In the meantime, Herr Weber will endeavor to get engagements here and there for concerts with me, and we shall then travel together. When I am with him, it is just as if I were traveling with you. . . . If my mother were not, as you know, too comfortably lazy to write, she would tell you the very same thing! I must confess that I much enjoyed traveling with them. We were happy and merry; I was hearing a man talk like you; I had nothing to worry about; I found my torn clothes mended; in short, I was waited on like a prince.

I have become so fond of this unfortunate family that my dearest wish is to make them happy; and perhaps I may be able to do so. My advice is that they should go to Italy. . . .

I will gladly write an opera for Verona for fifty zecchini, if only in order that she [Aloysia] may make her name; for if I do not compose it, I fear that she may be victimized. By that time I shall have made so much money on the other journeys we propose to undertake together, that I shall not be the loser. I think we shall go to Switzerland and perhaps also to Holland. . . . If we stay anywhere for long, the eldest daughter will be very useful to us; for we could have our own ménage, as she can cook.

Reading this letter, Leopold did not get any farther than that. His fingers clenched, blood rose in his face. "Nannerl!" he screamed.

Nannerl was doing the linen upstairs, but the tone of Papa's voice made her rush down the steps in a hurry.

"Here!" Papa yelled. "Read this! Your brother has lost his mind!"

Nannerl read and burst into tears. "Wolferl is in love," she sobbed.

"In love!" Leopold mimicked furiously. "He *thinks* he is in love, the silly ass! And what does your mother do? Says yes to everything!"

"Oh, no," said Nannerl, pointing to a hurried little note at the bottom of the letter. It read:

My dear husband! You will have seen from this letter that when Wolfgang makes new acquaintances, he wants to give at once his life and property for them. True, *she* sings exceedingly well, still we must not lose sight of our own interests. . . . He would not have listened to me . . . he prefers other people to me. . . . I remonstrate with him about this and that and about things I do not like, and he objects to this. . . . I am writing this quite secretly while he is at dinner and I shall close for I do not want to be caught. . . .

Father Mozart spent a sleepless night. The boy lacked discrimination. ". . . Her father resembles my father and the whole family resemble the Mozarts . . . ," he had written. Leopold shook his head. How could Wolfgang make his way in this world? He befriended everybody in exchange for flattery. Instead of finishing the work for de Jean, he had taken the Webers on a pleasure trip, jeopardizing the two hundred gulden the Dutchman had promised to pay for prompt delivery, and in addition to this unheard-of frivolity, he had shared the Princess' present with this girl. He gave presents away and expected his father to make up the deficit.

In the black night, Leopold saw his life-work crumble. He saw his son, upon whom God had bestowed a miraculous gift, ensnared by some fourth-rate singer and her calculating family, ending in starvation and disgrace. On his knees Leopold prayed for strength to lead Wolfgang back to the right path.

For the next two days he wrote. Slowly, word by word, entirely worn out, he drafted the noblest letter of his life. This was a different Leopold from the unpleasant and slightly ridiculous person of former years; he was pathetic now when, aging and deprived of his wife's company, his hands tied by a despised sovereign, he struggled for his child's best interests and tried desperately to protect him from a danger that mostly lay within the boy himself; when all he had to give—love, reason, anxiety, and the experience of a lifetime— was helplessly poured out on a few sheets of paper.

Leopold carefully avoided any allusion to Wolfgang's feelings for "that girl." He soberly discussed the difficulties of getting a novice singer on the Italian stage and, praising his desire to help the poor, even suggested what Wolfgang might do about it later on—a scheme skillfully designed to encourage his immediate ambition to make money and a reputation. He recalled to the boy their happy days together in the past. He flattered and implored, appealed to gratitude and duty, and finally ordered: "Find your place among great people. *Aut Caesar aut nihil.* Mamma is to go to Paris with Wolfgang."

This was final. Wolfgang accepted the verdict with adult dignity. He had never considered the project seriously—not at all, he feebly protested. Oh, yes, Papa came right after God, and must please think no evil of him.

But there were more letters. With the immediate danger forestalled, Leopold's old energies came back. With painstaking care, he pulled the boy's character to pieces; commented sharply on his search for kindness—which was "vanity"; on his natural behavior—which was "making himself cheap." An entire letter was devoted to his son's reprehensible attitude towards money.

Wolfgang became actually ill for two days. Recovering, he penned elaborate protestations of filial devotion. Coming tragedy was still hidden under emphatic assurances of mutual confidence and love. But there was one gap that could not be bridged, this gap of fundamental difference of character. Leopold's inelastic and bureaucratical mind kept him businesslike—even in matters of emotion; while Wolfgang, true son of his Austrian mother and her country, was thoroughly emotional—even in business.

Obediently, Wolfgang went about the preparations for the Paris journey, hiding his broken heart. If he had any comfort, it was the prospect of opportunities in Paris which might bring quick success and the possibility of early marriage.

He would leave Aloysia a present—an aria. He had a strange text on hand, a piece by Metastasio dealing with a king who had unknowingly sentenced his own son to death and could not explain the strange compassion he felt for the man he had condemned. *Non so d'onde viene* (K. 294) had originally been intended for Raaff; but now, while composing it, Wolfgang saw no king—instead, before his eyes was Aloysia, queen of his heart, and the compassionate words became words of love from Aloysia's blessed throat. The father-and-son problem was his, and sympathy was one of the moving forces of his passion.

"I won't study this aria with you, Luise," he told her. "Learn it as you think best. Your conception of it—let it be my surprise."

She sang it just as he had wanted her to sing it. He kissed her hand, deeply moved. "This is your best aria, darling," he said. "No one else shall sing it."

His friends heard the aria for the first time at Wolfgang's farewell concert at the Cannabichs'. Christian roared with joy when it was finished, and the players said that hardly ever had they been so deeply touched by a piece of music. The aria was Wolfgang's most personal confession, and it became Aloysia's *pièce de résistance*.

Boisterous March winds swept through the country. The streets were muddy as Wolfgang went to the Webers', and there was still a little snow left. Almost like the first time, Wolfgang thought sadly. It was to be his farewell visit. Papa's last letter still rang in his ears: ". . . In the future consult your own interests only and not always those of other people." There would be no one in Paris whose interests would be more important than his. He looked at his watch. Two hours only. The happiness of many months to come now squeezed into 120 minutes. Then nothing would be left but memories and impatience and looking forward.

"Oh, Wolfgang, we cannot believe that you are going!" Cäcilia, Josefa, Constanze, and Sophie gathered around him.

Aloysia tried to smile but her eyes were red. "Here, Wolfgang, I made them myself." She handed him two pairs of filet mittens and burst into sobs.

"This is from me," Fridolin broke in and cleared his throat. "Your music copied, some extra paper, and the plays of Molière. . . ."

"How can I ever thank you?"

"Thank us? Wolfgang, you are the greatest benefactor we've ever had. I've told your mother. . . ."

"Luise, once more, the aria, please!" Wolfgang's voice was choked.

Cäcilia beckoned to the three girls, who followed her out into the kitchen. Fridolin sat down in a chair near the window. The two young people at the piano were oblivious of his presence.

Non so d'onde viene—they both knew it by heart. They looked deep into one another's eyes, while he played and she sang. Wolfgang's heart was pounding; hers, however small it might be, was fully abandoned to the passionate melody. Never forget this moment, Wolfgang thought in despair. Never forget this voice. Outside the wind was blowing. The sky was bluish gray, neither pale nor dark, a cold and cruel sky.

When they had finished, Wolfgang's head fell forward on the piano and he burst into sobs. Fridolin silently left the room.

Aloysia was the first to speak. "That was wonderful," she exclaimed softly. She did not cry, but her cheeks were wet.

Wolfgang lifted his head. "Why can't we go on like this forever?" He sprang to his feet and embraced her stormily. She shrank. He had never dared to do this before.

"Won't you kiss me good-by?" he begged.

Her lips were cool and inexperienced, but they returned the pressure. His were hungry, passionate. . . . He took her by her shoulders and looked at her. Then he embraced her again, kissed her forehead, her eyes, her hair.

"Luise, there won't be any other girl for me. I shall work as I have never worked before. I shall come for you. It won't take long, darling. If you only wait for me. Will you wait?" She nodded. "And then we shall be happy, so happy! I shall write for you and you will sing for me . . . arias . . . opera. . . . Luise, darling, you have no idea how I love you!"

She pressed his hand.

He kissed her again, kissed the tears from her eyes. Then he set out to say something, hesitated. "Do you love me?" seemed so inadequate. He had asked her so often.

And with a throb in his throat he murmured: "Do love me, Luise —please, do love me!"

CHAPTER 13

ORDEAL

[1778]

FOR NINE AND A HALF DAYS Wolfgang and his mother traveled to Paris by carriage, victims of the tricks of spring weather. They stared out of the windows at the dull country-side, absorbed in their own thoughts. Frozen and thawed mud in turns made the horses stumble and the carriage shake. When sun-shine managed to split the fog, it shone on endless grayish brown acres. Trees stretched their bare arms towards the sky.

Wolfgang was glad to be on good terms again with Papa. Yet the sacrifice had been great. Aloysia, don't forget me, please. Oh, Luise, darling, wait until I come . . . I'll make a lot of money and then I'll take you to Italy. . . .

When Mamma broke the silence, she began to complain. She was cramped from sitting still . . . she had a headache . . . she was tired, bored, hot, cold. . . . Wolfgang comforted her. He even managed to be cheerful.

Two days before they reached Paris it began to rain. Torrents of water poured down from the skies, found leaks in the roof of the carriage, soaked them to the skin. The horses struggled through oceans of slush. Wolfgang's near-sighted eyes saw nothing but sheets of water. Everything, even his determination, even his love, was drowned in gray water and fatigue.

When have I been so tired before? He tried to remember. Oh, yes —eight years ago, on the trip from Naples to Rome. Papa was

putting me to bed in spite of the hurt to his leg. He was proud of me then. I had a contract. When shall I ever have a contract again? He shivered.

"Cold?" asked Mamma.

"No—just unhappy."

Their room in Paris was dark and unhealthy. Wolfgang saw at once that it would be impossible to bring a clavier up the narrow staircase. Mamma looked out of the window—nothing but walls of dirty stone, with a tiny strip of sky far above. Like a prison cell. . . . What would she do all day? There was hardly light enough for her to knit.

Wolfgang set about the awkward business of selling himself. He was glad to find that Wendling and the others from Mannheim had not yet left Paris. They had positions with the *Concerts spirituels,* and promised to introduce him to the director, M. le Gros, who just then had Raaff as his guest. They would also take him to Count von Sickingen, the Minister to the Palatinate, who had a large music library and might be able to do something for Wolfgang.

His great hope, however, was M. Grimm. He was Baron von Grimm now, boasting of a new Russian order and title. He lived at Mme. d'Epinay's *hôtel* in the fashionable Chaussée d'Antin. A frail, brown-eyed, soft creature, Mme. d'Epinay had conquered her shyness and become one of the most remarkable essayists of her day. Her salon assembled everyone worth while meeting. Mamma shrank at the thought of the loose-living folk Wolfgang would be forced to associate with, but she could do nothing about it.

Leopold had unbounded confidence in Grimm and his good-will. He sent him two long and over-candid descriptions of the family's situation, and kept urging Wolfgang to retain Grimm's affection by "a complete and childlike trust." These letters were a bad mistake on Leopold's part. Talent that got nowhere impressed Grimm as little as it would have impressed Leopold. Something must have gone wrong with the boy, he concluded, and his interest cooled immediately. Once he had been glad to present the child prodigies to the French snobs as a new sensation. But sponsoring a young and unknown artist from the provinces would entail asking favors on his behalf, and Grimm was not the person to go out of his way for anyone. He invited Wolfgang to his house and gave him a few letters; if good use were made of these opportunities, he would be happy to step forward as the young man's affectionate sponsor.

The fashionable private *hôtels* were now located in the suburbs. The distances were greater, and carriages more expensive to hire. Wolfgang did a lot of fruitless driving; people were not in, or they were busy and kept putting him off. Once he had to wait for an hour and a half in an unheated room with the windows open; and, when at last he was asked to play on some ill-tuned instrument, the hostess and her guests paid no attention to him. Never before had he been so utterly ignored. The child prodigy was forgotten, the young composer unknown. None of his music had appeared in print except some very early works and no one knew that he had almost three hundred compositions to his credit, including some operas; as for his piano-playing, it did not conform to the current French taste.

True artists are rarely good impresarios, and Wolfgang was no exception. Had he been more sophisticated, he would have hung his Papal cross around his neck and used his title of *Cavaliere;* he would have distributed compliments among ladies, and adopted hobbies and vices. French society could endure anything but boredom; and this moody dreamer bored them stiff. Pale and gloomy, he sat among celebrities and beauties—disapproval personified. He made no attempt to be agreeable or to hide his growing dislike of French ways. His good taste was offended by their frivolous attitude toward religion and marriage, and the mere mentioning of their idol Voltaire—and dying Voltaire was mentioned often—made him shudder. Strongly aware of his colorless appearance and his deficient literary education, he rarely opened his mouth; and, when he did, Grimm felt highly uneasy, in the virtual certainty that someone would be offended. "Arrogant German!" said some. "Poor boy!" said others. But neither anger nor pity could make Wolfgang acceptable to the Parisian *beau monde* of 1778.

For eight years now Marie Antoinette of Austria had been residing at Versailles, as Dauphine at first, and since 1774, as Queen. Married off at fifteen to a Prince only one year her senior—a young man who was shy by nature and awkward in appearance—a barrier arose between them which increased rather than diminished as the years went by. In her loneliness she turned to hysterical extravagance. While young Louis XVI pursued his favorite hobbies—hunting alone and pottering at handicrafts—dubious personages sneaked into the Queen's apartments for expensive entertainment.

Actually, one single person's lavish spending could not have ruined a country with a 20,000,000 population, had its finances not already suffered beyond repair through centuries of warfare. But the French, always hostile to foreigners, were quick to blame the light-headed young woman in Versailles who disregarded their stern Court etiquette and showed no interest in the well-being of her new subjects. The dissatisfaction of the impoverished people gradually turned into open threats.

Warning sounds, however, were drowned out in noisy entertainment. Nothing could prevent the Queen and her circle from enjoying themselves, and the well-to-do upper classes followed suit. Extremes in fashion and art ruled Paris; and a matter of fashion rather than of art was the *grande affaire* in music that was just then occupying French society—the famous Gluck-Piccini feud, which meant that the followers of a German and of an Italian were fighting in France over principles of opera composition.

To everybody's surprise and Grimm's extreme annoyance, newly arrived Mozart refused to take sides. In Vienna he had been deeply impressed with Gluck's *Alceste;* in Italy enchanted by the charm of the native stage. But he was too much of a musician to endorse fully Gluck's theory that drama should dominate opera, and too much of a dramatist to be satisfied with static arias made to order for individual throats. He was no innovator, no reformer, no adherent of one school or the other; he was Mozart—who wrote music instead of arguing about theories. He had come to Paris in order to make money, so that he could marry without annoying his father. He did not want to be bothered.

Since he could not mix with musicians without being drawn into the combat, he easily followed Leopold's advice to keep aloof. "They understand their work and I mine—that is enough." But it so happened that his potential sponsors, audiences, and pupils were ardent advocates of one party or the other. In order to get somewhere, an outsider needed diplomacy and a flair for intrigue—qualities that Wolfgang totally lacked. While third-rate musicians were making a fortune in France, Mozart was barely able to eke out an existence.

It took some time for him to realize that he was being brushed aside, cheated, exploited. In the beginning he had appeared very popular. Le Gros had put his piano at Wolfgang's disposal and asked him to compose eight numbers for a *Miserere* by Holzbauer and a *sinfonia concertante* (K. Anh. 9) for the Mannheim musicians. A famous ballet master from Vienna wanted to do an opera with him. The Duc de Guines might re-introduce him to Marie Antoinette. The Duke played the flute and his daughter the harp and they ordered a concerto for their two instruments (K. 299)—instruments that Wolfgang detested.

As a result of intrigues the *sinfonia concertante* disappeared from the schedule. The opera plans never materialized; all that resulted was a little ballet music, *Les Petits riens* (K. Anh. 10) given with a Piccini opera. As for the Duc de Guines, he did not take Wolfgang to Versailles, but asked him to drill his hopelessly untalented daughter in composition, so that she could write her own harp music. Wolfgang loathed the lessons with the stupid, lazy girl. "Do you think everybody has your genius?" wrote Leopold, imploring Wolfgang to be patient. But Mademoiselle became engaged, and the lessons were discontinued. Wolfgang never received his full fee.

Gradually Grimm became more and more impatient with Wolfgang's constant criticism. Poor people had no right to be choosy or over-sensitive. Success had to be won, no matter how, and reluctance to play the game was preposterous, disgraceful arrogance. Had it not been for Mme. d'Epinay's pleading and the promise he had made to Leopold, Grimm would have given up the young man altogether.

The Mannheim friends were recalled in May with only Raaff staying on in Paris. For this, Wolfgang was grateful, since with Raaff he could talk about Aloysia. He was worried over the fact that her letters had been few and brief. Whatever the explanation, he began to realize that he must get back to her quickly—and speed depended on making money.

Summer came, and a hot one it was. They had moved to better quarters near the Boulevard. Mamma met a German musician and his wife, the Heinas, with whom at least she could talk in her own language. Raaff came to see her frequently. He called her *Frau Mutter* and sang for her. Still, Anna Maria was lonely and unhappy. Wolfgang's patrons rarely invited her, since she did not know French. Both mentally and physically she was ailing. Her usual medicines were almost exhausted, and she felt she ought to be bled. But it was hard to find a surgeon for that purpose; bleeding was going out of style. People had such advanced ideas about everything. The new medical theories were just as crazy as that idea of a "lightning conductor" which the United States Minister, Benjamin Franklin, was trying to introduce. They said it protected people— but if a person was destined to die . . .

Mamma spent her days waiting for Wolfgang—for news, good news, better news. When he stumbled into the room late in the evening, she would raise a tired head, and worried eyes would search his face. Wolfgang would absent-mindedly kiss her hand and forehead, and, without speaking, fling himself on his bed and stare at the ceiling. There was a crack in it that fascinated him. It was shaped like a sharp, unpleasant profile that he knew—the Mufti's! Since December, Papa had kept mentioning that the post of organist in the Salzburg Cathedral was available. No—anything but that! Whenever Wolfgang thought that the walls of Paris were crushing him, he had only to look at the crack in the ceiling.

Late in May, Mamma was better, and her good spirits came back.
She even ventured a trip to the Louvre. With eagerness she followed
the political news of which there was plenty those days. She, of
course, was primarily interested in the imminent danger of war
between Austria and Prussia over succession in Bavaria (if shooting
spread to Bavaria, how would she be able to get home?), but the
rest of France was much more concerned with the conflict going on
between Britain and her colonies in America. Most people in France
were interested in seeing the colonies victorious and Britain defeated.
Only last year the Marquis de Lafayette had gone over to help the
Americans; recently they had sent Mr. Franklin to Paris as their
Minister; and early this year there had been a treaty of alliance
signed between France and the colonies.

"I've just finished writing to Papa," said Anna Maria one day to
Wolfgang, as he lay tired and worried on the bed. "Don't you want
to add a few words?"

He didn't much feel like writing—it was always the same old
story. However, he began: "I am tolerably well, thank God, but I
often wonder whether life is worth living. I am neither hot nor
cold, and don't find much pleasure in anything."

Neither hot nor cold . . .

Two months had sufficed to generate in Wolfgang a fervent
hatred not only of French people but also of French music. He
found the language unfit for singing, and his nerves shrieked when
he heard French singers whine out wonderful Italian melodies.
Opera buffa performances were bad, and as for the Paris *opéra
comique*—he shrank from thinking about it. But, even without
Papa's explicit advice, he would have made full use of his ability
to imitate. So the French liked trifles? He wrote brilliant piano
variations on French chansons, with tricky passages for the virtuoso.
His feelings went into sonatas, a group that includes the popular
one in A major, with the *Rondo alla turca* (K. 331).

Raaff had arranged Wolfgang's reconciliation with Le Gros, with
whom he had not been on speaking terms since the affair of the

sinfonia concertante, and Le Gros had ordered a symphony for one of his concerts. Wolfgang had not written one in four years. His *Paris* Symphony (K. 297) was composed early that June; it is short and brilliant, cut according to the fashion of salon music for amateur ears. When he played it to Raaff and Grimm, to learn whether he had hit the right note, the two men were greatly pleased. As he wrote it, Wolfgang had been angrily determined to attract attention. The *premier coup d'archet?* Opening a movement with a bang? At the beginning, yes. But the final allegro started with two violins, very softly: the audience hushed in surprise. Then the forte set in suddenly, and they took a deep breath of relaxation and cheered. A pleasing passage from the first movement was re-introduced at the end: loud bravos and *da capos.* So he had tricked the French into applauding him? For the first time in many months he was happy. He treated himself to a large portion of dessert, said the rosary he had promised if everything went well, and went back to his lodgings. He would write to Papa immediately. There was a long letter still unanswered, scolding him about his bad mood, talking at length about the vacancy at Salzburg. He had better reply tonight, in this good frame of mind.

He found Mamma in bed. Strange . . . she usually sat up for him. Her cheeks were so pale. When he touched her, she opened her eyes and closed them quickly. "I don't feel well, Wolferl. My head —the light . . ." Wolfgang extinguished the candles and undressed in the dark.

The headache was worse the next morning and Anna Maria had to stay in bed. Her fever rose; she shivered, her teeth chattered. Wolfgang was in despair. She looked so apathetic—she didn't even complain. This was different from the other attacks of illness she had recently suffered. Clumsily—for he was not very clever with his hands—he applied cold compresses and moistened her lips. He was trying to persuade her to let him call a doctor. "I don't want a French doctor," she replied feebly yet stubbornly to all his suggestions. For two days and nights he tended her, taking no rest himself.

Now he *must* call a doctor—a German doctor. But how to find one in Paris, in the middle of the summer? Herr Heina knew some Germans, of course; but he had not called for the last two days. Wolfgang could not possibly leave Mamma and go away for hours to look for someone at random. Finally he heard the familiar steps on the stairs. Wolfgang hurried outside and put his finger on his lips. "She is so ill," he whispered, and broke into a fit of sobbing on the friend's shoulder. Heina tiptoed into the room and searched Anna Maria's face. She was not aware of his presence. "I'll find you someone," he said quickly, and left.

Two more days elapsed before the doctor came—two days during which Wolfgang sat and stared, desperate. Close to him, Mamma breathed heavily, turned restlessly from one side to the other as if in great pain. She must be very sick, he thought—so sick that perhaps she will die. Die . . . die . . . the idea seized him with full violence.

He had never seen anybody die, never seen a corpse. In the Mozart family there had been a good deal of talk about death. Leopold, clumsily and pathetically, had lectured on death while discussing religion. Wolfgang had mostly felt curiosity. How was it? How did death come?

Perhaps the hands grew cold . . . the eyesight grew dim . . . the hands . . . the eyes. . . .

But these were Mamma's hands, these good, warm, smooth hands, so tender and comforting . . . and these were Mamma's eyes, these grayish-blue eyes that were so much like his own. . . .

It was to his mother that death was about to come . . . to Mamma. . . .

A sudden dreadful anguish overcame him. "Mamma!" He cried it aloud. On her bed, Anna Maria made a slight move.

"Mamma!"

"Did you say something, Wolferl?" She opened veiled eyes. "If you want to talk to me, please don't whisper. There is such a ringing in my ears."

So this is how it starts, with the ears. . . .

The German doctor was old and unsentimental. Mamma desper-

[1 1 3]

ately longed for a drink of water. He prescribed rhubarb powder in wine and a nurse. Neither helped.

Forty-eight hours of suspense went by. When at last the doctor returned, all he had to say was: "I fear she will not last out the night. Better see that she makes her confession."

Wolfgang raced through the night trying to locate Heina, who might be able to find a German clergyman. Stumbling, sweating, crying, covered with dirt, he found him at the outskirts of the city. Then he dashed into Grimm's house. Grimm and Mme. d'Epinay were sympathetic, but all they could do was to send their own doctor.

The French doctor was politer and less hopeless. Mamma's breathing became calmer and she responded with a slight pressure when Wolfgang took her hand. Wolfgang bent forward and shouted: "I have met Heina with a German priest who wants to hear me play. They are coming tomorrow morning."

Anna Maria nodded slowly. She knew. There was no use pretending.

Heina kept his promise and came with the priest. Anna Maria seemed to be quite satisfied to make her confession and receive the Sacrament and extreme unction.

The symptoms of improvement had been deceptive. Anna Maria drifted towards death. Wolfgang moved about like a lifeless automaton. The nurse silently did the little that could be done.

It was on June 30 that she became delirious. The succeeding three days were sticky with heat and, for Wolfgang, black with despair.

At twenty-one minutes past five on the afternoon of July 3, she became quite still. Wolfgang pressed her hand, spoke to her, touched her arm. She had lost all sensation.

It was a matter of minutes, perhaps, some hours at the most. But Mamma could not go just like that, without saying good-by to Papa, to Nannerl, to Salzburg. She could not rest in the soil of a country she dreaded. Wouldn't she be frightened through all eternity?

And he had to talk to her. It might not take long—but it was terribly important.

Wolfgang tried to concentrate. If Mamma came back to consciousness, he would have to tell her right away . . . fear seized him that it was too late. . . .

What was it that he had to tell her? In these bygone weeks they had been silent so often. . . .

Oh, yes, he had to tell her: "I love you, Mamma," nothing but that, but many times, as many times as it could be said in a lifetime. There had been misunderstandings. Sometimes he had been impatient with her. He had expressed himself wrongly. He should have told her about his affection instead of arguing. Mamma probably knew that he loved her. But how could he be sure without asking her?

Anna Maria's features became emaciated.

It's death, Wolfgang thought. It's death. It would only take seconds to ask the question and to have her nod. This was his punishment—that he could not ask her the question of both their lives.

"I tried to do my best, my very best," he muttered in apology.

Mamma did not move. She could not hear him, he remembered.

But perhaps she would open her eyes again, for one second only, and at one single glance she would know all he could not say or ask. . . .

He watched her eyes for hours. Suddenly—it was as if she would open them again—and then her breathing stopped.

They buried her the next morning in the cemetery of St. Eustache. Her modest belongings, carefully wrapped by Heina and Wolfgang, were sent back to Salzburg later.

CHAPTER 14

CROSSROADS

[1778-79]

O N THE VERY NIGHT of Mamma's death, when she was lying on her bed with all the traces of pain gone and with two candles lighted beside her, Wolfgang had written to Leopold. His eyes blinded with tears, his hands shaking, he did not cry out his despair to his father. He was determined to be brave.

"I have very sad and distressing news to give you," he started out. ". . . My dear mother—

—is very ill. . . ."

Then followed a brief account of her illness, submitting to the will of God as Papa would have done, adding an awkward retraction that there was still hope. And, with a superb effort of self-control, he turned to other subjects.

Then he wrote to Bullinger, asking him to prepare Leopold for the blow. Papa should see a friendly face when he heard the worst. "Watch out for my dear father and sister for me," Wolfgang implored.

After the funeral, Wolfgang did not know what to do. He could not stay in this room, where he had spent three weeks of agony. Sensitive Mme. d'Epinay understood without being told, and a few days later Wolfgang found himself in the Chaussée d'Antin. He was given the sickroom of the house, and within its bare walls he sat and stared, wondering what to do next.

A few weeks before, he had refused the only acceptable offer that had been made to him in a long time; the Chapel at Versailles had wanted him as an organist, had offered a good salary and a six months' vacation a year. It would have been an ideal arrangement, but Wolfgang had preferred his full freedom to all the obvious advantages of a position near the French Court. Now his funds were exhausted. Pupils owed him money—and he owed money to Grimm. Small sum though it was, he saw no prospects of earning it.

As the memory of the last weeks began to fade a little, the picture of Aloysia returned to his mind. Mourning and hope, grief and love, became fused into one overpowering emotion—desperate longing.

His attempts to arrange an engagement with Le Gros for Aloysia had failed; so, in order to be with her, he had to go to Germany. From Mannheim had come the news that the musicians, if they wanted, could join the Court in Munich. Would the Webers be able to afford the trip? His own chances in Munich were not bad. Papa kept trying to negotiate a position for him there, supported by Padre Martini and some Mannheim friends who had already moved. If nothing came of it, there must be other places where they needed a Kapellmeister—and a prima donna.

"What shall I write to your father?" asked Grimm one morning late in July. "What do you want to do?"

The more Wolfgang depended upon Grimm, the more unpleasant their relations became. Grimm grew hopelessly impatient with Wolfgang's lack of decision. He complained about Paris—and stayed. He said he dreaded Salzburg—and outlined the conditions under which he might return. He did not know what he wanted, except, of course, that he wanted Aloysia—Aloysia and opera, whether at the ends of the earth—or even in Salzburg.

"I wish he had half his talent and twice his energy," Grimm then wrote to Leopold. That letter destroyed Papa's last shred of hope for his son's future in Paris.

With all the wiliness at his command, Leopold included Aloysia and opera in his schemes to bring Wolfgang home. There was talk about a new company in Munich to cultivate opera in German; they might want a composer who knew how to conduct. Hieronymus was having troubles with his Italian male soprano and might want a prima donna instead; if Wolfgang accepted the vacant post in Salzburg, he and Leopold might take Aloysia under their wings, and, when the Webers came, they would all live together—there was room enough.

This sounded convincing. Despite the roving life to which Wolfgang was accustomed, and his sometimes heady plans for conquering the world, at bottom he had a strong tendency toward home and family life. He had almost despaired of bringing about an understanding among the people he loved best, and the possibility now of finding Aloysia at home, of doing rewarding work with her—this was something to look forward to. On the other hand, he still mistrusted the Archbishop, and he was reluctant to live in a small town without opera.

His letters drove Papa mad with their alternate yeses and noes, until, on August 31, Leopold reported the Salzburg situation satisfactorily settled: Hieronymus was now kindly disposed toward Wolfgang, would pay him five hundred gulden a year, and would let him leave Salzburg whenever a contract called him away. However, Wolfgang continued to waver during an entire month. Letters from home kept coming. From his arsenal of moral pressure, Papa drew the words: "Everything depends on whether . . . you want to see me dead or alive . . . ," and from his arsenal of love, "Everyone is longing to see you again. The Chief Steward offers you his horses, and Dr. Prex his fine little bay; Louisa Robinig her love . . . your sister her friendship, love, and service; and our maid Theresa all thirteen of the capons she has bought for you. . . ."

That did it. Thirteen capons! And in another letter Papa had enclosed the complete list of Mannheim musicians who would go to Munich, and there was Signor Weber's name. Why should he be a hanger-on in Paris, when back home everybody awaited him so anxiously, and at Christmas he might be sharing his capon with Aloysia?

There were still proofs to be read of sonatas he wanted to present to Elector Karl Theodor's wife, and there was money to be collected.

Wolfgang only collected good wishes and regrets, but these he took at their face value, and he would not have made up his mind, had not Grimm practically forced him out of Paris. Solemnly he handed Wolfgang a ticket for the mail coach, telling him that it was the fastest (which it wasn't) and pompously bidding him not to think of repayment.

The sonatas remained uncorrected, the money was lost. And, when on September 26, Wolfgang boarded the coach, it was to learn that the trip to Strassburg would not take five days, as Grimm had told him, but twelve. As the vehicle rumbled out of the city gate, Wolfgang sent a vague look back in the direction of the cemetery of St. Eustache. It was the only spot in Paris to which his thoughts ever returned in love.

Wolfgang's behavior during this fall of 1778 seems curious at first sight. All his plans had been shaped with Aloysia uppermost in his mind; and now, with reunion almost tangibly near, it took him three months to travel the five hundred-odd miles from Paris to Munich, where the Webers now were.

Obviously, his happy-go-lucky fatalism and tendency to act at the spur of the moment came to the fore as he traveled farther and farther away from the greatest ordeal he had yet faced. And, although he would scarcely have admitted it to himself, he was delighted to be free, actually free to do as he pleased, for the first time in his life. He could have seen Aloysia within two weeks, three at the utmost. But he needed a breathing spell. After Munich, there was Salzburg. After Aloysia, the Mufti.

The carriage rumbled and groaned. A fellow traveler had a contagious disease. Wolfgang's fury against Grimm increased hourly. After six days of bone-shaking, he and another traveler left the inhospitable vehicle and proceeded to Strassburg in a hired coach. Wolfgang decided to stay and give some concerts, insignificant in the point of earnings but valuable as excuses to offer Papa. Then the fall rains set in and interrupted communications; Papa grew frantic, thought him stranded, ill, or dead.

While in Strassburg, Wolfgang received the news that Aloysia had found occupation in Munich. The Minister of War, Count Hardeck, had become her sponsor. Overnight he had made of her a prima donna at a fee of one thousand gulden a year. Wolfgang was both pleased and wretched; he could not help reflecting that he would now be deprived of a career with her. Gone were his dreams.

And with them had gone every reason for his returning to Salzburg.

So he simply changed his schedule and went straight to—Mannheim. He was the romantic Wolfgang, in search of memories. He was the disappointed Wolfgang, escaping to the only place where he knew he was respected. Nowhere but in Mannheim had he been so happy, since his early childhood days.

He stayed at Mme. Cannabich's, and Raaff was there, on his way to Munich. It was rumored that the Elector might return to Mannheim, and Wolfgang was urged to remain and wait. Here he was no defeated boy, but a worthy and important person. His music was called the best in town.

His self-confidence returned. So, too, did his creative energy return. Wolfgang settled down to compose *Semiramis,* of the fairly new melodrama type which fascinated him. It would bring him forty ducats and take only two months. He started a violin concerto and discussed an opera project. He also took on some pupils. All this would provide money enough to keep him until he should find a permanent appointment in Mannheim or Munich.

But Leopold foamed with rage. Ignored by his own son! Wolfgang had an obligation in Salzburg! Thunderbolt after thunderbolt was sent by mail. Exasperated to submission, Wolfgang packed the fragment of *Semiramis* together with his other manuscripts, and left Mannheim after heartbreaking farewells.

However, he had begun to see things from a different angle. Before Salzburg, there was Munich. Before the Mufti, Aloysia. He would be in Munich on Christmas Day. By New Year's they might be married.

What if she did not want to marry him? Impossible! shouted one part of his ego. Might well be so, whispered another. And at once Wolfgang found himself doing the queerest thing: he wrote and asked Bäsle to meet him in Munich. The Archbishop wouldn't permit him the detour to see her in Augsburg, he wrote hypocritically, but ". . . Make a point of being there [Munich] before the New Year. . . . Perhaps you will have a great part to play. . . ." To him, this letter had a double meaning: Bäsle would certainly enjoy being a bridesmaid, but if things went wrong, she might be still more glad to offer consolation. To Bäsle, the letter had but one meaning; she made herself as pretty as she could manage, and left for Munich in happy anticipation.

In any journey it is always the final hours that are longest, and this was especially true for the eighteenth-century traveler in an uncomfortable coach. The struggling horses dragged heavily over ice and snow. Wolfgang kept looking at his watch. He counted hours and milestones.

In the early afternoon, with the daylight already growing dimmer, the coach jolted into the streets of Munich and stopped at the Webers' house. The windows were lighted and shadows flitted across them. There were many people within—wasn't it like an engagement party? Waiting for the bridegroom to arrive?

Wolfgang's heart leaped ahead to certainty: Aloysia did love him, and they were going to marry.

He entered. Fridolin was first to see him. He embraced him, kissed him warmly.

Over in a far corner of the music room, with Raaff and two other gentlemen, stood Aloysia. She was wearing a long white dress of heavy brocade, with a red rose on it. . . . She looked very beautiful . . . and very much preoccupied.

Hastily Wolfgang made a move to arrange his hair. He greeted Cäcilia and Josefa—Aloysia did not look in his direction—and then he stood before her.

"Merry Christmas, Luise," he said tenderly, "and a very happy New Year."

[121]

"Thank you." Her look was remote and cool. With a bored routine gesture she held out her hand to be kissed.

Wolfgang paled while the two beaux stared at him with an ironic sneer, at his red suit crumpled from the trip and the black buttons which were worn for mourning in France.

"Luise," Wolfgang stammered.

"Gentlemen," she burst out, "have you ever seen *this?*" She pointed at the buttons. "The latest Paris fashion!" Her laugh was shrill.

The floor seemed to sway beneath Wolfgang's feet. His love had not only been repulsed, it had been ridiculed. For a second, he observed Aloysia with a cold look. No, this was no more his Luise. There was something new about her, something that made her— just like everybody else. But what it was he did not know.

He bowed slightly and turned around. Aloysia's sarcastic smile flickered out, and she stood watching him uncertainly. Perhaps she had gone too far. . . .

Slowly he went to the piano and seated himself, waited until everybody was looking at him and listening. Then, instead of the Christmas carol they expected, he yodled a new and popular ditty, coarse and of unmistakable meaning.

There was a nervous titter from someone, then all the guests began to laugh uneasily—Aloysia loudest of all.

Without looking at her, Wolfgang rose from the piano. Fridolin rushed toward him, very disturbed. Wolfgang patted his shoulder. "It's perfectly all right," he said. "The only thing I need is a drink of v-e-r-y f-r-e-s-h w-a-t-e-r."

Wolfgang had a long, confidential talk with Fridolin. Aloysia had certain obligations to Count Hardeck. It meant a career for her, and perhaps for Josefa.

Wolfgang began to understand a little better. He should have realized something of this long ago. Aloysia's scant and evasive letters—the family suddenly living in luxury—Mme. Cannabich's elaborate explanations. . . . Why hadn't they told him the truth?

Bravely he stayed on with the Webers and tried to meet the new situation philosophically. Aloysia was an unequaled interpreter of his music. They would work together, amuse themselves together, and she would never know how he really felt.

As he sat opposite her at the dinner table, telling the latest gossip from Paris, he watched her every movement eagerly. He coached her and finished the aria he had begun for her—as his wedding gift. He worked with Josefa, and gave a few music lessons to Constanze. They all got along well. And, though he was at first quite unaware of it, Aloysia's new prima donna habits helped him overcome the crisis. This was no longer the girl who had dreamed of her first success in one of his operas.

At nights he wept into his pillow—for Mamma, and for Luise, and for his illusions. Where would he find love?

Bäsle had arrived. There were jokes, giggles and tears. Bäsle, too, wept for her illusions. But she still hoped a little.

Munich had become a super-Mannheim. It now boasted the finest musicians in Europe, the best theater, the boldest artistic schemes. *Alceste* by Wieland and Schweitzer was the feature of the season, and waiting for its performance was a good excuse for Wolfgang's staying. He presented his most recent violin sonatas, which finally had arrived from Paris, to the Electress, and Cannabich and Raaff pulled all the strings at their command.

But Papa threatened to come to Munich in person to fetch his obstinate son who for the sake of "gay dreams" was cheating both his father and his employer. Indeed, said Leopold, the Archbishop might take back his promises. If only he would, sighed Wolfgang to himself.

But he might just as well go back to Salzburg. If only he had not to go alone. He needed someone to soften the shock of the moment when he would get out of the carriage without Mamma; and someone to distract the conversation from the Webers. Bäsle!

If Bäsle came along, Leopold might not talk about Aloysia. He might think that it was Wolfgang who had changed his mind. He could not admit to Papa, not right away, that he had failed triply: as a son, as an artist and—as a suitor.

Leopold wrote that he would be delighted to have his niece come. As for Bäsle herself, she needed little urging. Chattering and giggling, she sat next to Wolfgang in the post chaise and happily saved him from remembering who had sat next to him when he had left Salzburg.

CHAPTER 15

DRUDGERY AND DELIVERANCE
[1 7 7 9 - 8 1]

HOME received Wolfgang with open arms. A roost full of capons, his nicely arranged room and the clavier for which he had asked were waiting for him. Leopold's skillful interpretation had placed Wolfgang in the position of an urgently recalled, indispensable artist. Papa had decided to refrain from reproaches. He was glad to have the boy back, after all.

Mamma's picture hung in the living room. When Wolfgang stood before it, Nannerl fell sobbing into his arms. This gap could not be filled; nothing could replace the gay voice, the undisturbed "don't worry," the thousand small goodnesses that had come from this simple woman. Although they all assured each other emphatically that it had been Mamma's destiny to die, the pointed friendliness around Wolfgang only increased his certainty of guilt. He felt like a criminal on probation.

The Archbishop was convinced that he had been very generous in his offer to young Mozart, but now he expected him to apologize for his long delay in returning home. Wolfgang bravely penned a humble letter, but in reality he was stubborn from the outset. No sign of appreciation came from either side. The atmosphere became tense, then openly hostile. In no time, Wolfgang was more than ever a stranger at the Court of his own sovereign.

Part of his service routine consisted in taking meals with the Archbishop's retinue. They all had disgusting table manners and spoke foul language. The red Court livery which made him one of them burnt on Wolfgang's body like fire.

Bäsle played her part beautifully; her cheerfulness helped overcome the embarrassment of the first days. She talked family and small-town gossip with Leopold, always with a clever touch of admiration for the old man. For the first time in many months, Papa found himself laughing. In her presence, even Wolfgang seemed to forget that he still loved Aloysia hopelessly and hated the Mufti. Papa and Nannerl decided between themselves that they would be quite content if the two young cousins were to marry. But Wolfgang did not give it a thought. He amused himself with Bäsle but she did not fascinate him. Calmly he let her return home to Augsburg after a few months, and they never saw each other again.

Wolfgang felt happiest when he sat at home and wrote music. Then he forgot the past, the present, and the future, and surrendered himself completely to the voices within him. Mozart always said that Salzburg frustrated his inspiration. This might have well been true if he had lived there uninterruptedly. But the quality of the music which he produced during the Salzburg months or years seems to indicate that he needed these involuntary periods of rest in the quieting atmosphere; perhaps also the very fight for recognition in his hometown stimulated a passionate effort to give his best.

Most of his music at this time was written in connection with his church services. Of the two masses, both in C major, the so-called *Coronation* Mass (K. 317) has become Mozart's most popular church composition besides the Requiem.

For Nannerl and himself he wrote a concerto for two pianos (K. 365) and a violin sonata (K. 378). Also dating from this period are three symphonies, the well-known *sinfonia concertante* (K. 364) for violin and viola, occasional pieces, and songs.

There was a theater across the street from the Mozart house on the Hannibalplatz, which all three in the family—theater-crazy as they were—watched avidly. In the fall of 1780, a new tenant took the place over, one Emanuel Schikaneder, a big heavy fellow with a fat face and bombastic gestures. An adventurous theater man he was, with a gypsy's intuition, who loved the spectacular for its own sake and had a shrewd understanding for popular tastes. He would pick up actors for minor roles on street corners and in coffeehouses, because something in their appearance or mannerisms had struck him as unusual. He would write entire scenes, and finally entire plays, around mechanical tricks. (Much later, Mozart was to compose some of his most precious pieces—the scenes of the genii in *The Magic Flute*—in order to allow Schikaneder to show a new flying device.) Schikaneder's love for extravagance and thrills would later increase to the point of mania and lead him to a tragic end in the insane asylum.

Schikaneder was a fascinating new friend. Soon the three Mozarts had free admission to all the performances in the theater, where they saw a hodge-podge of tragedies, comedies, operettas, and farces. The company was a poor one, mostly actors who knew how to sing. They could not possibly do Italian opera—and so Schikaneder condemned the general predilection for it as unpatriotic. Once again Wolfgang was taken with the idea of *Singspiel* in German, the more so as he understood how effective it could be in the hands of a good producer.

It seemed an eternity since Wolfgang had written for the stage. He had started to work on a *Singspiel* in the then fashionable oriental setting, and the part of it he finished was later published under the name of the heroine, *Zaide* (K. 344). Now he rummaged among his old manuscrips and found two choruses written in 1773 on his short visit to Vienna. They had then been intended for a freemasonic play, *Thamos, König in Ägypten,* which Schikaneder now put on his program. Wolfgang revised the choruses and wrote a few more numbers (K. 345).

The acquaintance with Schikaneder lasted only a few weeks. In October, 1780, a surprise offer came from Munich. The friends there had done good work. Wolfgang had an opera contract.

The subject was *Idomeneo, Rè di Creta* (K. 366), a version of which Mozart had seen in Paris as a child; the plot was the Old Testament story of Jephtha and his daughter, changed to a Greek setting; and the present librettist was the semi-Italian Salzburg Court chaplain, Abbate Varesco.

Varesco fancied himself a great poet, but he had no dramatic sense at all. The original plot, already discouragingly involved, had been made bearable by effective dramatic devices; these, however, were smothered in endless and boring recitatives. Mozart knew at once that substantial changes would have to be made, but he had to wrestle with Varesco over every single word. Nothing, however, could diminish his enthusiasm for the assignment. *Idomeneo* represented not only his re-entrance onto the stage—it was his re-entrance into the world. Feverishly he set to work and composed as much as he could in Salzburg.

After he had left for Munich, Papa became his ambassador at Varesco's studio. Good diplomat that Leopold was, he proved just as stubborn and difficult as the poet himself. He was the ideal intermediary between Wolfgang, who wanted to write dramatic music, and Varesco, who had written learned dialogue. Father and son talked it over in long letters, now of extreme importance to the historian, as they show the high degree to which Mozart had already developed his insight into the requirements of the stage. Eventually the libretto was brought into a form which did not interfere too seriously with Mozart's ideas about opera.

So this was Munich again, and here they were: the Cannabichs, the two Wendling families, Raaff, Lang, Ritter, Ramm—everybody except the Webers. Wolfgang had already heard that Aloysia, accompanied by her family, had gone to Vienna to take a high-salaried appointment at the National Theater. He hardly cared. He had once believed that he would be permitted to follow both the voice of his heart and the call of his genius, enriching both by serving both. But he had asked too much. Now—though this is the part that he can scarcely have guessed—he was riper for the experience; the romance had introduced him to a grown man's emotions.

Musically and emotionally he had served his apprenticeship. Musically and emotionally, *Idomeneo* was his first mature opera.

More news of the absent Webers was awaiting him in Munich. First, a big shock: Fridolin had died. Aloysia had got him a position as a ticket-clerk, but in a few weeks he had suffered a stroke. Aloysia, deprived of the only person in the world for whom she really cared, had found the five-woman ménage unbearable and had run away—without bothering over the question of support for her mother and sisters. Cäcilia had been forced to take in boarders, while Aloysia had rented a comfortable apartment all her own where she had entertained her fiancé, the actor Josef Lange. They had married recently, whether with or without Count Hardeck's blessings, nobody knew. Probably Aloysia had treated the Count no better than she had treated Wolfgang when there was nothing more he could do for her.

"So she is Mme. Lange," Wolfgang said thoughtfully. "Is he very much in love with her?"

"Must be so," was the reply. "The marriage has cost him dear. Cäcilia made Lange pay the debts she contracted after Fridolin's death. You see, Aloysia was still a minor, so she could not get married without her mother's consent. And Mother made her conditions."

What an awful thing to do, thought Wolfgang; but he was not really interested. What was this man Lange to him, or his family affairs? He had an opera to write.

He had taken quarters in the Burggasse, providing also for Papa and Nannerl if they could manage to come to the performance. Here, in spite of a mild attack of illness, he buried himself in his work. It simply *had* to be good. It *had* to be a success—a *sensational* one.

While he wrote the third act, the first two were already being rehearsed. Raaff was Idomeneo, and Wolfgang's problem child. He was sixty-four, no longer in full command of his voice, and as bad an actor as he always had been. But he had been instrumental in getting Wolfgang to Munich. Now, as a token of friendship and respect for his gray hair, he demanded musical compromises which Wolfgang would not have made for anyone else in the world. The other tenor was elderly, too, and, in addition, arrogant. The male soprano was young, but he could neither act nor sing; Wolfgang had to coach him like a baby. Except for the two Wendling women who sang the parts of the two female rivals, the cast was hopeless, and the music written for these singers naturally suffered from their ineptness.

But there were the choruses, introduced into this *opera seria* after the pattern of Gluck; and there was the Munich orchestra, now the best in the world. Wendling, Ramm, Ritter, and Lang were all first-desk men, and Christian Cannabich conducted. After each rehearsal they cheered and embraced Mozart. Limited by the shortcomings of the singers, Wolfgang made the orchestra the medium of his dramatic ideas. There was no economy in *Idomeneo*. "Overwritten," said nagging critics after the performance. Overwritten? A rich flow of wonderful music. There were small phrases, and fragments of phrases, in every single instrument, varied, repeated, balanced against each other. Wolfgang gave fully of himself, out of all that had been pent up during years of dreariness interrupted only by tragedy.

Not only Raaff, but also Leopold had to realize that there was a limit to the musical compromises Wolfgang was ready to make. Papa still conceived of art as merely a service to please the public. "Don't forget the popular," he would warn; "I mean the kind of music that tickles the long ears." "There is music for everybody in my opera," Wolfgang would cheerfully reply. "For everybody— except the long-eared."

In the midst of composing and rehearsing, in November, 1780, came the devastating news of Empress Maria Theresa's death. Leopold feared that the performance would be called off, but he was soon relieved to learn that official mourning would last for six weeks only, and after that *Idomeneo* could be given.

The dress rehearsal fell on Wolfgang's 25th birthday, January 27, 1781. Two days later came the première. Wolfgang—ill, excited, and overworked during the preceding weeks—found himself suddenly quite calm. He knew he had done a good job. Leopold and Nannerl had arrived, bringing Wolfgang's best clothes for the coming Carnival, and accompanied by a crowd of Salzburgers. Salzburg had conquered Munich, and was showing its pride. Munich, very naturally, felt rather second-hand. A local paper commented dryly:

On the 29th of last month the opera *Idomeneo* was given for the first time in the new opera house here. Lyrics, music and translation are of Salzburg make.

However, there was still something in the opera Munich had contributed. The review went on:

. . . The scenic settings, among which the view of the port and Neptune's temple are the most outstanding, are masterpieces by our famous theater architect, Herr Kammerrath Lorenz Quaglio, and have aroused everybody's admiration.

Mozart always held *Idomeneo* particularly dear, but try as he might he could not again bring it to the stage except for an amateur performance in Vienna, in 1786. Because of its dramatic shortcomings, its beautiful music is mouldering in the archives. In 1931, for the celebration of the 150th anniversary of the première, a number of revisions were tried, among them one by Richard Strauss for Vienna, and another by Wolf-Ferrari for Munich. Neither was a lasting success.

Happy and tired, Wolfgang indulged in the pleasures of the Carnival. He was respected and popular. Leopold, who had been writing melancholy letters for so long, became ten years younger. The camaraderie of the Mannheim *bohémiens* swept him off his feet, and he did not miss a ball, nor a concert, nor an opera.

Wolfgang was more hopeful than ever that he would be retained by the Court at Munich. He had made friends with the Countess Baumgarten, the Elector's present favorite, and presented her with one of his two new arias for soprano and orchestra. He showed the Elector his church music (maybe a vacancy would occur in this field) and wrote for him a *Kyrie*. To his friends he dedicated a serenade for thirteen instruments (K. 361) and a quartet for strings and oboe (K. 370); and in his happy mood he wrote two charming little songs to mandolin accompaniment.

Leopold himself advised his son to stay on in Munich, although his leave of absence had expired weeks before. Hieronymus had gone to Vienna, to pay a state visit to the Emperor after the death of Maria Theresa. In an effort to shine in all his splendor, the Archbishop had moved there with a huge retinue, eight thorough-bred horses and part of his furniture. He would not come back too soon. So the Mozarts stayed on in Munich, cherishing vain hopes that the Mufti had forgotten all about them.

CHAPTER 16

FREE!

[1 7 8 1]

THIS, however, turned out to be wishful thinking. The Archbishop would not have forgotten anything that could help him to eclipse the other princes assembled in Vienna. Who except Hieronymus had in his retinue a musician who had been received by the late Empress? But let the boy come alone. The father-and-son team might play some trick on him. They had many friends in Vienna, and the Mufti soon realized that he himself had none.

So, by the end of March, Wolfgang received an order to come to Vienna immediately. Leopold was told to return to Salzburg.

Wolfgang was both miserable and happy. Vienna was the last place where he wanted to appear in the red livery of a servant. Aloysia was there, a prima donna. She, and the Mesmers, and Prince Kaunitz, the Emperor himself—all would be witnesses of his humiliation. But it was still Vienna. If ever he was to be free, this was the time and the place.

When the spire of St. Stephen's Cathedral appeared on the horizon, every trace of his uneasiness vanished. With an ironic bow he accepted the scolding for his prolonged stay in Munich and learned that he was to live in the same house with the Mufti, near the Dome, which was meant to be a distinction. The long table where he took his noonday meals was headed by the valets. ". . . at least I have the honor of sitting above the cooks," he wrote bitterly to Salzburg. He had to play for His Grace's guests, line up with the other musicians when they passed by, and spend his mornings in the anteroom waiting for orders.

Whenever he had a moment to himself, he went to the Webers'. They lived only a five-minute walk from the Cathedral, in a house called *Zum Auge Gottes,* on St. Peter's Square. Mme. Weber radiated maternal kindness, and he wept on her shoulder. "Why don't you quit and stay with us?" she asked. For her, this would be killing two birds with one stone. Her business—taking roomers—was going poorly, and three of the daughters were still unmarried. She noted with pleasure that Wolfgang was seeing more and more of Constanze, now eighteen and the least attractive of her brood. With Josefa devoting herself entirely to singing, Constanze had taken over the household duties and was shown off at her best in Wolfgang's presence. She liked music, and she was gay and companionable. Wolfgang could talk to her about Aloysia. "I was a fool," he admitted to his father in a letter. "She is false and coquettish." But he could not help adding that, fortunately, her husband's notorious jealousy prevented him from seeing her too often.

Through the concerts which Hieronymus arranged, he met leading nobles, renewed old acquaintances, made new ones. That he wore livery did not harm his reputation as he had feared it might. Everyone disliked the Mufti, and sympathized with Mozart. There was Prince Kaunitz, less influential now than under Maria Theresa's reign, but highly respected as elder statesman; there were Prince Gallitzin, Count Cobenzl, Countess Thun, and Countess Rumbeck, the last of whom became his pupil on the spot. The ladies offered to distribute tickets for him if he wanted to give a concert. Wolfgang felt like a schoolboy when he had to reply that "his master" would not permit it.

It was for a good reason that Hieronymus consistently withheld permission for Wolfgang to do anything outside of his service. Contrary to the prescribed etiquette, young Mozart, at a concert that the Archbishop had his musicians give at Prince Gallitzin's, had walked right past the valet to whom he was supposed to report and had gone directly into the music room to greet their host, whom he had known for years; had indeed found it quite natural to behave as though he belonged to the illustrious crowd. What was still worse, the illustrious crowd had found it natural, too. Hieronymus did not like this at all.

So he not only refused permission for Wolfgang's own concert, but also wanted to prohibit his appearance at a benefit given for widows and orphans. This was an occasion well worthy of the Church's support, and the Mufti's attitude provoked a storm, which finally forced him to yield.

Wolfgang was "quite delighted with the Vienna public," as he wrote home. "I had to begin all over again because there was no end of applause. . . . I assure you this is a splendid place, and for my métier the best spot in the world!"

On April 8, His Grace arranged a concert for the nobility. Wolfgang was ordered to compose a rondo for violin (K. 373) and another for soprano (K. 374), both with orchestra, and a sonata movement for the Salzburg Court violinist Brunetti and himself. He worked through the night and, as there was no time left to write down his piano part, he improvised it at the concert. He received no extra remuneration for this rush job—and on that very evening there had been a musicale at Countess Thun's which he had had to miss; the Emperor had put in an appearance and had sent fifty ducats each to the performing artists. Well, the loss of this present was a point Papa would be able to appreciate.

If he had not been afraid of his father, Wolfgang would have quit then and there. Papa suspected something of that sort and wrote hymns in praise of financial security. For his sake alone Wolfgang stayed on.

But finally it seems that Wolfgang tried to provoke a scandal. He performed his inescapable duties with open hatred and negligence. He gradually skipped his appearances in the anteroom except when sent for, but stayed in his room and wrote music instead. He missed the noonday meals with the valets and cooks and went to dine with whomever he liked. And he made it very plain that he would try his best to establish himself in Vienna.

Hieronymus' sense of pride was badly hurt, and he never lost an opportunity to vex Wolfgang. But in Vienna, Mozart had the upper hand. The Viennese spoiled their darling and promised to move heaven and earth for him, if he would only decide to stay.

Twice Hieronymus had yelled at Wolfgang: "Get out of here, rascal, scoundrel. . . ."

Twice Wolfgang had controlled his temper. He had thought of his father. But presently, when the Archbishop's musicians were no longer needed, they were to leave their quarters. Unlike the others, who were given ample time to make new arrangements, Wolfgang was not notified of the day when he was to move. He was forced to pack at a moment's notice, and went—to the Webers'. "Where else should I go?" he said to himself—although he would have been very welcome at the Mesmers'.

Leopold raged and ordered Wolfgang home. Wolfgang became very skillful at inventing excuses for both Papa and the Archbishop. Wolfgang's ruses gained him two more days; three more days; another three. Every hour was precious.

"His Grace wants you to take a parcel home to Salzburg when you go tonight," said a valet to Wolfgang, when he presented himself on the morning of May 9.

"Is it urgent?"

"Yes, very."

"Well, I regret to lose the privilege of serving His Grace, but I cannot start before Saturday. Since I left this house, I have had to live at my own expense, so it is obvious that I cannot leave Vienna until I have collected some money to pay what I owe."

The valet Schlaucka had overheard the conversation. "Listen, Mozart," he said, "if I were you, I'd tell him that the coach is already full. That's a better reason. He'll be mad at you anyway."

Mozart looked at the man thoughtfully. More than once Schlaucka had witnessed his pretty interviews with the Archbishop. He was a friend.

"He'll be mad at me, whatever I do, only . . ."

"Hush," said Schlaucka. And Wolfgang was confronted by his furious master.

"When are you leaving, fellow?" he shouted.

"I intended to go tonight, but all seats were taken."

"You are the worst rascal I know . . . no one serves me as poorly as you do . . . you better leave tonight or I shall write home and have your salary stopped. You're getting five hundred gulden, you . . . you rascal . . . you miserable fellow. . . ."

At first Wolfgang listened with indifference. There was no use in trying to stop this torrent of abuse. Only a Prince of the Church shouldn't lie, he thought. He had never received the full amount of five hundred.

"Idiot!"

"So Your Grace is not satisfied with me?" Wolfgang's face was very red. "Idiot!" was too much.

"What, you dare to threaten me, you scoundrel . . . rat. . . . Get out of here . . . I don't want to have anything to do with such an impertinent wretch. . . ."

"Nor I with you!"

At last! Almost in spite of himself, it had slipped from Wolfgang's trembling lips.

"Get out!"

"I certainly will! You'll have it in writing tomorrow!"

Burning with humiliation and delight, Wolfgang found himself running out on the street. What would Papa say? But he had been insulted and this was a disgrace to his father, too! If Salzburg should consequently be made unbearable for Leopold, Wolfgang felt sure he could make enough money in Vienna to bring his father and sister to this delightful city, and the old man could at last enjoy freedom and leisure.

Vienna! Mozart looked around. The city had never been so beautiful. The air was radiant with light. Gay sounds floated in the atmosphere. Houses gleamed and smiled. Trees and shrubs bloomed. Every stem was a string, every leaf a sounding-board. Wolfgang's head swam with music. This was Vienna, conceived with ear, eye, and heart, sung by bright voices, played on fiddles formed like the hills about the city. There, the laburnum tree. Laburnum, translated, means "rain of gold." A rain of gold would descend upon him, coined money for his pocket, and uncoined gold for the happiness of his heart.

And St. Stephen's pointed its finger straight toward Heaven.

But first he had to hand in his resignation. Mozart came right down to earth. How silly to file an application acknowledging that you had been fired! He became actually ill from excitement. The next day he took his written resignation to the Chamberlain, Count Arco, together with the money he had received for his return trip. Neither was accepted.

Three subsequent memoranda were suppressed by Arco and sent back to Wolfgang without comment. The Count had known the Mozarts since childhood and he fundamentally meant well. Also, he might have lacked the courage to clinch the matter with his Prince. He tried to mediate; he talked to Wolfgang and wrote to Papa. Leopold tried to scold the rebel into reason. But Wolfgang had never been as firm as he was now. Should he seem a coward, and the Archbishop a worthy prince?

Meanwhile summer was coming on, and Hieronymus was ready to return to Salzburg. Wolfgang decided to present his resignation himself. He drafted another petition "in the most pleasant way imaginable" and set out for the hated house. But in the anteroom, Count Arco blocked his way. After a short but hot argument, the Count settled the matter by catapulting Mozart through the door and down the stairway with a well-aimed kick. Wolfgang foamed with rage. But his long training in respect for the apartments of His ungracious Grace made him take to his heels, lest he might have to kick back right in the Archbishop's antechamber.

Wolfgang no longer cared about his formal dismissal—the kick

was sufficient. Apparently his resignation was never otherwise acknowledged, for two years later friends warned him against visiting Salzburg lest the Archbishop might send him to jail.

He was blazing with hate and revenge, and the flames were readily fed with memories of past insults. As he could not expect to get satisfaction from the Archbishop, he would have it all out with that Arco, that stupid underling. He decided to write him a letter containing a solemn warning that the kick would be returned on the next possible occasion, even if it had to be done in public.

Leopold stopped Wolfgang from mailing this letter. It was the last order his father was able to enforce. Wolfgang had emancipated himself from Salzburg once and for all—and not only from the Archbishop, as Papa knew only too well. . . .

CHAPTER 17

VENTURES IN VIENNA

[1781]

FOR THE FIRST TIME in his life, Wolfgang was fully responsible for himself. He had opposed Papa, convinced of his ultimate success. His talents, of whose extent he was entirely aware, should at least provide him with a modest living and protect him against insult. And Vienna was indeed the best spot in the world for him.

It is misleading to refer to Mozart as a German, although he himself occasionally did so in his letters when he was driven to defend himself against competitors who spoke Italian or French. History changes the meaning of words. The idea of nationality was vaguer in his period than it is today, and in the case of the later Germany and the Austrian possessions the picture appears confusing at first sight. For, it had almost become a tradition that the hereditary Austrian monarchs were elected German Emperors, thus combining the fundamentally different offices in one person. Popular characteristics, however, were strongly distinct even then, and Mozart's personality had nothing in common with what has come to be considered typically German since the "forging" of Bismarck's Reich under Prussian leadership in 1871.

Mozart had the Austrian's likable qualities and shortcomings. Nowhere but in Vienna would he so courageously have taken the step for independence. Here he felt at home. The Viennese lived in happy illusions. Their gift of jesting at their own expense removed bitterness from satire, tragedy from the tragic aspects of their own lives. Their tendency to accept anything as long as it satisfied their fancy was an attitude natural to Wolfgang. It was a heritage from his mother which he had never before been permitted to develop.

If he had resembled Leopold rather than Anna Maria, his life would have been easier, but he would not have been Mozart. However, without Papa's training he would not have been Mozart either. He might easily have become one of those long-forgotten wholesale producers of pleasant music, had not his affectionate critic at home conveyed to him at least a fraction of his own discipline. Wolfgang owed much to Papa, and he knew it. He thanked him by leaving Mannheim for Paris, and Paris for Salzburg; by suffering insults until he could not longer tolerate them; by infinitely patient letters after the final step was taken, trying to convince the old man that he had done right. Although the shops of Vienna were full of beautiful things, he sent Papa the first thirty ducats he could spare.

Leopold's displeasure, however, was not to be appeased. He could not forgive Wolfgang for having grown up.

Musical life in Vienna, which had been impeded by Maria Theresa's increasing melancholy, gradually came into full swing again after the official mourning for the Empress was over. Austria was on the road to recovery after decades of warfare. Her losses were bitter, her gains of doubtful value, but her populace rejoiced in the novelty of peace. The Emperor could not be expected ever to become generous; more disturbed than he would admit by developments in France, he was driven to thrift, even austerity. But land-owning aristocrats from Hungary and Bohemia who had palaces in the capital resumed lavish spending; the prosperous bourgeoisie had created a bridge to the titled classes; and the generally comfortable atmosphere prevented even the underprivileged from hating the rich. There were the wide meadows and woods of the Prater east of the city, watered by a multitude of branches of the Danube river; here Court and nobility did their hunting and parading under the eyes of colorful crowds. In the same district lies the Augarten, a great park which the Emperor had thrown open to the public, with a castle in which he sometimes lived.

Emperor Joseph was full of good intentions. Whereas his mother had carefully avoided any departure from traditional regulations, he made himself the champion of progress in a number of reforms. He reduced the strength of Church control over land, education, and the like, and introduced all sorts of freedoms. He set aside certain hours in his daily routine for personal audiences with his subjects. He rubbed shoulders at public functions, much to Mozart's shocked surprise. But Wolfgang was no less delighted than the rest of the Viennese, when the Emperor permitted one Marinelli to open a regular *Hanswurst* theater in the Leopoldstadt, of the kind the late Empress had not tolerated for reasons of propriety. Joseph himself visited the new theater, and the buffoon had to perform at Court.

Mozart's immediate plans were to earn his living by giving piano lessons, and this would make him known as a composer also. Busily preparing for the winter, he stayed on with the Webers. Cäcilia shrewdly complied with his domestic wishes. He made music with Josefa, whose voice developed remarkably well, and sometimes Aloysia came to visit with her husband. Then there was Constanze, the Cinderella, hard-working and often scolded, but a congenial listener and a good storyteller herself. Wolfgang seemed to overlook the unpleasant atmosphere in the noisy, untidy apartment, resounding with constant quarrels, and he also overlooked gossip spreading. So he was genuinely surprised when he learned, late in July, that he was supposed to be marrying one of the girls.

The news, of course, came from Leopold. Papa was having a bad time anyway. Nannerl, almost resigned to remaining an old maid, had suddenly fallen in love with a penniless swain. Wolfgang had made a fool of him, and the Court people looked at him askance. Now some Salzburgers returning from Vienna brought reports about the frivolous life Wolfgang was leading, and Leopold believed every word of it.

Wolfgang was very much hurt. So Papa trusted strangers more

than he trusted his son? Why didn't he stand up for him? He took it so much to heart that one day he had to write: ". . . I do beg, dear father, that you will spare me such letters in the future. . . . They serve only to irritate my spirit. As I am now constantly occupied in composing, I require both a cheerful mind and a heart at rest. . . ." He could not afford to be upset and disturbed.

Lessons with Countess Rumbeck enabled him to pay for his room and board and the few extra things he needed. At first he had only three pupils. Later, others also came to him: Countess Zichy, Countess Palffy (in all secrecy, for she was the Mufti's niece), the wife of the bookseller von Trattner, and Fräulein von Aurnhammer, who played charmingly but was fat, ugly and, to her own misfortune, very much in love with Wolfgang. If she expected sentimental responses to her advances, all she got was a professional reaction— a sonata for two pianos (K. 448) which she played with Wolfgang at a reception in her father's house. His pupils helped him to get subscribers for the publication of six violin sonatas, two old and four new, which were enthusiastically announced and reviewed. And early in the spring, Countess Thun had brought about the possibility of an opera contract.

At her house Wolfgang had met some important people: Baron Gottfried van Swieten, Director of the Court Library; Count Rosenberg, whom he had known in Florence and who now managed the Court Theater; and Stephanie, Jr., playwright and supervisor there. Wolfgang had played *Idomeneo* for them and had shown *Zaide* to Stephanie. There was no chance for either, but Stephanie reconsidered an old plan of adapting *Belmonte und Constanze,* one of many dramatic versions of an oriental tale, by Bretzner, Leipzig merchant and playwright. From this collaboration sprang *Die Entführung aus dem Serail* (K. 384).

Stephanie was commonly called the "evil genius of the Vienna stage," but Wolfgang had no cause to complain about him. He proved a docile collaborator.

On August 1, this letter went to Salzburg:

Stephanie brought me a libretto the day before yesterday . . . very good indeed. . . . I intend to write the symphony, the chorus in the first act and the final chorus with Turkish instrumentation. . . . I eagerly hurry off to the writing table and remain seated there in the greatest delight. The Grand Duke of Russia is coming here . . . the Emperor and Count Rosenberg are soon expected, and their first question will be whether anything new is in preparation. . . .

Not only the Grand Duke of Russia, but the Duke of Württemberg and his family were also to come to Vienna in the fall. Stephanie and Wolfgang expected to earn their laurels if they finished the opus in six weeks.

This haste was no hardship for Wolfgang. He was so happy about the opera that he sat down immediately and did two arias and a finale without a break. Not even three months had gone by since his break with the Archbishop, and already he had a splendid opportunity.

He was to write for the most brilliant audience of the time. Every note would be a kick back at the insolent Arco—that nobody! Every burst of applause would be a hissing of Hieronymus—a censure on his stature as a human being.

He had good singers to write for. It was the company that had been assembled in 1778, for which he had tried to obtain an assignment before going to Paris, and to which Aloysia belonged. Joseph II had recalled Rosenberg from Florence to manage the new theater; now he intended to make it a stronghold of domestic production, both in drama and opera. By 1781, the company could boast of being able to compete with any long-established Italian troupe.

In spite of trying weeks ahead of him, Wolfgang moved. Papa had been urging him to do so and Cäcilia had concurred "in order to stop gossip." He took lodgings on the Graben, practically across the street from the *Auge Gottes*. For reasons of economy he had taken a small room that overlooked the back yard, thus denying himself the view of the broad long square, then planted with trees, the picturesque old fountain and the column in memory of the

[145]

termination of the plague, the cupola of St. Peter's and the spire of St. Stephen's towering above the roofs. There was no one to talk to, no one to mend his clothes. Wolfgang never had lived alone, and he did not like it. He needed a mother or a sister—or a wife.

All this Cäcilia knew, and her kind advice to Wolfgang had been just another strategic move to catch the fish that was already rising

to the bait. When he visited them (as he now did almost daily) she was all motherly kindness. But she had lately taken to drinking hard, and the sound of her quarrelsome voice haunted his dreams. Constanze was too simple to have a part in her mother's game. She suffered honestly. When she was alone with Wolfgang, she would fall sobbing into his arms—and once more compassion became the moving force. . . .

Leopold seemed to consider the Weber situation settled, and Wolfgang was careful not to allude to it any longer. So, as before, he sent his father detailed reports about the opera, valuable documents on his ideas about dramatic writing. ". . . I have already indicated to Stephanie the words that I require for that aria [Osmin].

Indeed I had finished composing most of the music for it before Stephanie knew anything whatever about it. . . . Osmin's rage is rendered comical by the accompaniment of Turkish music. . . ." It was also made comical by Wolfgang's giving him coloraturas to sing, unnatural to a bass. Mozart instinctively understood that any device can be made to appear comic by using it in an incongruous setting.

". . . I have sacrificed Constanze's aria to the flexible throat of Mlle. Cavalieri . . . endeavored to express so far as an Italian bravura air will admit of it . . . I should say that in an opera the poetry must necessarily be the obedient daughter of the music. . . . Why do the Italian comic operas please, with all their wretched poetry! Because music rules there supreme. . . . It would be perfect if a good composer could be found who understood the stage . . . and combined with that true Phoenix—a clever poet; then no misgivings would be entertained about the applause even of the unlearned. . . ."

Always when Wolfgang reread these letters before sending them off, he was quite surprised at himself. Why, they were real discourses! He was perhaps too modest to suspect that he himself was this "good composer who understood the stage"; the "clever poet" lived on the Graben like himself—but Wolfgang didn't know that—either.

CHAPTER 18

TWO CONSTANZES

[1 7 8 1 - 8 2]

ALTHOUGH WOLFGANG HAD DENIED any idea of marriage in the letters he wrote during the summer, he was definitely engaged by the end of the year. Cäcilia Weber was not the person to be distracted from her objective. Constanze had to marry Mozart—or rather Mozart had to marry Constanze.

He seemed to be very fond of her, but he had hinted more than once that Papa must be taken into account—Papa who wrote those giant letters for which he came so nervously on post-days. Papa had already interfered with one romance; Cäcilia was not going to let that happen twice.

After Fridolin's death, the legal guardian of the Weber daughters was one Johann Thorwart, inspector of the Court Theater. Obsequiously submissive to superiors, and rude to subordinates, he had managed to make himself indispensable to Count Rosenberg. He was therefore a considerable factor to be reckoned with by an aspirant for an operatic career in Vienna.

This doubtful personage, whom outsiders considered smart and insiders unbearable, was the perfect partner for Cäcilia Weber. They understood each other without many words, and indeed many words were not necessary when Wolfgang was so open about everything. Cäcilia shrewdly tricked him into a discussion with Thorwart at her house. With the double authority of guardian and theater official,

Thorwart blustered a demand that Wolfgang express himself clearly on the subject of marriage.

"I have the very best intentions," Wolfgang asserted. "But I cannot get married without my father's permission, and he does not know a thing about the whole affair."

"Well, I suggest that you inform him at once," frowned Thorwart.

"I am afraid my father will not consent unless I have a fixed income," Wolfgang answered bravely, "and I think it would be wiser not to provoke his refusal. Just give me a little time. My affairs are bound to take a good turn."

Thorwart leaned back in his chair and focused his attention on a large diamond ring adorning his fourth finger. "I will give you all the time you want, son," he finally replied out of the corner of his mouth. "But, of course, you cannot expect Madam Weber to let you see Constanze until you have made up your mind."

There was an interlude of hypocritical protests from Cäcilia, which Wolfgang took at their face value, and bombastic insistence by Mr. Thorwart that Wolfgang must protect Constanze's reputation, either by marrying her or by not seeing her. Wolfgang suddenly felt that he simply had to see her and that there was only one thing left to do—in spite of all the trouble it would mean. His pitiful firmness vanished, his mind became confused, and by the end of the session he found himself signing a paper which read: "I bind myself to marry Mlle. Constanze Weber in the course of three years, and if it should so happen, which I consider impossible, that I should change my mind, she shall be entitled to draw on me every year for three hundred gulden."

Dramatically, Constanze tore up the paper as soon as the door closed on Thorwart, with Cäcilia standing by, furious but helpless.

Wolfgang was beside himself with happiness and tenderness. She really did not need the paper. Now he knew more than ever that he would never forsake her.

But the news had to be broken to Papa. At first, Wolfgang merely hinted at it, until Papa anxiously demanded an explanation. Encouragement to talk was all Wolfgang had wanted; he became

very matter-of-fact—the best way, perhaps, to reach an understanding with his father. There was nothing in him of the romantic
dreamer of the Aloysia period, who had eagerly advocated love-
marriages among the penniless, when he wrote:

I never have been in the habit of taking any charge of my linen or
clothes, etc., and I think nothing is more desirable for me than a wife.
. . . I am forced to spend a good deal owing to the want of proper care
of what I possess.

But now, who is the object of my love? Do not be startled, I entreat.
Not one of the Webers, surely? Yes, one of the Webers—not Josepha, not
Sophie, but the third daughter, Constanze. . . . She is the martyr of the
family . . . the kindest-hearted, the cleverest, and, in short, the best of
them all; she takes charge of the whole house, and yet does nothing right
in their eyes. . . .

She is not plain, but at the same time is far from handsome. . . . She
is not witty, but has enough good sense to enable her to fulfill her duties
as a wife and mother . . . she is invariably very simply dressed . . . and
she can, herself, make most of her things . . . dresses her own hair,
understands housekeeping, and has the best heart in the world. I love her
with my whole soul, as she does me. . . . I shall never cease to entreat
your consent to my rescuing this poor girl. . . .

Leopold was thoroughly fed up with Wolfgang's passion for
rescuing Weber women. Again Leopold raged, prayed, and wept

as he envisaged his son trapped by these uneducated vagabonds. Such people should "sweep the streets in irons like criminals, with a tablet hung around their necks and marked *seducers of youth!*" His written outbursts were carefully destroyed by Constanze in later years. Wolfgang's answers were desperate efforts to win his consent. Meanwhile Constanze, at Wolfgang's instigation, sent to Salzburg timid little notes self-conscious in spelling and grammar, awkward little presents, and advice on fashions. Nannerl, half won over, replied and thanked her—but not Leopold.

The poor results of this writing campaign opened a second front to Wolfgang: Madam Weber. Thorwart, contrary to his promise to keep the affair a secret, had given it wide publicity. Everybody, including the Emperor, now considered Wolfgang Constanze's fiancé. He could not have changed his mind without serious harm to his reputation. Seeing him thus bound to his word, Cäcilia deliberately tormented him as she had tormented Lange before his marriage to Aloysia. Poor Constanze was treated as an outcast. Wolfgang became more determined than ever to rescue her.

At his importunate request, one of his pupils, a Baroness Waldstätten, engaged the girl as a home nurse to give her shelter for a month. Cäcilia could not be entirely blamed if she did not want to see her daughter in this house. Its atmosphere was too free for a young unmarried middle-class girl who could not afford to become the center of gossip. When Constanze finally returned home, she was treated worse than ever.

Wolfgang was upset about it, but he could not afford to be moody. Too much was going on in Vienna. There were many chances for one who knew how to grab them, but the competition was keen. He rose at six, worked from seven to nine, then went about his teaching until one. The big midday meals he often had to attend took up most of the afternoon, but they were part of his business and also helped him to save money. Unless he was going to a concert or a musicale, he wrote again until nine, then went to see Constanze. He would stay for an hour or two, depending on Cäcilia's moods or on his "patience in bearing them," after which he continued to compose until one o'clock in the morning. This was a strenuous life, leaving him only five hours of sleep.

And the first disappointments soon developed. In spite of the Emperor's meager regard for Gluck and his favorite prima donna, the famous Bernasconi, three Gluck operas had been chosen for the entertainment of the visitors from abroad. Wolfgang was told that the performance of *Die Entführung* would be postponed until some time around Easter. Another chance also vanished. The young Princess of Württemberg—prospective bride of the Emperor's nephew, Archduke Francis—needed a music teacher. The Princess would have liked to study with Wolfgang but Court Composer Salieri, an Italian, was assigned to the post.

Antonio Salieri, only six years Wolfgang's senior but already holding almost the highest position a musician in Vienna could attain, considered the choice very natural. He did not know that for the first time he had crossed the path of one whose ghost would haunt him until the last hour of his life. Wolfgang, however, was strongly aware of Salieri. He watched the Court Composer with anxious curiosity. "The Emperor thinks Salieri all-in-all!" he sighed in a letter. What business did this Italian have to tamper with opera in German? His *Der Rauchfangkehrer* had already been given in April, while *Die Entführung* was postponed indefinitely.

Time and again Wolfgang was told of favorable comments the Emperor had made about his playing and no one doubted that an appointment would result eventually. But Joseph seemed to consider the assignment of an extra man an unpardonable luxury. Moreover, he could not help feeling that Mozart's music, as well as Haydn's, was too modern. None of their compositions were ever played in his daily chamber music sessions, and Wolfgang suspected that he was appreciated as a concert pianist only.

That the Emperor appreciated him as such, there was no doubt. The famous pianist Clementi had arrived from Italy just in time to help Joseph solve the problem of how to entertain his visitors with something new. Apparently in one of his spells of sarcasm, the Emperor thought it would be good fun to pit two pianists against each other—just a milder form of cockfighting—and made a bet with the Grand Duchess that young Mozart would win. On Christmas Eve, Wolfgang was summoned to the Emperor's apartments. He was so elegantly groomed that Clementi first mistook him for a courtier—which was just the effect he was always trying to create. They took turns and then they played together. Wolfgang seemed to have won. The Emperor was highly pleased and sent him fifty ducats.

No appointment resulted.

At Baron van Swieten's musicales Mozart became acquainted with the music of Handel and Bach, which opened new worlds to him. In musical life van Swieten was the M. Grimm of Vienna, but socially he was much better than that. His father, private physician to Maria Theresa and her family, had enjoyed her unlimited confidence. Some of the general respect for the father, which almost amounted to superstition, was enjoyed by his son, who was Director of the Court Library, whose hobby was music, and whose opinion nobody dared to contradict. During a prolonged stay in Berlin, van Swieten had acquired Handel and Bach scores and was proud to introduce them in Vienna. Wolfgang took some of them home, and copied them for practice like a novice. In the evenings he played them to Constanze.

"Haven't you written any fugues?" the girl asked.

"No," answered Wolfgang, surprised, for, although he often played fugues, he had not bothered to write them down. Constanze loved fugues, she said, and would he please write one for her. Wolfgang started many of them during this spring of 1782. Some were for two pianos so that they could play them together. Many remained fragments—as did almost anything he wrote for Constanze.

Mozart's love went into his opera. Much has been written about the extent to which Wolfgang identified himself with Belmonte in *Die Entführung* and his Constanze with the Constanze in the plot. It certainly was a strange coincidence that brought him this libretto, which mirrored his own situation and his own sentiments

[153]

in oriental disguise, at just this period of his life. It was not for
nothing that he later used to call his marriage "The Abduction
from the *Auge Gottes*." Easy and tender is this music, a fairy tale
with the fragrance of spring flowers.

The performance was finally commanded by the Emperor for
July 16. It was a hot and sticky day and many people had already
gone to the country, but the house was packed.

There was tremendous applause after every number, and many
da capos. Perspiring and happy, Wolfgang kissed the Emperor's
hand. "Too beautiful for our ears, my dear Mozart," commented
Joseph, "and *very* many notes." (Why did this Mozart and this
Haydn always cover the singers' voices with the orchestra?) Wolfgang bowed: "Just as many, Your Majesty, as are necessary." Salieri
would have never given such a bold answer. The Emperor did
not take it amiss; he liked this little man, and liked his music,
even if it was sometimes rather wild.

"*Die Entführung* is full of beauties," said Cramer's *Magazin der
Musik,* the leading musical periodical. "It surpassed by far the
expectations of the public and the author's taste."

Six years later Goethe stated: "All our endeavors to limit our-
selves to simple and restricted means became fruitless efforts when
Mozart appeared on the scene. *Die Entführung* outdid anything
else."

And long after Wolfgang's death, Constanze's cousin, Carl Maria
von Weber, remarked: "In *Die Entführung* Mozart's experience in
art had reached its maturity and the impulse to his later works
came from his experience in life."

There was a financial side to the matter, too. "To Mozart,
Wolfgang, 426 gulden 40 kreutzer for the composition of the
music," reads an old bill in the theater archives. This was no
more than the Emperor used to send an artist for a single evening.
The theater made a fortune and so did two German publishers
who printed the piano scores. Wolfgang lost the latter income by
his laxity in business affairs.

Die Entführung was the first of Wolfgang's operas to be given concurrently on the big stages of Central Europe. There were many performances in Vienna. In Prague it started the Bohemians' enthusiasm for all of Mozart's music, and in due course there were provincial performances in Baden, a health resort about twelve miles south of Vienna, and even in Salzburg, on which occasion the Archbishop could not help but admit that the opera was good. Within the next few years, practically all German stages had *Die Entführung* on the program despite the unfavorable reaction of the author upon whose play the libretto had been based. "A certain individual named Mozart," he complained in his local paper, "has had the insolence to misuse my drama, 'Belmonte and Constanze,' for an opera libretto. I herewith protest solemnly against this infringement on my rights and reserve further steps to myself. Christoph Friedrich Bretzner, author of *A Little Tipsy*."

His success made Wolfgang sure of himself. He no longer doubted that he could support a wife and children. Constanze had again gone to live with the Baroness, and Cäcilia threatened to send the police to bring her daughter home. Only an immediate marriage could prevent disgrace.

The Baroness provided the money for the marriage contract and on August 4, there was a quiet ceremony in St. Stephen's Cathedral. When they were pronounced man and wife, both burst into sobs of emotion. The Baroness gave them a supper. The only ones present were Cäcilia and Sophie, Herr von Thorwart, and two witnesses. It was a quiet day, almost a sad one.

Leopold's grudging consent, with a formal blessing and a statement that Wolfgang could expect no further support from his father, arrived on the morrow.

CHAPTER 19

"THE SALZBURGER RASCAL IN VIENNA"

[1782]

NATURALLY, with no money, there could be no wedding trip. But some economic miracle of the kind that keeps poor people going, enabled Wolfgang to find an apartment and pay for it. It was in the house on the Hohe Brücke where the Mozart family had stayed twenty years before.

They were two children jumping into marriage. In spite of the domestic virtues which Constanze had been made to display for Wolfgang, she did not know the first thing about running a household. Her character was still forming; fairly gifted and very superficial, she acted according to her environment. Her second husband, a Danish diplomat, turned her into a paragon of efficiency. But an efficient wife would have caused Mozart to flee in despair. . . .

Constanze has often been criticized as the wrong wife for Wolfgang. She was a "Weberische," with little self-control, subject to the whims of her changing moods. Never to her dying day did she realize to whom she had been married, nor could she ever live up to being, or having been, the companion of a genius. Perhaps this was because Wolfgang did not give the impression of working very hard when he was composing. Constanze's husband was no unshaven, bad-tempered artist wrestling with fate, but a man who lived affirmatively, who wrote music for his own pleasure and the enjoyment of others, who appreciated all the niceties of human existence. Handsome dress coats, buttons, ruffles, shoe buckles, were the objects of his particular weakness. He had remained an ardent devotee of dancing, and Constanze often declared, joking, that it meant even more to him than music.

Wolfgang could be himself with Constanze in their gentle and gay companionship. The romantic call of his soul found no echo in life, so he poured it into his music. It was Constanze's most valuable contribution that she did not interfere.

Mozart did not so much need someone to inspire him for his work as to save him from overstrain. Constanze did this very well. She was lazy by nature. Although unable to prevent her husband from keeping his long hours at the piano, to which he had been accustomed from childhood, she could be a persistent little devil when it came to persuade him to quit his writing table, wrap up their lunch and take her outdoors. Wolfgang, who had never before been permitted the least unnecessary expenditure, however much he earned, adored his wife for the pleasure she got out of modest entertainment and the little trifles he could afford to bring home. When their fortunes ran low, she never nagged. Good-naturedly, she would pack their trunks again and move to cheaper quarters. Although moving was something fairly unusual in Vienna among married couples, they moved four times in their first year of marriage and many more times thereafter.

More and more the subtle and sensitive character of Mozart's music grew toward perfection. Twenty years of study and experience had given him superior technical certainty. The requirements of the craft had become natural to him, his choice and treatment of artistic devices spontaneous and effortless. His uneven temperament, which since his childhood had been reflected in sudden changes of mood in his music, made him search longingly for "the happy medium—truth in all things"; not even his most emotional passages were permitted to disturb classical balance and clarity. In life, Wolfgang's mercurial spirit often prevented him from attaining this ideal, but here the balance was, so to speak, achieved through his natural decency.

Under his influence, Constanze gradually lost the quarrelsome "Weberisch" disposition and developed the better side of her character. She later made a good mother for her two surviving sons. Although her tendency to imitate the levity of social entertainment then prevailing in Vienna had troubled Wolfgang before their marriage, she was a very good wife. The serenity of their life together was never really clouded.

Wolfgang could have done worse than to marry Constanze. An ambitious woman like Aloysia would have dominated him beyond endurance. And in spite of his full acceptance by the high nobility, social prejudices were still too strong to permit him to marry one of the young ladies he met in those circles. Many rich bourgeois and minor nobles would have been glad to have him as a son-in-law, but this might have been a strenuous life and not at all amusing. And he would always crave amusement as in his very youthful years. "I can't help it, I must poke fun at someone," he wrote to Constanze in one of the darkest moments of his life.

It was summer when he left the Archbishop and it was summer again when he got married—a beautiful season, but very unprofitable for a free-lance musician. From the very beginning, a trip to Salzburg was planned. Wolfgang was anxious to have his father meet his wife and Leopold had urged them to come. He felt that the personal introduction of his daughter-in-law might make a more favorable impression in Salzburg than her letters. Constanze herself eagerly expressed the wish to embrace her in-laws, but at heart she was terribly afraid.

But hard as he tried, they could not get away. In the fall, the Russian Grand Duke passed through Vienna again on his return trip and this time he was to see *Die Entführung* under the composer's direction. In November, they sat with their trunks already packed but were stopped by bad weather. Wolfgang felt he could not expose his wife to it, as she had just confessed to him that she was expecting a child. The trip was postponed until spring.

The Vienna season was gay. Hardly had Wolfgang settled down when he found himself surrounded by a circle of merry friends. When winter came, they all went dancing together. In a wonderful red dress coat with fancy buttons, a gift of the Baroness—Wolfgang had been so funny in his despair because he could not afford it—his graceful figure and fine powdered head would show up wherever there was any dancing to be done.

Wolfgang loved to write little burlesque sketches for the young, gay crowd around him. *The Salzburger Rascal in Vienna* was one of them.

But he did not always write jokes. "I should like to write a book, a short criticism of music," he wrote to his father bitterly. Work in Vienna was not easy. Tastes changed with amazing speed. People were no longer as interested in the best as in the new and thrilling. Nonentities attracted audiences to the Italian theater, while German opera was on the decline. *Die Entführung* seemed to remain in lonely splendor. Another libretto had been offered to Wolfgang, but it was atrocious. Umlauff, who had set it to music, had been hissed off the stage. In the meantime Wolfgang taught, played, and composed piano music—three piano concertos within a few months, "very brilliant, pleasant to the ear and natural," just as the Viennese wanted all music to be just then. He gave his own concerts and was frequently invited to assist at those of others. The programs were very long. This public, not yet overstrained by daily life, wished to get its money's worth.

More often than not, the Emperor was present. Prince Kaunitz was said to have told Archduke Maximilian that people like young Mozart were born only once in a century. Gluck, hardly recovered from a paralytic stroke, had asked him to dinner twice; Haydn introduced him to Prince Esterházy, who spent the winter in Vienna with his retinue; Prince Gallitzin had engaged him for all his concerts; van Swieten highly praised his instrumentation of fugues; publishers became interested in his works . . . and still the Emperor offered no appointment.

Early in the fall, just a few weeks after he was married, Wolfgang had buried himself in French and English grammar and had written to Le Gros. In spells of discouragement he sometimes played with the thought of leaving Vienna, only to abandon it in the same breath.

This time it was Papa who urged him to stay put. Hardly recovered from the shock of Wolfgang's marriage, Leopold was greatly worried by his son's restlessness only a year after he had declared that Vienna was the one and only place in the world for him. Maybe the Baroness Waldstätten could mother him a little.

"He is too impatient, too hasty," Leopold complained to her, "and will not bide his time. Two opposing elements rule his nature; there is either too much or too little, never the golden mean. Who will prevent him from pursuing his present career in Vienna, if only he has a little patience? Kapellmeister Bonno is a very old man. After his death, Salieri will be promoted and will make room for someone else. . . ."

Yes, Salieri. . . . Little did Papa know.

Salieri, picked up by the late Court Conductor Gassmann and supported by him, while Wolfgang was the protégé of kings and queens, became Gassmann's successor eight years later while Wolfgang had to leave Vienna empty-handed. Then the shrewd Italian became a devoted disciple of Gluck, his only real competitor, who now allowed him to use his name as a collaborator on an opera for Paris. It was undoubtedly Salieri's influence that Gluck did no more for Mozart than invite him to dinner. And now the Italian even jeopardized a fixed income for Wolfgang. When it turned out that he was unable to teach piano as well as voice, the Emperor had asked him to suggest someone else as a piano teacher for the Princess of Württemberg. This time the Princess actually asked for Mozart, but Salieri recommended an obscure musician named Summer.

That Italian established himself as a dictator. Soon the theater would again be completely italianized. A French group had been dismissed because one of the actors had offended the Emperor while his guest at Schönbrunn; *Singspiel* was gradually killed by silly librettos and permanent quarrels in the company. Joseph had had two attacks of fever in the fall; he was a sick man and yielded easily to persuasion. Salieri said that Italian opera would solve all the problems, and no one contradicted. So why not have Italian opera?

Rosenberg sent messengers all over Italy to round up singers, and they brought the best they could find. Among them were an Englishwoman and an Irishman who had studied at Naples: Nancy Storace, tall and fair, her dark voice contrasting most attractively with her appearance, and Michael O'Kelly, a highly gifted tenor who tried his own hand at song-writing. With them came Nancy's brother Stephen and young Thomas Attwood, both composers.

Wolfgang had never lost his weakness for the British and a friendship was soon struck up among the five, with Attwood becoming his pupil, and his most promising one at that. However, Nancy's presence meant severe competition for Aloysia. Aloysia was among the few of the German group to amalgamate with the Italians, and these few found themselves confronted with unfriendliness and intrigue. Aloysia came often to the Mozarts' and wept on Wolfgang's shoulder. Besides, she was very unhappy in her marriage. Josef Lange made disgraceful public scenes because of his jealousy, and her name was dragged through the gossip columns of the papers. An affectionate friendship developed between her and Wolfgang. She gradually began to appreciate the full worth of the man with whom she had thoughtlessly toyed; she made it a point of singing his works, and, new and striking as they were, such an exquisite interpreter was almost as important to Wolfgang as the supply of his music was to her. Now she and Adamberger, the first Belmonte, approaching their debut in Italian opera with justifiable stage-fright, asked Wolfgang to write them a few arias to be introduced in the Anfossi opus in which they were to sing.

This procedure was not unusual, but whatever Wolfgang did seemed to raise a storm in the Italian teacup. He wants to correct Anfossi, they complained, and the success of Aloysia's arias (K. 418, 419), made things only worse. As for Adamberger, Salieri in person had talked him out of singing his (K. 420).

A real clash might have ended in an understanding, but there was no open conflict between Mozart and Salieri. The Italian was no villain, only a shrewd and cautious schemer. Later he was to be very helpful to young Beethoven, Schubert, and Liszt. In Mozart's time, however, he was still a fairly young man with an unusually high position which he felt he might have to defend against this young fellow from the provinces, who found ready audiences wherever he appeared. Gossip-mongers took care of the rest. Polite, very polite, in personal intercourse, Mozart and Salieri haunted one another in their imaginations. Wolfgang's aversion gradually reached the point of mania and embittered his life until his very last hours. He never knew how afraid Salieri was of him.

"Every nation has an opera of its own, why should not we Germans have one also?" Wolfgang wrote to Papa and, at the same time, feverishly pored over hundreds of booklets friends had sent at his request from—Italy. The Italian singers were excellent; Count Rosenberg had vaguely encouraged Wolfgang as to his prospects with Italian opera.

But all these librettos were not worth editing. Where would Mozart find a poet?

CHAPTER 20

SUMMER 1783

"YOU SHOULD MEET my young friend Mozart, Abbate,"
Baron Wetzlar addressed a diabolic face above a dandy's
raiment. The Baron, one of Wolfgang's numerous ex-land-
lords, had become very friendly.

The diabolic face nodded vaguely. "I am always delighted to
meet one of your friends. I have heard about him. An excellent
pianist, they say."

Abbate Lorenzo da Ponte, newly-appointed Court Poet, liked
to be addressed—though not to be dressed—as a clergyman. His
lean face, with its high, hollow cheeks, thin lips, eagle's nose and
shaggy eyebrows looked devilish indeed. Born in the Venetian
ghetto, he had been turned into a Catholic when he was fourteen,
and later had become a priest.

Young Lorenzo changed his mind after the ordination. He had
learned Italian and Latin rapidly and had become a wizard at
translating verses from one into the other. His dexterity in writing
was remarkable. Feeling that he could do better in a worldly career
than in the Church, he first established himself in Venice, where
he taught Italian until he was banished for immoral conduct and
socialistic propaganda. Then he toured the rest of the continent
in a series of breath-taking adventures. Down and out, he finally
came to Vienna with a letter of introduction to Salieri. Soon after
he was presented to the Emperor.

"Have you ever written for the stage?" asked Joseph II, amused
by da Ponte's appearance and personality.

[163]

"No, Your Majesty," answered the Abbate, regretting at the same moment that he had told the truth and perhaps spoiled a chance for himself. But this was just what the Emperor wanted to hear. The routine playwrights were dull and exhausted. "Fine, we shall have a virgin muse," he smiled, and da Ponte was named Court Poet.

He buried himself in librettos to see what it was all about, and when he had read a hundred of them, he found that he could do better. He had a sharp, quick mind and knew his world. There was no character he felt unable to depict to perfection, because he had dealt with them all at some time in his life.

It was in Vienna that he had met Baron Wetzlar, also a scion of a Jewish family, recently ennobled and very wealthy. He could discuss things more openly with Wetzlar than at Court or with Salieri.

"An excellent pianist indeed," Wetzlar confirmed. "But not only that. An excellent composer."

"I have heard his German opera," replied da Ponte. "A fine piece of music. Too bad that the company is folding up. But Italian opera to the Italians, eh?"

"Mozart is the coming man, my dear Abbate. You know the Emperor . . . it's his privilege to change his mind . . . I think you ought to meet Mozart. . . ."

The Abbate became thoughtful. Yes, it was not wise to stake one's fortunes on a single card.

"I am greatly indebted to Signor Salieri," he replied bombastically, "and I am going to be loyal to him. But only narrow-minded people could speak of disloyalty if I were just to meet another composer and discuss opera with him, as long as it does not interfere with my work for the Signor Maestro Court Composer."

"So I can arrange the meeting?" Wetzlar was eager.

"No arrangements, please," declined the Abbate. "I am sure to meet Maestro Mozart some day, quite accidentally. . . ."

The Baron beamed. "I hope, Abbate, that you will honor me with your presence at my party a week from tomorrow."

"I want you to meet one of my friends," said Wetzlar to Wolfgang and dragged him through the crowded reception room to the opulent buffet. "This is Abbate da Ponte. You ought to know each other. . . ." He handed Wolfgang a plate and disappeared.

Mozart was too embarrassed to be talkative. This was a surprise indeed. He had seen the Court Poet before and had made some biting remarks about the Abbate's mannerisms and his all too obvious efforts to make a graceful appearance. Everything about him seemed affected: the dancing gait, the dandified clothes, the way he wore an incredible quantity of trinkets as a savage tribesman might have worn the bones of his victims—even the heavy Venetian accent. Only the strong lisp was not rehearsed. The story had it that the gallant Abbate had lost all his teeth through the medical advice of a jealous surgeon.

They started talking about one thing and another, with Wolfgang trying to be unusually cautious. After all, da Ponte was Salieri's man. The Abbate admired Wolfgang's flawless Italian.

"Well, I've been to Italy three times," Mozart replied aggressively. "And I have written *opera* there."

A short silence followed. Then da Ponte said: "It will take me two more months to finish a libretto for Signor Salieri. Perhaps we might discuss something after that. . . ."

The plate almost slipped from Wolfgang's trembling hand. This was incredible, miraculous, the Heaven-sent solution of all his problems, the certain victory over Salieri. The Italian Court Poet his librettist. . . . Confusedly he stammered something about looking forward to it very much indeed, while the Abbate, highly satisfied with the effect he had produced, addressed another visitor with his well-rehearsed diabolic smile.

Da Ponte. . . . But soon Wolfgang recovered from the shock. These Italians were just a bunch of tricksters. This was nothing but a trap and he, with his un-Italian naïveté, had nearly walked into it. Salieri and da Ponte were conspirators. They had agreed that Mozart should be prevented from seeking a collaborator for an opera while waiting for the Signor Court Poet to write one for him. But he would outsmart them both. If Salieri had his Abbate, he, Mozart, would have an Abbate, too. Papa could easily manage to reconcile Varesco and have him send suggestions for an *opera buffa* right away. While the two Italians would think he was waiting and dreaming futile dreams, he would finish an entire opera better than they could ever hope to write.

So Wolfgang wrote to Papa, and Varesco got busy.

When the first sketches came from Salzburg, Wolfgang's belligerent mind was distracted by cheerful preparations for a happy event in his family. On the morning of June 17, Constanze gave birth to a fat little boy. At her bedside, with mother Cäcilia and the midwife fluttering about the room, sat Wolfgang with music paper spread out before him. When the first weak cry came from the baby's lips, his father had just written the last notes of a string quartet (K. 421).

Wolfgang could not very well visualize himself as a father. Often before the baby arrived, he had thought that it might be time for him to become very dignified. The picture he had of fathers completely disagreed with the picture he had of himself. He made a few unsuccessful attempts at dignity and then gave it up. If some bossy female had not always been watching, he would have fooled around with son Raymund Leopold (Raymund being Baron Wetzlar's first name) all day long.

When Constanze had sufficiently recovered from her confinement, little Raymund was left in the care of someone out in a suburb, and by the end of July the young Mozarts had started on their long-overdue trip to Salzburg.

Leopold's letters had been anything but cordial, and the young people met with a cool reception. Papa could not forgive Constanze for crowding him out of his son's heart, as he believed. He still felt that Wolfgang owed him everything and that she deserved nothing. And although Baroness Waldstätten had assured him that Constanze was not like the other Webers at all, he could not bring himself to accept as a Mozart the woman who had given birth to his first grandson and heir.

For three months, four uneasy people lived together: Leopold stubborn and embittered, with Nannerl afraid of his moods and nothing more than just polite; Wolfgang over-sensitive; and Constanze hopelessly clumsy. To increase the discomfort, Leopold had students staying with him, and their very presence was a grim reproach to his son. Wasn't he ashamed to let his father labor like that in his old age? Instead of supporting him as he had promised, he had exchanged a good position for an incompetent wife.

They went out to see old friends. The friends, too, were a disappointment. Wolfgang had changed, they decided, and to Wolfgang they now appeared intolerably provincial. Michael Haydn was the only exception. He was eager to hear all about Vienna and his brother, whom he secretly envied. Michael Haydn was not feeling well, and asked Wolfgang to ghost-write a couple of duos for violin and viola (K. 423, 424) for him which Hieronymus had ordered. Wolfgang willingly complied with his request. If the Mufti had known!

The Archbishop made no attempt to harass Wolfgang as some friends had feared. He ignored Wolfgang's presence and he also ignored Leopold's request to have his son's new mass (K. 427) performed in the Cathedral. Wolfgang had made a vow to write a mass for Salzburg if he brought Constanze there as his wife. He had planned it ambitiously and had started to work on it in January with enthusiasm. But it shared the same fate as other works connected with her—it remained a fragment. Together with parts of older church music, the mass, later transferred into the oratorio *Davidde penitente* (K. 469), was performed on August 25, at St. Peter's, with Constanze singing the soprano part.

Only later did the distressed parents learn that at about the same time their first-born had been buried in a small suburban cemetery. They never found out whether the carelessness of his guardians had caused the baby's death and whether their presence might have saved him.

Drearily the summer went by. Shortly before Wolfgang and Constanze left Salzburg, a trivial incident brought the smoldering fire of mutual aversion to a sudden blaze. Leopold used to show everybody a collection of trinkets acquired during Wolfgang's child-prodigy period. Constanze had long coveted at least one small memento and finally, after Papa had repeatedly ignored her hints, she asked for one. Thereupon Leopold exploded. Hadn't he made it very plain that they had nothing to expect from him? Did Constanze perhaps intend to by-pass this decision by appealing to sentiment?

Constanze lost her temper for the first and last time in Papa's presence. Wolfgang diplomatically diverted the scene to the only field of common understanding, his new opera. He brought Papa right back from the family tragedy into the comedy of *L'Oca del Cairo* (K. 422). This was the libretto Varesco had suggested. It was a comic paraphrase of the Trojan horse story and offered many funny situations and dramatic impossibilities. Wolfgang had already started to compose, and Papa was again left the doubtful pleasure of arguing with Varesco after Wolfgang had gone away.

Wolfgang had always left Salzburg with relief, but never as gladly as this time. On their way home he played the organ in the Lambach monastery and in Linz he composed a symphony, commonly called the *Linz* Symphony (K. 425), on a few days' notice for a soirée at Count Thun's, the father-in-law of his pupil in Vienna. He was overflowing with new ideas, happy, and very much in love with his wife. A strange presentiment told him that he had been to Salzburg for the last time.

CHAPTER 21

THE FAVORITE OF VIENNA
[1 7 8 3 - 8 5]

FOR THE NEXT THREE YEARS, Mozart was the rage of Vienna. Encouraged by his successes of the previous winter, he took a chance on subscription concerts on a wider scale. Repeat performances of *Die Entführung* helped to keep him in the public eye. His mornings were crowded with lessons, the afternoons with composition. In the spring of 1784 he had twenty-two appearances in about five weeks. Just as his serenades had once opened the hearts of all Salzburg to him, his piano playing now made him the most fashionable young artist in the capital.

He caught to perfection the spirit of a beautiful and beauty-addicted society. In these three years he wrote the greater part of his masterful piano concertos, and he was their best interpreter. Mozart had grown into artistic maturity. The enthusiastic response of his audiences was a constant source of power. Every concert he gave, every note he wrote, was a bitter fight against his strongest competitor: the man he had been the day before. He wanted to do better every day, and he wanted his listeners to do better, too.

An atmosphere of privacy prevailed even in the public concerts of that time. Everybody knew everybody else. A common love of music bridged discrepancies of birth or education, even of mentality. There were nearly always the same faces in the boxes and everybody felt at home.

In the public concert hall on the Mehlgrube, in the theater, in the spacious salons of the palaces, the slender, exquisitely dressed man with the pale face and sparkling rings on his beautiful hands was a conspicuous figure. Whenever the Emperor put in an appearance, His Majesty was likely to make a favorable remark about the brilliant young musician.

Less favorable were the remarks that young Dr. Barisani made about Wolfgang's health. The doctor had known him since their childhood days in Salzburg together and was aware of his previous illnesses. Mozart's bad posture and pallid face were tell-tale signs of irregular hours and a sedentary occupation. Dr. Barisani prescribed fresh air and exercise.

Wolfgang thought it over. He was willing to work standing up, but not to engage in anything which required non-musical concentration. He became increasingly distracted, as though living in a fog of sounds. So they compromised on billiards and horseback riding. Wolfgang bought a billiard table, and took to long morning rides in the Augarten after leaving a tender little note for his wife. When Constanze was well enough, she, too, rose at five o'clock and Wolfgang took a morning walk with her instead. This had become the fashion in Vienna, with the Emperor giving the cue.

Gradually Wolfgang, who had never had any particular feeling for nature, longed increasingly for flowers and trees, probably because he had now become a city dweller. He had always loved animals and usually kept a little dog or birds. Once, in the spring of 1784, he encountered a marvel. From within a pet shop he heard a starling whistle that seemed to be the theme of his G major piano concerto (K. 453); he had written it only five weeks before. No, it couldn't be. But there the tune was again, and it *was* the concerto. Wolfgang rushed into the store, seized the cage, paid with eyes and ears glued to the little bird, hardly counting the change. "Vogel-Stahrl" became an important member of the Mozart household. When it died three years later, Wolfgang was in great distress. Solemnly he buried it in a garden behind his lodgings, under a stone with an epitaph he wrote himself.

It had not taken long for Wolfgang to enlarge the circle of his acquaintances. The nobles in whose salons he performed never made him feel like a hired entertainer. Yet, for all their kindness, they were sponsors rather than friends. This distinction, however, did not exist with the minor nobles, who mixed readily with the better bourgeois. There were the Trattners, the Aurnhammers, the Ployers, the Wetzlars, the Greiners, the Keesses, the Mesmers. In most cases the friendship developed through instructing or composing for the lady or the daughter of the house; but these were privileges he granted them rather than a favor they did for him, and they paid very well. Under these circumstances, Wolfgang did not feel like looking around for a broader field of lesser paying pupils, which was to become a crucial point later in his life. He would rather teach for nothing, as in the case of poor but gifted little Johannes Hummel, whom he took into his house, perhaps stimulated by a sentimental desire to repay a debt to fate for the lucky circumstances of his own child-prodigy career.

Every Wednesday evening there was open house at the Jacquins'. Freiherr von Jacquin was a celebrated botanist, living near the Botanical Garden in the suburb of Landstrasse, which Maria Theresa had founded. While the older set discussed science and literature, the younger crowd gathered around Gottfried and Franziska, well educated and talented young people. To this carefree social intercourse, posterity owes a variety of small pieces: instrumental, or vocal with accompaniment. The scoring was small, owing to the occasions, and limited to woodwinds. Wolfgang grabbed at the opportunity to write for the clarinet, his favorite instrument since he had first used it in 1771 in a divertimento written during his second Italian trip for some private concert. It was probably in the circle around the Jacquins that he now met the brothers Stadler: Maximilian, a distinguished church composer and Abbé, and Anton, a lighthead, clarinetist and Freemason. Wolfgang's weakness for Anton, which was to cost him dearly when he least could afford it, was due to the combination of Anton's fine virtuosity on the clarinet and his adherence to the order. For, at about the same time Wolfgang ran into Ignaz von Born, a renowned scientist and masonic leader. Wolfgang was fascinated with the impressive rites and their implications. He joined the order late in 1784, and, a loyal fellow-brother to his dying day, wrote many compositions for his Lodge.

A most surprising piece of news had come from Salzburg in the summer of 1784. Nannerl, who had been almost resigned to celibacy after her unfortunate passion for Mr. Penniless, had announced her marriage. She was thirty-three, a fairly old bride for those days when girls were usually married off in their teens, but the groom was no callow youth either. Johann Baptist von Berchtold zu Sonnenburg was a dignified widower with five children and a Magistrate of St. Gilgen, who lived in the very house where Anna Maria Mozart had been born. Wolfgang sent his sister a joking little poem a few days before the ceremony, but thereafter there was hardly any correspondence between them. Somehow they had become strangers. They had nothing in common but memories.

Leopold was left alone in the big house with no one to take care of him but faithful Theresa. Wolfgang suggested that he resign from his post and come to live with him in Vienna, but the old man had been used to being in service all his life and stayed put to the very end. Also, he perhaps did not feel like being at the mercy of his daughter-in-law.

In September, 1784, a second son, Karl Thomas, was born to the Mozarts in the Trattner house on the Graben. A few weeks later the young family moved to larger quarters at Schulerstrasse 846, a two-minute walk from St. Stephen's. Therese von Trattner, however, remained Mozart's pupil and lifelong devotee. Before moving, he wrote for her the famous piano sonata in C minor (K. 457) as a sort of farewell present, and subsequently, as an introduction to it, the Fantasy in the same key (K. 475).

Moving was quite a business, with the billiard table, the piano, the baby, the dog, and the starling. In their new dwellings, they tried to introduce a spirit of order and system. Wolfgang even went so far as to start entering his income and expenses in a little book and keeping a catalogue of his works. The account book didn't last long. . . .

The billiard table was placed in the center of a big room with a desk standing at the window. The green board became a magnet. Someone would dash into the room at any hour of the day and ask for a game. Wolfgang usually won (because he practiced secretly, with Constanze—hadn't Dr. Barisani ordered exercise?) and this gave him the greatest of pleasure. Between shots he continued to work. This was what amazed people most about him: the complete detachment of his musical thoughts.

With so much space at his disposal, Wolfgang made a habit of having weekly chamber music sessions in his own house and charging a nominal entrance fee. His service for the Archbishop had given him a strong aversion to fiddling, but here he readily took a hand in performing his own works, or Joseph Haydn's, or whatever came into his hands.

Haydn himself showed up whenever he was in Vienna. The mutual devotion of these two has become proverbial. It is the perfect symbol of the really great finding one another in a world of petty jealousy. The nickname of "Papa," which was Wolfgang's invention and which Haydn has retained ever since, therefore has a double meaning. Wolfgang looked up to his friend, twenty-four years older than he, as he had not looked up to anyone since the days of Padre Martini.

But Haydn learned a great deal from Mozart, too. His style grew easier, fuller and more melodious after he came to know Wolfgang's music. He admitted it to everyone, and pointedly stepped into the background in favor of the younger man whom he considered to be greater than himself. Many years after Wolfgang's death, the dignified old man would still burst into tears when Mozart's name was mentioned.

But there were other musicians who spoke less well of Wolfgang; the friendship of the two "modernists" gave these a welcome point of attack. Once, when listening to a Haydn quartet, one of them sourly remarked to Wolfgang that he would not have written it like that at all. Thereupon Wolfgang scornfully snapped back: "Nor I— do you know why? Because neither I—nor you!—would have been able to write it."

Such tartness was not wise and did not make friends for Wolfgang. But he was too naïve to recognize sweet-sour cordiality for what it was worth, nor did he realize how quickly public mood might change. Undisturbedly, he indulged in the pleasure the Viennese got from his music, and in his own pleasure of writing for them. The nonentities of the concert stages did not yet dare to throw a stone at the declared favorite, but the compliments on their lips were poisoned—they kept at a distance and waited for their time to come.

Varesco had turned out to be impossible. He would not listen to suggestions and after a few months Wolfgang gave him up. He also dropped *Lo Sposo deluso* (K. 430), another Italian opera he had started. Its libretto was equally bad, and he could not afford to waste his time.

The Salieri-da Ponte team was working on their first opera together (which was also da Ponte's first stage opus), when vigorous competitors began to loom up. Giovanni Paisiello and Giuseppe Sarti would pass through Vienna, Paisiello returning to Italy after eight years as music director at the Russian Court, Sarti on his way from Italy to St. Petersburg to take over. Both had written a number of operas which had been performed in Vienna. Paisiello in particular was kept in the spotlight. His *Il Barbiere di Seviglia* was based on Beaumarchais' play, and Beaumarchais, in Paris, had finally succeeded in staging its sequel, *Le Marriage de Figaro,* after a fierce three-year fight with censorship.

Salieri considered it fortunate that Gluck managed to have their "joint" opera, *Les Danaïdes,* performed in Paris in the summer of 1784. He felt that his reputation in Vienna was still hurt by the success of *Die Entführung*. The call to Paris would undoubtedly impress the Viennese, for it always meant more in Vienna to be recognized abroad than to be successful at home. So Salieri left for

Paris and his new librettist, da Ponte, had to face an aggressive enemy, Abbate Casti, alone.

Casti, a sexagenerian like Count Rosenberg and his friend from bygone days in Florence, had the reputation of writing and living in a rather slippery way. This did not hurt his prestige as a great poet, however, nor had it prevented him from acquiring a highly privileged position at the Russian Court.

Joseph had hardly heard of the presence of Paisiello and Casti, "two of the greatest geniuses alive," when he summoned them to the next levee, and asked them to do an opera together for the Court Theater. So, while da Ponte waited for Salieri to return, Paisiello and Casti produced *Il Rè Teodoro,* based on a chapter from Voltaire's *Candide.* It was an excellent opera, and it was given the best cast and magnificent costumes and settings. The première, on August 23, 1784, was a tremendous success. Wolfgang was overwhelmed with enthusiasm and heartache. Memories of the night of *Mitridate* came back, when he had faced an opera audience for the first time, confident, enthralled by the atmosphere, hardly aware of difficulties. At 28, Walfgang began feeling very old. Moreover, he was not well. Exposure to the fresh air after the stuffy atmosphere of the theater made him severely ill for weeks. Dr. Barisani had to come every day.

Salieri returned in the fall, worn out and, as da Ponte angrily remarked, musically "frenchified." He hurriedly finished their opera and had it produced on December 6. The performance brought boos and hisses, a hypocritical statement by Casti that da Ponte was indeed a great lyric poet and could hardly be expected to know the stage too, while Salieri swore that he would rather cut off his hand than ever set a single line of da Ponte's to music again. He immediately lined up with Casti, while poor da Ponte went about his dull routine in a bad temper, wondering whether he would ever again find anyone to set to music what he wrote.

Wolfgang, in the meantime, taught, composed, played the piano and billiards, and felt rather out of it all. In the various houses that he frequented and through da Ponte himself, whom he occasionally saw in the English set, he heard all about the inter-Italian struggle.

These Latins were ready to poison one another over trifles but formed an insurmountable barrier against any outsider.

So there was nothing to do but get ready for another concert season. Papa had announced his visit to Vienna for the midwinter, and Wolfgang and Constanze prepared for it like soldiers for a general's inspection. The place was practically inundated in scrub-water, and Wolfgang went sighing about a distasteful task—the writing down of music. He always loathed this job; for him, a piece of music was finished as soon as it was ready in his head. But he had one of his most crowded concert seasons ahead of him, and besides Papa ought to see how much he had worked.

Leopold arrived on the morning of February 11, 1785, apprehensive and ready to turn on his heels at the first sign of friction. He was prepared to find poor Wolfgang living in a mess of dirt, diapers and unwashed dishes, with his manuscripts used as wrapping paper, like Joseph Haydn's before his escape from conjugal martyrdom. Constanze and Wolfgang greeted him warmly and dragged him as quickly as his old gouty feet would carry him to the little bed. There was Karl Thomas, as well-washed as babies could be in those days. To Leopold's delight, his grandson was a perfect copy of Wolfgang and as jolly as Wolfgang had ever been. Everything else, too, in this house seemed to be Mozartish rather than Weberish. Thoughtfully, Leopold examined the immaculately clean apartment, the kitchen, the billiard table, and stopped inquisitively before a piano with a pedal he had never seen before. "I had it made for me," explained Wolfgang. "It is carried to most of my concerts." Leopold looked at him startled and continued his sight-seeing.

"How much is your rent, Wolfgang?" "460 gulden." "So, so." "But that's a bargain, Papa. Herr Stephanie is paying five hundred for a much smaller place, because he is living on the Michaelerplatz near the theater. People are such snobs. When I take the short-cuts, I can be at the theater in ten minutes." It appears that you don't have to be there very often, Papa wanted to say. To his own surprise, he kept quiet instead.

Wolfgang had the first of three subscription concerts on the

Mehlgrube that very evening. He was constantly leaving Papa and rushing to the window in the music room, where a copyist worked with flying fingers on a new piano concerto, the famous one in D minor (K. 466), which he was going to play. As usual, he had written it down in the last minute.

When he came on the platform, he bowed conspicuously up to the box where Papa was seated. Many eyes turned to the old man with his still handsome face, dressed in the pathetic remnants of once fashionable gala clothes. In the intermission people flocked around him, introduced him to others, and they all claimed to know him or to have heard of him. Leopold secretly glanced at his daughter-in-law. But her natural, unpresumptuous ways were disarming, and the Mehlgrube, with its friendly audience, was hardly an appropriate battle ground.

The next day an unusual celebration took place at Schulerstrasse 846. Haydn had become a Freemason the night before, and he and two other brothers were to come and play three new quartets of a series of six, among them the so-called *Hunt* Quartet (K. 458). In 1781, Haydn's new string quartets had stimulated Wolfgang to resume writing in that form. Early in 1785, he had hurriedly finished the series in order to play them with the friend who, as he said, had taught him how to write them; later he dedicated them to Haydn with words of deep affection.

Now, on the 12th of February, 1785, the two Papas were to meet. "I tell you before God and as an honest man," said Haydn solemnly, "that your son is the greatest composer I know—either in person or by name." And more casually he continued: "He has taste, and, what is more, the most profound knowledge of composition."

Leopold murmured embarrassed words of appreciation. But to himself he said that if he were to drop dead this very minute he would know that he had not lived in vain.

There were many more concerts, and Wolfgang's music filled Leopold's eyes with tears of delight. The serenity and clarity, the beauty of the interplay of instruments in these piano concertos revealed his son's art to him as never before. While Wolfgang played, flashes of bygone days danced behind Papa's eyes. The first music lessons, Schönbrunn, Versailles, St. James Park . . . the Accademia and the Vatican . . . opera houses in Italy and Munich . . . they were all his doing and from them had sprung to life every single one of the wonderful creations that poured from the magic fingers of that little man who was his son. "Papa comes right after God" . . . the piano sang to Leopold. There had been nasty scenes and nasty letters . . . but all this did not matter any longer . . . God has performed a miracle and placed it in my hands . . . a quarter of a century ago he had said it for the first time. He had almost forgotten it since, but now he knew . . . God *has* performed a miracle. . . .

". . . Bravo Mozart!" shouted someone, and the voice was swelled by waves of applause. It was the Emperor standing in his box and waving his hat.

Wolfgang's successes and Constanze's unexpected efficiency melted Leopold's icy stubbornness. Once Wolfgang made 559 gulden at a single concert—almost as much as Leopold's yearly salary. Even though hostile to the Webers on principle, Papa was less rude to Constanze than he had intended to be, and he went to see Aloysia who sang for him. And to her great surprise, Nannerl read: "We lunched on Thursday the 17th with your brother's mother-in-law, Frau Weber. . . . I must tell you that the meal, which was neither too lavish nor too stingy, was cooked to perfection. The roast was a fine plump pheasant and everything was excellently prepared. . . ." Prejudices of seven long years had vanished with a nice piece of pheasant on Leopold's plate. . . .

"We never go to bed before one o'clock. Every day there are concerts; and the whole time is given up to teaching, music, composing and so forth. . . . If only the concerts were over! It is impossible for me to describe the rush and bustle. Since my arrival [four weeks before] your brother's pianoforte has been taken at least a dozen times to the theater or to some other house. . . . If my son has no debts to pay, I think that he can now put two thousand gulden in the bank. Certainly the money is there, and so far as eating and drinking is concerned, the housekeeping is extremely economical."

So Leopold wrote. . . . However, Wolfgang did have debts to pay, and he hardly ever managed to put money in the bank. But even though he did not know this, Papa became apprehensive. He noticed that little habits that he had vainly criticized when Wolfgang was young had developed conspicuously. His son had grown into a very nervous person, unable to sit still. He tapped with a foot or drummed with his fingers and he grew increasingly distracted, misplacing parts of his music and forgetting important things. Leopold noted with amazement that at table he was so absent-minded that he twisted his napkin around, forgetting to eat, or that he would cut his fingers with the knife, so that Constanze had made it a habit to cut his meat for him. He also wondered at Wolfgang's teaching methods. Usually Wolfgang would play for his pupils, claiming they would learn more if they listened to him than if he had to listen to them. Leopold considered this to be a kind of impatience too. And Wolfgang was as hypersensitive as he had been when a little boy. If someone said a word while he was playing he would stop immediately. People loved him—but would it last? If it did not, then all his little peculiarities would work to his disadvantage.

One day Papa and Wolfgang talked about themselves like good old friends. Leopold no longer upbraided his son for being lazy, but urged him to "try to be patient . . . don't expect everything to happen in five minutes . . . learn to be diplomatic . . . learn to appear tolerant . . . and, for Heaven's sake, don't be too blunt. . . ."

And then came a crucial question: "Wolfgang, I have the impression that you neglect your religious duties?" True, Wolfgang admitted, he was not going to Church as regularly as before. But this had nothing to do with his belief in God. Then he gave Papa a lecture on Freemasonry. "I have composed nothing for the Church because there is so little opportunity now," he said, "but I am always composing for my masonic brothers and am never too busy to do it."

As they went on talking, Papa saw with amazement how Wolfgang's eyes shone when he said that death was the ultimate truth of life, and that our wanderings on earth were only trials and preparation. Leopold became first interested, then thoughtful, finally enthusiastic. He, too, needed a new object for his religious impulses, since the Service in Salzburg had become so uninspiring. Before he left Vienna, he entered Wolfgang's Lodge. A new tie had been created between father and son. When Leopold held his worn hands over his grandchild's head in his farewell blessing, there was no formality, nor were their future letters unpleasant. Their freemasonic allusions, however, caused Leopold to burn them all, while his were destroyed by Constanze after Wolfgang's death, in petty resentment.

CHAPTER 22

"*FIGARO*"

[1 7 8 5 - 8 6]

WOLFGANG could never be happy without an opera contract. But he had grown tired of wrestling with Italians. He wanted to write another *Entführung*. Something simple, in German.

Another theater, the Kärntnerthortheater—thus named because of its location by one of the city gates, the Kärntnerthor—had been amalgamated with the Court Theater and was in the stage of redecoration. German and Italian opera would be given there by turns. Wolfgang watched the preparations with suspicion. The old and inefficient management had been retained. No big income was expected from the enterprise and instead of top-flight singers, actors would be hired who knew how to sing if they had to. And Wolfgang bitterly recalled how actors had been paid not so long ago. In addition to a minimum fee, they were given bonuses for special performances—for every slap in the face, for every time they were pushed down the stairs or drenched with water and—for every aria they sang. And the lustiest kick, the wettest coat and the loudest aria would bring just a modest income. Director Anton Klein of Mannheim had sent Wolfgang a Rudolf von Habsburg libretto some time before, but Wolfgang had hardly taken the trouble to read it. "It looks as if they were trying to ruin German opera altogether," he sighed in his letter, an angry outburst against German-speaking people who refused to think, act, speak and, above all, sing in their mother tongue.

Meanwhile the trio Rosenberg-Salieri-Casti went about their schemes to drive da Ponte out of his position. Lorenzo da Ponte had not dared to go near the Emperor since the failure of his first opera, but, when the warm season came, he managed to meet him one morning in the Augarten "by accident." The Emperor stopped him: "You know, da Ponte, your opera is not that bad. You must summon up your courage and write another."

For some time Lorenzo walked the streets of Vienna, thoughtfully, until one day his feet carried him to Schulerstrasse 846, first floor. Wolfgang was standing at his desk, a billiard cue in one hand, a pen in the other.

"For Heaven's sake, Signor da Ponte," he exclaimed. "It is nice to see you again."

"What have you been doing all the time?" questioned da Ponte.

"Oh, nothing. Playing, teaching, composing. Look what I have here."

Lorenzo took the manuscript Wolfgang handed him, and spelled in broken German: *"D-a-s V-e-i-l-ch-e-n"* (K. 476).

"Do you know it? A lovely little poem, by Herrn von Goethe, of Weimar."

Lorenzo looked at the song more closely. Its simplicity was touching. He asked: "Have you many more like this?"

"I have written a few recently," Wolfgang replied and his eyes clouded. "You know, that's my only chance not to forget how to write for voice. Want a game?" and he handed a billiard cue to da Ponte.

"No," said Lorenzo abruptly and put the cue back in its stand. "I want to talk to you about our opera."

"About what?"

"Why, child, this isn't so hard to understand," Lorenzo said and his bony hand grasped Wolfgang's arm. "If Your Highness will condescend to write an Italian opera, My Humbleness will be honored to supply the words."

Wolfgang blinked at da Ponte as through a mist. "Signor Court Poet, this is the nicest thing that has happened to me in many years. . . . Listen, it isn't the first of April as far as I know?"

Da Ponte laughed and flung himself on the sofa. Wolfgang drew up a chair. His fingers drummed nervously on the billiard cue. "But they won't perform what I write. . . ."

"Nor what *I* write, child, unless you do the music." And he gave a sarcastic account of what was happening to him every hour of the day, and of his conversation with the Emperor. "You let me handle it," he concluded. "We shall get it performed, but it must be good."

"What do you want it to be about, Abbate? Any bright idea?"

"No," admitted da Ponte. "All these Italian plays are rubbish. I want something witty, fast, with a big part for Benucci, and Nancy and Michael must be in it too, of course."

Wolfgang opened a door. "Stanzi!" he called.

Constanze came in and shook hands with da Ponte. "What do you think, Stanzi?" asked Wolfgang. "Would Benucci make a good Figaro?"

"Wolfi, please, don't start that all over again," Constanze whined. "You wear me out."

"Why?" da Ponte almost shouted.

"Because ever since he got hold of that play he has gone crazy. He talks about it morning, noon and night, and how he would compose this scene and that, and I think it's useless to talk so much about things that can't be done."

"But why can't it be done?"

"Because the Emperor has just forbidden the play, as you very well know," Constanze remarked dryly, "and I don't believe in writing for the shelves."

"Oh, if that's all. . . ." Lorenzo took a deep breath and seized Wolfgang's hands. "Listen, both of you. If I can manage to get a persecuted librettist and a taboo composer on the stage, I will get permission to adapt a forbidden play. It's just the way of putting things. . . ."

[183]

"You could really manage," Wolfgang asked, "to take it all out . . . I mean the revolutionary business, the offense to our audiences?"

"But certainly, Wolfgang, leave it to me. We are going to write a first-class musical comedy, and they'll have the time of their lives. Signora Mozart, this was the best idea your husband has ever had. . . ." Lorenzo's voice almost cracked with excitement.

"You ought to talk it over with someone," Constanze suggested meekly.

"All right," Wolfgang agreed. "Let's see what Wetzlar has to say."

Arm in arm, mischievously smiling like conspiring children, Wolfgang and Lorenzo walked up to Baron Wetzlar and asked him to abandon his guests for a moment. In a corner of his spacious music room, what may be called the superior perfection of Italian comic opera was settled.

"My wife is a little anxious," Wolfgang ventured, "because the Emperor does not want the play."

"The King of France did not want it either," Wetzlar put in. "And that was the best publicity it could possibly get."

Wetzlar then offered to pay da Ponte for the lyrics and have the opera produced abroad if it proved impossible to get permission to give it in Vienna.

"No," said da Ponte. "I do not want to take advantage of your kindness. I suggest that we go ahead without telling a soul and when we are ready I shall take it to the Emperor myself. In case things go wrong, it will be a great relief to us to know that you are ready to step in."

In the meantime, both Lorenzo and Wolfgang hoped, they might have further opportunities to establish a favorable atmosphere between the Emperor and themselves.

They set to work right away. "As I wrote the words, Mozart set the music to them," da Ponte claimed in his memoirs, and "everything was ready in six weeks." This is doubtful, but hardly ever before or after did Mozart devote himself so completely to a single task. Every afternoon the awkward figure of the playwright hurried across St. Stephen's Square, oblivious of his appearance and of the slush spattered on his clothes by the noblemen's carriages. Every afternoon Wolfgang would eagerly seize the scripts Lorenzo brought him and roar with delight. Hardly allowing him to read what he had written, Lorenzo would drag Wolfgang to the piano to hear what he had composed.

Both were greatly pleased with each other. Da Ponte was an excellent playwright despite his lack of experience. Papa back in Salzburg found the play too involved for adaptation, but da Ponte managed to cut and compress it beautifully, and wrote splendid verses which were much more than mere imitation, as he claimed with exaggerated modesty.

The coming season brought both Lorenzo and Wolfgang assignments from the Emperor; these interrupted their work together but advanced them both a step further in Joseph's favor. Quite unexpectedly Mozart was asked to write a few musical numbers for a one-act comedy in German, *Der Schauspieldirektor* (K. 486), to be given on a double bill with an Italian operetta by Casti and Salieri at the Orangery in Schönbrunn, an occasion arranged to show off the Emperor's best singers and actors to the Governors of the Netherlands on a State visit. Da Ponte was assigned librettist to Vincente Martin y Solar, a young Spanish composer sponsored by the Ambassadress of Spain. Their opera met with such a success that it almost brought about Lorenzo's—resignation. For the manner in which Rosenberg and Casti congratulated him was so offensive that even the hard-boiled Abbate felt unable to stand these hostilities any longer.

He went to the Emperor, firmly determined to take leave. But "You must strike while the iron is hot," Joseph said before da Ponte had even opened his mouth. "I want to hear another opera from you, with Martin's music."

He was much surprised when his Court poet reported soon after that he was about to finish an opera, not with Martin but with Mozart.

"Don't you know," said Joseph, "that Mozart is an excellent

instrumentalist, but that he has written only one opera here and nothing remarkable at that?" He had not changed his mind about *Die Entführung*.

"Without Your Majesty's support," da Ponte tactfully replied, "I too should have written only one play in Vienna."

"What is it about?" asked the Emperor.

This was the crucial moment.

"An adaptation of *Figaro,* Sire."

"Don't you know, da Ponte, that I have forbidden that play?"

"Yes, I do. But in writing a libretto and not a comedy, I had to leave out many scenes, and I managed to omit everything which might offend the refinement and decorum of an entertainment at which Your Majesty presides. Besides, as far as I can judge, the music is very good."

Joseph did not answer immediately. Moments of torturing silence. . . .

"All right," said the Emperor finally. "I trust your good taste. You may have the score copied." And with that he held out his hand to be kissed.

Lorenzo ran down the stairs so quickly that the footman whom the Emperor sent after him could not catch up with him. So Joseph sat down, wrote a few lines in person, sealed the letter and had it dispatched.

Wolfgang was working when Lorenzo burst in, hot, excited, out of breath.

"We've made it, child, we've made it!"

"What?"

"The Emperor. . . ."

There was a commotion outside and an Imperial lackey was shown in. Ceremoniously, "A message from His Majesty," he announced, handed Wolfgang a letter and disappeared.

Wolfgang broke the seal so hastily that he almost tore up the note.

"Lorenzo," he shouted, "he wants to see the score!"

Constanze and da Ponte somehow managed to put the trembling Wolfgang into his Court clothes. He almost ran all the way to the

Hofburg. Then he played to Joseph for hours. And like lightning out of a clear sky, the Imperial command fell upon Rosenberg to prepare for a performance of *Le Nozze di Figaro* (K. 492).

Then began a fight for priority. Both Salieri and Righini, another Italian, had performances scheduled. To Rosenberg's permanently hostile attitude against da Ponte was added the annoyance that he had been by-passed. "The contest raised much discord," relates O'Kelly, "and parties were formed. Mozart was as touchy as gunpowder and swore he would put the score of his opera on the fire if it were not produced first. His claim was backed by a strong party, while Righini was working like a mole in the dark."

The Emperor decided in Wolfgang's favor and *Figaro* was put into rehearsal. Benucci was Figaro, Nancy was Susanna, O'Kelly sang the double parts of Don Curzio and Don Basilio.

O'Kelly, who had plenty of opportunities to hear *Figaro* in many lands in the following decades, makes the bold statement that "never was opera more strongly cast." During the rehearsals, Wolfgang was on the stage in a gold-laced cocked hat and crimson pelisse, giving the time of the music to the orchestra and instructing the singers. "I shall never forget this little man's animated countenance when lighted up with the glowing rays of genius," O'Kelly wrote. "It is as impossible to describe it as it would be to paint sunbeams." Never before, not even during the *Idomeneo* rehearsals, had Wolfgang been so entirely possessed with something he had written. He found so much of what he himself had experienced in Beaumarchais' lively characters, and he had not observed Paris society for nothing. Lorenzo's cool sarcasm and his gift for sharpening dramatic effects were a perfect foil to Mozart's more emotional mind. The frivolous plot amused the gallant Abbate, and he, too, was a passionate intriguer. Working with him, Mozart managed to accomplish what he had been striving for ever since he had started to write opera: characterization. With the mastery he had achieved in the treatment of instruments and with his lifelong training in writing almost any kind of music, he created the finest balance imaginable by using the orchestra to describe the situation and the voice to portray emotion. The duets and ensembles are interwoven in the plot, supplying conversation which had hitherto been given to the recitatives alone. In Mozart's ensembles, every singer has a perfect melody which could just as well be sung alone. The finale of the second act alone would suffice to make of *Figaro* a landmark in operatic history.

Lorenzo soon had an opportunity to put his flair for intrigue to work. Cabals had by no means stopped. The Salieri clique, after unsuccessful attempts to convince the singers that this music was beneath their contempt, went to Rosenberg and reported that the author had introduced a ballet into the opera. This was contrary to the Emperor's order, as he had banned it from his theater. The ballet, in *Figaro,* is an important dramatic requisite, since it gives the background for a mute play between Susanna and the Count which establishes the plot of the final act. Da Ponte probably took it for granted that the Emperor would see the artistic implication and permit the exception to the rule.

Nothing could have pleased Rosenberg more than this failure on the part of Lorenzo to comply with the Emperor's wishes. He summoned the poet, happiness in his heart, sarcastic indignation in his manner.

"So the Signor poet has introduced a ballet into *Figaro?*"

"Yes, Your Excellency."

"Doesn't the Signor poet know that the Emperor won't have ballets in his theater?"

"No, Your Excellency."

"Well, Signor poet, I tell you so now."

"Yes, Your Excellency."

"And what is more, I tell you that you must take it out, Signor poet."

"No, Your Excellency."

"Where is the ballet scene?"

"Here, Your Excellency."

"This is what we do." Rosenberg took the two sheets of the play containing the scene, and threw them on the fire. "You may go, Signor poet."

Lorenzo went, nay, ran, to Wolfgang, where he had to tackle a second problem: calming his collaborator. Wolfgang wanted at least to give the tell-tales a thrashing or to send the rest of the score after the two sheets.

"Give me two days, Wolfgang," da Ponte begged. "Only wait until the dress rehearsal. Don't worry. But, for Heaven's sake, write the overture."

Wolfgang finally promised that he would not burn the score for the next two days, but neither would he write the overture until everything was settled.

Da Ponte succeeded in having the Emperor and his escort come to the dress rehearsal. When they came to the critical scene, the orchestra stopped, the singers stopped, everything was as silent as in a grave. In this vacuum, Susanna and the Count were gesticulating.

"What do you think that means?" the Emperor asked Casti who was sitting behind him.

"I don't know," smirked Casti. "Your Majesty ought to ask the poet."

Da Ponte silently handed Joseph the manuscript in which the scene had been fully restored. The Emperor looked up with astonished disapproval. Lorenzo remained significantly silent. The Emperor turned to the Count. Rosenberg stammered: "There are no dancers in our theater, since Your Majesty doesn't want them."

"So let them come from somewhere else. Ask da Ponte how many he needs."

Thus reprimanded, Rosenberg was more than ever determined to make *Figaro* a failure, while Wolfgang happily sat down and completed the overture on the evening of April 29. The première was on the first of May, and never, at least O'Kelly says so, "had one beheld such a triumph. The theater was packed and so many numbers had to be repeated that the time of the performance was nearly doubled."

It did not, however, go off without mishap. Some of the singers, in league with Rosenberg and Salieri, deliberately spoiled the first act. They sang off pitch, missed their cues, omitted lines. In her box, Constanze clenched wet hands. After the first act, da Ponte paced the floor backstage in a rage, while Wolfgang stormed up to the Imperial box, to explain.

The Emperor had a fine ear, both for music and rebellion. Wolfgang did not have to say much. And while the stage hands were setting up the Countess' bedroom for the second act, an Imperial aide-de-camp, followed by a pale and meek Rosenberg, appeared behind the drawn curtain, and a lackey knocked at the doors of the dressing rooms to summon the singers. When they all stood around him in a half circle, the officer announced:

"His Majesty is very much displeased with tonight's performance. His Majesty wishes it to be known that it will depend on the progress of the show whether or not the Italian theater will be continued tomorrow."

Wolfgang fell back on a chair in the wings with a prayer of thanksgiving on his lips, while Lorenzo felt moved to an outburst of loyalty to the entire dynasty of Habsburg.

CHAPTER 23

WELCOME TO PRAGUE
[1 7 8 6 - 8 7]

ROSENBERG, more angry than ever, did not give up. After a few performances of *Figaro, da capos* were prohibited "in order not to overstrain the singers." The Count found easy excuses to avoid repetitions of the opera. Single performances were scheduled only when public curiosity demanded them with too much emphasis to be ignored.

It was summer again, and only small earnings came Wolfgang's way. The pittance of 450 gulden he had received for the opera had disappeared.

Though the Emperor had gone to unusual lengths on *Figaro's* behalf, he had plenty of other things on his mind besides music. Joseph spent the summer in Laxenburg, then well out in the country, where he moved when it became too hot even for Schönbrunn. The castle was surrounded by hunting grounds and gardens, ponds and pavilions. They had parades and fireworks to which the peasantry was admitted. His Majesty was a wizard at making himself popular without spending money; he simply opened to the public, entertainment which had hitherto been reserved to the privileged. The Italian company had accompanied him and performed in a little theater of exquisite beauty. The singers had sumptuous apartments and their own horses and carriages. They lived like princes, while Mozart walked the sunbaked streets of Vienna, wondering how to collect the money for the landlord and shopkeepers, and for Constanze's coming confinement.

O'Kelly came back to the city in the fall, tanned and healthy and full of mischief. But one day he wore a sad look and announced that

his mother back home in England was in bad health and that he would have to leave by the end of the Carnival.

"Why don't you come along, Wolfgang?"

"Leave home?"

"Yes, and make all the money you want."

Wolfgang hesitated a moment, then said quietly: "Look, Michael, ten years ago a childhood friend wanted to keep me in Salzburg because it was home. I told him then that my home was where I could make music, and that I had to go and find it. I did find it here. I wrote *Figaro.*"

"But you could return later, and be acclaimed like all these other people who have come here from foreign countries. And maybe you will not want to return. In England there'll be no Salieris and Rosenbergs, you know, but O'Kellys, Storaces, Attwoods. . . ."

Wolfgang was deeply moved. "I've been an arch-Englishman at heart ever since I went to your country as a child. I'll think it over."

He thought it over. England at that time was said to be a musicians' paradise. But Constanze could not be expected to stay behind, nor could they travel with two children. And although they were on much better terms with Cäcilia who had behaved handsomely during Constanze's confinement, Wolfgang did not trust her household well enough to leave the babies at her mercy. But he might try Papa. His house was large enough.

Leopold, however, had grown resentful again. The short-lived success of *Figaro* had brought it home to him that this son of his was financial ineptitude personified. Such a person ought to remain independent until he had a fixed income. All Papa's anger at Constanze came to the surface again. Was he now supposed to take care of her children as he had formerly taken care of Wolfgang's debts?

But, by the time Leopold's "clear and instructive" refusal arrived, there was only one child in the Mozart household. Little Johann Thomas Leopold had not lived even a month. The baby's death and the shattering of his hopes to go to England drove Wolfgang into a nervous breakdown. He was unable to fight. The future looked hopeless.

The start of the season was hopeless indeed. Wolfgang had fewer pupils than ever; there was less public reaction to his music. He had just been a bird of passage. He and *Figaro*. . . .

Lorenzo fared better. He was safely anchored. It would have taken orders from the Emperor not to appoint, but to dismiss, him. Besides, Casti left Vienna in the fall and Rosenberg was less aggressive towards da Ponte, who, together with Martin, had written the greatest hit in years. *Una Cosa rara* had snappy, popular melodies and offered no problems. Its success became proverbial, even a jest on suburban stages, encouraging extemporizations such as "This ducat is for Madam's ticket for *Cosa rara,* for she has only seen it forty-eight times." No one asked for *Figaro,* and after its ninth performance Rosenberg happily sent the score to the archives.

Figaro was the turning point in Mozart's music. From then on he ceased to think of his audiences, of what might please them and of what he might receive in return. He wrote for himself. And *what* he wrote was too complicated for the Viennese. Just as Italy had deserted him when he gave himself instead of easy entertainment, now his beloved Vienna turned away from his somber, worried, disappointed face to the happy and carefree.

Into this depressing atmosphere dropped a few encouraging letters from Prague. One of them was a joint note from orchestra musicians and music lovers. Prague had gone mad over *Figaro* and wanted a visit from the composer.

Prague was jealous of Vienna. The city had a high and very special culture, less exposed to foreign influences and therefore more uniform. There had even been periods in bygone days when Prague had definitely outdone Vienna. Even before Smetana, Dvořák, and Gustav Mahler, Bohemia had given remarkable artists to the world, and Bohemian orchestral musicians were much in favor for their excellent training. Music was obligatory in the country schools; a child who excelled was granted a scholarship by an aristocrat, who took him into his service later. The Bohemian nobility made a point of having only servants who could play at least one instrument and could uphold their reputation for having the best private bands in Europe. As a result, whoever had a large staff of servants had an orchestra as well.

The manager of a small, but skillful troupe that had hitherto played on Count Thun's private stage, a certain Bondini, rented the new, big National Theater on Prague's Fruit Market in 1783. Permanently in financial difficulties, Bondini was easily convinced that the production of *Figaro* might solve all his problems. *Figaro* does not make excessive demands on the voices of the singers, and therefore does not require stars. What it does need above all is perfect musicianship, precision, and a sense of humor. These qualities Bondini's company possessed to a high degree. And while Mozart was almost starving, *Figaro* made Bondini a well-to-do man.

Now, to their dismay, people in Prague learned that their favorite composer was neglected in Vienna. And when Mozart answered that he and his wife would be glad to come, their enthusiasm knew no bounds.

In the coach, Wolfgang's inclination to go to England grew stronger. The taste for traveling came back as he looked out into the breadth of the countryside which he had missed for so long. In the creaking carriage sat Constanze and her oldest sister's fiancé, court violinist Hofer, who went with them. They chatted while Wolfgang looked out at the cold, dreary landscape. Gradually their voices and the painful noise of the coach driving over poor roads dwindled to a distant accompaniment of a great song, the song of trees, snowbound meadows, ever-green pine forests.

Wolfgang's expression changed. Constanze saw it. She gave Hofer a sign to be silent, pointing to her husband's strange look. Then, she hastily opened a portfolio, and handed Wolfgang sheets of music paper. There were already many such sheets in the portfolio, covered with hurriedly jotted notes. They were pages of a musical diary which he kept, little musical items, fragments of melodies, which came to him in the mood of the moment.

Wolfgang scribbled on for some time, then suddenly music gave way to playing; a game in which his fellow travelers of fact and fantasy would have their share. Tension relaxed. He smiled cunningly.

"Why doesn't Sagadarata go faster?"

"Who?"

"Why, Sagadarata. Our dear servant Joseph out there. Don't you understand me, Schabla Pumfa?"

"Oh, Wolfi, I don't want you to call me that," Constanze whined. "Stanzi-Marini is much nicer."

"No, Madam, it can't be helped," Wolfgang replied in a serious tone. "From now on you are Schabla Pumfa."

"Then you are Punkititi, because you are so puny, and that's coming to you," Constanze snapped back in comic anger. Wolfgang laughed. His wife was the only one who could refer to his smallness without hurting him.

"Now I'm offended. I want a name, too." Hofer put in.

"You may call yourself Rozka Pumpa."

"And Gottfried?"

"Hikkiti Horky, and his sister Dini Mini Niri, and his brother Blatterizzi. . . ."

". . . and Fräulein von Aurnhammer?"

"I'm polite and won't give her a name, but Freistädtler who composed those songs for her can be called Gaulimauli. . . ."

And so they went on *ad infinitum,* until Constanze exclaimed in despair: "We have forgotten to give a name to doggy!"

"Isn't Goukerl funny enough?"

"No!"

"Then call her Schomanntzky."

"That will be funny, Punkititi, when I call 'Schomanntzky!' all over the Augarten!"

Their happy mood did not leave them until they arrived in Prague, with stiff limbs, but merry as children. When Wolfgang was playing the buffoon it meant that all was well with him.

Count Thun lodged the party comfortably in large rooms where they even found a good piano. The very evening of their arrival they were taken to a party at Baron Breitfeld's. His balls had gained wide fame for their gathering of feminine beauty. In the anteroom they heard familiar tunes—from *Figaro.* An orchestra played, and Wolfgang thought that this was part of his well-arranged reception. But, upon entering the ballroom, he realized that they had made dance music out of his opera. To the bravura arias of his heroes, happy Prague society danced their quadrilles, waltzes, minuets, German dances. Mozart was a little surprised at first, but then he was delighted. In a new coat with fancy buttons, in white stockings and shining shoes with large buckles, very pale and thin, his rich blond hair carefully powdered and fastened with a jeweled ribbon, he stood in a corner with Constanze and wondered about Prague.

It took him three days to get over a feeling of bashfulness. What happened in Baron Breitfeld's ballroom happened all over town. In court yards, street musicians fiddled—*Figaro;* on the streets schoolboys whistled—*Figaro;* from ground floor apartments came music—*Figaro;* every amateur played—*Figaro;* every newly arranged piece of music was based upon—*Figaro.* And finally, on January 17, he heard *Figaro* itself at the theater. It seemed to be a condensation from the music all over Prague.

On the 20th he conducted it himself, and in between he gave a concert, that brought him one thousand gulden. Contemporaries remembered that never before had the hall been so crowded. The enthusiasm almost burst the walls. Wolfgang played his new symphony in D (K. 504), thereafter called the *Prague* Symphony, which he had composed in somber moments just a month before, significantly without a minuet. He also played a piano concerto and variations, and as an encore he improvised. Encore . . . encore . . . effortless, in spite of hours of playing, his hands wove more and more patterns of unique loveliness on the keys. . . . "Figaro!" a bold voice yelled. Easily, Wolfgang found a transition to *Non più andrai,* the favorite aria everywhere, and gave it twelve variations which ended in an uproar of applause.

Bondini beamed. This young man was his savior. He did not leave Wolfgang's elbow. And when, after the second performance of *Figaro,* exhausted but happy, Wolfgang casually remarked, "It would be gratifying to write an opera for such a public," Bondini's eyes opened wide. "Do you really mean it, Maestro?"

Wolfgang hadn't thought it over seriously . . . but why not? "I might," he said vaguely.

Bondini wondered, and sighed. Wasn't this a smart introduction to complicated business negotiations? "I'm afraid I won't be able to pay your fee."

But that had not been the cause of Wolfgang's vagueness. He had just been tired. "Don't worry about that," he said. "I wouldn't charge you more than I would receive in Vienna. One hundred ducats."

"So you would write an opera for us, for one hundred ducats?" Bondini was still incredulous.

"Yes. Your company is good, and your public even better. They deserve it."

Shortly thereafter, a contract was signed for an opera to be performed next season and the event was celebrated with a large quantity of beer.

Now Wolfgang was in Prague with nothing in the world to do—on a real vacation. He indulged in an orgy of pleasure. He did not write a single note except a group of dances (K. 509) for a private party. Women competed for his attention, men for his company. A train of admirers followed him everywhere. Wolfgang and

Constanze danced throughout the night and slept until lunch. Neither of them could get enough of it.

It suddenly came to Constanze that she had never really enjoyed herself before. She had not done much traveling or vacationing; she had never been away with her husband, except on that trip to Salzburg which she preferred to forget. At home, there had been housekeeping, illnesses, childbirths, baby sitting. In Vienna, she was merely taken for granted and sometimes she could not help wondering whether at bottom she had not remained the "Weberische" in society.

But in Prague, Maestro and Madam Mozart were the toast of the town. Constanze was a coquette at heart. She loved compliments, and her black eyes could look frivolous and tempting in return. She had more money than ever to spend on herself. She wore exquisite new dresses and looked prettier than she had ever dreamt she could.

"What have you done all evening?" Wolfgang would ask her with an assumed air of severity when they finally started home. Then Constanze would look at her husband's face, dimly lighted by the dawn. "Wolfi, what have *you* done?"

"Why, there was this young woman, but, Stanzi, you remember, the one in the pink dress with cream lace, she is a scream when she is embarrassed. . . ."

"Wolfi, you bad boy, you made her blush?"

"I can say so," he laughed. "But what about you? Who made you blush?"

"Nobody, Wolfi, really nobody."

"Stanzi, you were a wall-flower? Shame on you!"

"No, Wolfi, I was no wall-flower at all," Constanze would giggle, "but in Prague I forget how to blush."

CHAPTER 24

DISILLUSION

[1 7 8 7]

T HE PRAGUERS urged Wolfgang to stay. While writing his
opera he might make substantial money from concerts. Yet
Wolfgang decided to leave. Though Prague had bestowed its
gifts upon him in heaping measure, he still wanted to conquer
Vienna. It was perhaps the same stubborn ambition that had almost
kept him in Paris in spite of, or because of, mighty competitors. If
he should fail again in Vienna, for all Imperial bravos and gracious
empty gestures, his competitors would at least not be able to say that
he had withdrawn defeated to the provinces. Then he would go to
another, even greater, capital—to London.

Back in Vienna, he found Michael O'Kelly about to leave, and
the rest of the English set going with him. It was a painful farewell.
With streaming eyes, Nancy sang a beautiful scena with rondo
(K. 505), words from *Idomeneo,* which Wolfgang had composed
anew for her as a souvenir. The lovely singer had a prized appointment at Drury Lane Theater, while Stephen, who had written two
operas for Vienna, hoped to have one ordered for his home town.

"We'll meet again," the Britishers asserted. "We'll get you a fine
contract in England, or at least a guarantee for your expenses." They
would see Papa on their way through Salzburg and talk it over with
him.

They came to Salzburg and saw Leopold. Their caravan attracted
general curiosity and aroused Papa's pride. There were Nancy and

Stephen, their mother, O'Kelly, Attwood, and a dog, plus heaps of luggage, all packed into two carriages with eight horses, and a servant riding in front of them. Leopold took them sightseeing. Nancy performed for the Archbishop who sent her a handsome present. The social part of their stay was a success—the mission for Wolfgang dissolved in words.

Mozart remained in Vienna, and soon discovered that his return from Prague was as unnoticed as had been his absence. People were still running to see *Cosa rara,* which had moved to the Leopold-städter Theater after Nancy's departure, and was now performed in a German version.

The champion of opera in German at the Court Theater was Baron Dittersdorf, who had already had his third Singspiel performed since the previous summer. Dittersdorf too was a Knight of the Golden Spur, but he made better use of it than Mozart. As music director for the Prince-Bishop of Breslau, he had his own theater, and his music was as easy as his manners. Dittersdorf and Mozart were very fond of each other. They liked to talk and play chamber music. It was perhaps no mere coincidence that Dittersdorf named one of his operetta characters *Hieronymus Knicker* (*Knicker* meaning miser, the nickname the Salzburgers had found for their sovereign), whereas the title of his most popular *Singspiel, Doktor und Apotheker* became a much-quoted saying of Wolfgang whenever he spoke of illness.

Dittersdorf had the Emperor's ear. But though he was willing to support Mozart's claim for better work, he, too, was disturbed by the novel trend in Wolfgang's newer compositions.

"I have met no other composer with such a wealth of ideas," he once told Joseph. "I wish he were not so generous with them. He does not permit his hearers to breathe. . . ."

"Too many notes. . . ." The modern Emperor with the old-fashioned ears was obviously proud of this statement. He honored Dittersdorf with another. "I have drawn a parallel between Mozart and Haydn. Mozart's compositions are like a golden snuff box made in Paris, and Haydn's ditto, made in London. Both are beautiful, the former for its adornments, the latter for its simplicity and finish."

The Emperor obviously did not appreciate adornments. Soon after the sensation of *Figaro* was over, he was overheard saying that he still preferred Martin so far as opera was concerned. He was not alone in his judgment; others were just as conservative. "It is a pity," reads a contemporary criticism, "that Mozart goes too far in his intention to write new music, wherein the heart has nothing to gain." The publisher who had hitherto printed most of his instrumental works made excuses after customers had returned the last quartets "full of errors"; and so did minor firms.

There was still the opera contract for Prague—the one bright spot in the dark picture. Right after his return, Wolfgang had asked da Ponte to do the libretto. Lorenzo scratched his head. "It is tough," he said. "I am overrun with inquiries ever since the success of *Figaro* [he meant *Cosa rara* but did not want to say so] and I am pledged to do operas with both Martin and Salieri. . . . With Salieri, yes, we've made peace. . . . But I won't let you down. What about the subject?"

"I don't know," Wolfgang admitted. "My mind is a blank. In Prague I was too busy dancing and here I am too busy worrying. Whatever you say will be all right."

He was indeed worrying. The mood of the previous December returned, blacker than ever against the light serenity of the days in Prague. The falsity of earthly things filled Wolfgang with melancholy, caused him to withdraw more and more from society into his masonic Lodge. From Bonn came the news that young Count Hatzfeld, thirty-one years old like himself and a friend from childhood, had died; and from St. Gilgen that Papa, tortured by gout and rheumatism, was conspicuously declining in health. Death and mysticism . . . they were constantly in Wolfgang's mind. Their shadow spurred his impatience to the extreme . . . impatience to die, strangely mixed with an impatience to live all that was worth living.

DISILLUSION

I have now made a habit of being prepared in all affairs of life for the worst. As death, when we come to consider it closely, is the true goal of our existence, I have formed during the last few years such close relations with this best and truest friend of mankind, that his image is not only no longer terrifying to me, but is indeed very soothing and consoling. . . . I never lie down at night without reflecting that, young as I am, I may not live to see another day. Yet no one of all my acquaintances could say that in company I am morose or disgruntled. For this blessing I daily thank my Creator. . . .

This was written to Leopold on April 4. Then, in quick succession, came two of Mozart's greatest and most personal works: his string quintets, in C major (K. 515) and G minor (K. 516), heralds of the two symphonies in the same keys of the following year.

Meanwhile, in a poor musician's home in Bonn, a deathly sick mother bid farewell to her sixteen-year-old son. "This young genius ought to be supported so that he could travel," a newspaper had already written a few years before. "He might become another Mozart." So the young genius set out for Vienna with money scraped together by some sponsors. Once when Wolfgang came home with a few friends, he found him waiting in his anteroom. Mozart looked askance at the stocky fellow, with his wild black hair and pockmarked face. He was strangely prejudiced against ugly people.

"My name is Beethoven. Ludwig van Beethoven," the visitor introduced himself. "I am sixteen years old . . . I wonder whether you would permit me to play for you."

Awkwardly he produced a letter of introduction.

Mozart was in a hurry. They had come in only to pick up Constanze for a bowling game on the Jacquin skittle ground . . . he was in no mood to listen to a strange pianist . . . he didn't even want his own pupils to play . . . it was boring . . . but sixteen years . . . at sixteen I was in Italy . . . I was with Papa . . . he is all alone . . . a man is very hopeful at sixteen . . . these thoughts shot through his head and "I am pressed for time," he said, "but since you came all that way, you might just as well play right now."

Beethoven went to the piano. He had thoroughly studied Mozart's music and started a concerto.

Quite good, Wolfgang thought, just good . . . bowling would be much better . . . the only entertainment he could afford because it cost him nothing . . . they all wanted him to help others, but nobody helped him . . . nobody. . . .

Beethoven, while he played, noticed with despair that Wolfgang grew increasingly distracted. He had traveled so far to hear his judgment, and now Mozart hardly listened. He made a final effort: "Would you care to hear me improvise on a given theme, Maestro?" It was bold to ask Mozart, the master of improvisation, such a thing, but what was he to do?

Mozart gave a sigh of relief. Now it would soon be over. He went to the piano and played a theme.

Passionately young Beethoven set to work. His fingers grasped Wolfgang's attention and drew it to the keyboard. As he played, he watched Wolfgang's eyes light up, his face grow tense. Mightily, sweeping, Beethoven's playing filled the place. Constanze and the friends appeared on the threshold. With fervent impetus, drenched with perspiration, scarlet in the face, Beethoven brought the improvisation to an end.

"That surpassed all my expectations," Wolfgang said after a long silence. And, turning toward the group still standing in the door, motionless: "Watch out for this young man. He will make a noise in the world one day."

For some time, better news had come from Salzburg. Leopold had improved. Wolfgang hoped to see him in the summer. Then, suddenly and unexpectedly, a letter reached him on May 29. Papa had died.

Wolfgang broke down completely. It was fortunate that the Mozarts had just moved to a friendly place at Landstrasse with the Botanical Garden as a perfect outing place and the Jacquins as neighbors. Gottfried Jacquin tried to cheer up Wolfgang as best he could, but he was not very successful.

Beethoven returned and asked for lessons. But Wolfgang declined. He was too sad, too unsettled, too preoccupied. Beethoven went back to Bonn, to his dying mother. He and Mozart remained strangers.

But fundamentally they had more in common than they would ever have realized—the sensitive, well-bred man with the fierce eyes whose "Do you love me?" was in his every melody, and the stocky lad raised under distressing circumstances who once, deaf and lonely, was to cry out a desperate apotheosis of Joy. But never would Beethoven have acquired Mozart's musical tact, his aristocratic subtlety of discrimination. Though only fourteen years Wolfgang's junior, he already belonged to a different age.

CHAPTER 25

GENIUSES OF SIN
[1 7 8 7]

ONCE UPON A TIME there lived in Sevilla a noble cavalier whose name was Don Juan Tenorio y Salazar. He was so handsome and so bold that no fair maiden could resist his charm, whether she were a king's or a peasant's daughter, whether a young girl, a married woman, or even a nun. The daughter of the Commander of Ulloa was young, beautiful, and innocent. But Don Juan made his eyes shine and his voice sound so that hers became blind and mute. She ran away with him, but her father came after them with a naked sword. Don Juan drew his weapon and pierced the old man's heart. He was buried in the Church of St. Francis under a shining marble tomb, topped by his monument on horseback. Don Juan deserted the maiden and left her mourning at her father's grave. There were other women upon whom he cast his eyes, and there was one among them more beautiful than any he had known before. While he was pursuing her, she lured him into the church. Strange figures sprang from behind the pillars and Don Juan was killed. The monks disposed of his body secretly and rumors were spread that the sinner had been sent down to the eternal sufferings of hell by the father's statue come to life with thunder and lightning to take fierce revenge.

This is the story of Don Juan.

From the mouths of the people and through the centuries the legend and its variants traveled over the stages of Spain, Italy, and

France. As a ballet by Gluck and an opera by Righini it came to the Vienna theater, as a play by Molière it was on Mozart's shelf, and a report about the sensational success of its most recent version in Venice had reached da Ponte's studio.

Da Ponte loved topics in which he could describe what he would like to be. And he found Don Juan—in Italian *Don Giovanni*—perfectly suited to Wolfgang's passion for realistic acting.

"You won't be able to do it," warned the Emperor, when his Court Poet reported that he was going to write three librettos at the same time.

"I should like to try, Sire," replied da Ponte. "I shall work in the morning for Martin, in the evening for Salieri, and at night for Mozart, and I will feel as though I were reading Petrarch, Tasso, and Dante simultaneously."

The Emperor liked learned parallels.

Da Ponte's memoirs about this period are even more unreliable than usual. They were written in New York, in the 1820's, for a public that had just gone wild over *Don Giovanni,* which Garcia had introduced for the first time in America. He claimed to have finished the first two operas and nearly two-thirds of *Don Giovanni* in sixty-three days. As usual, Wolfgang worked on the music as Lorenzo went along. He discussed the libretto, acquainted himself with his characters and started to compose. He wrote little else during the summer; from May through August, in irregular intervals, there came a few songs, a satirical divertimento *Ein Musikalischer Spass* (K. 522), a four-hand piano sonata (K. 521), which he sent to Gottfried's sister, a violin sonata in A major (K. 526), his most famous one, and the popular *Eine Kleine Nachtmusik* (K. 525), reminiscence of his serenade period.

Shortly before his scheduled trip to Prague, he had a big shock—young Dr. Barisani suddenly passed away. Another death. . . .

The journey in mid-September was not as jolly as the previous one. Constanze was pregnant again, and they had four-year-old Karl with them. The landscape this time was touched by the coming of autumn: golden brown acres, leaves turning to red, peasants in colorful garb at work.

Wolfgang was in a state of creative excitement. His nostrils quivered, his fingers drummed scales and chords or now and then reached hastily for one of the loose music sheets. He wrote in such a hurry that nobody but himself could have deciphered his scrawl. It was like some kind of musical shorthand. But when the Mozarts arrived in Prague, a good deal of *Don Giovanni* (K. 527) had been sketched.

Bondini showed them the rooms he had reserved on the Kohl-markt. "Signor da Ponte will live across the street," he cheerily announced. "You can discuss the opera from your windows. And right around the corner there is a little tavern with very good wine and food," he added. He knew Wolfgang's weakness.

Lorenzo arrived a few days after Wolfgang, and they both took full advantage of the neighborhood. When one would appear at the window and shout something about a line, or a verse, or a cue, the other would unfailingly shout back: "We had better discuss it downstairs." "Downstairs" meant an incredible quantity of wine, beer, ham and cheese. Lorenzo, chewing away, would say: "Now, Wolfgang, imagine I am Don Giovanni [Wolfgang grinned] and you are Zerlina and you are engaged to a nice peasant, but here I am in my big castle and I put my irresistible smile to work on you . . . what would you say to me?"

"I don't know," Wolfgang would answer seriously. "We had better ask the waitress, the sturdy blonde over there." The waitress was very serious too, and very instructive.

But hardly a week after he had arrived, Lorenzo received a letter from Salieri reminding him sharply that he was a Court Poet working on a libretto for the Court Composer, and that they had to finish *Azur* for the forthcoming marriage of Archduke Francis to Elisabeth of Württemberg. Da Ponte had to return to Vienna at once lest he risk his position; that meant leaving Wolfgang with a most important scene, Leporello's narrow escape in the second act, a

confusing fragment. It would also mean missing the rehearsals and the première.

Gloomily they sat in a corner of their tavern discussing what they could do about it in a hurry, when the door opened and a strange figure entered. Da Ponte blinked, then sprang to his feet. Cataracts of Italian filled the place. "I am here with Maestro Mozart," Wolfgang heard da Ponte say. "We are doing an opera for Bondini. Wolfgang"—and he drew his friend to the table—"I want you to meet Signor Giacomo Casanova de Seingalt."

Wolfgang stared. Was this the legendary conqueror of women?

The sexagenarian looked a hundred years old. His features were sharp and dilapidated, his bones covered with a livid skin, his eyes like those of a bird of prey, almost lidless and piercing. Women are strange, Wolfgang thought. He was a specter, but tall—oh, so tall. . . .

The tall specter bowed. It was a careful, well-studied motion. Acting, thought Wolfgang, typical Italian acting, very impressive but slightly overdone.

The specter's face showed what was intended to be a smile. Then a voice sounded, somewhat ringing as the stories said, but the bell seemed to have suffered a crack: "Delighted, *Cavaliere* Mozart."

Wolfgang had almost forgotten his title. So Casanova knew about him? Of course he did. The pathetic old man in virtual exile up in the mountains followed the goings-on in the world with curiosity and envy. Casanova relished the sound of the title. It bolstered his self-esteem. He had fallen on evil days.

His self-esteem had suffered almost continuously since his spectacular escape from the Leads in Venice. After years of an unsuccessful race through Europe, he finally returned to Italy. Constantly he got into trouble, constantly he had to fight, mostly impolite bailiffs —and the bailiffs mostly won.

Applying for civil service employment in his native Venice, Casanova got the doubtful assignment of stool-pigeon in charge of public morals. Besides, he became a spectacularly unsuccessful author. His marriage in Paris with a well-to-do girl of mediocre reputation did not outlast his wife's fortune. In Vienna, where the withering gallant had gone to hunt for luck, he was at first disdained by everyone, but finally he found a sponsor. The tremendously wealthy Joseph Karl Emanuel Count Waldstein-Wartenberg, Imperial and Royal Chamberlain, was attracted by Casanova's reputation and offered him a refuge of sorts, a nominal assignment in his castle at Dux, Bohemia. There the pensioner indulged in illusions of his past and future. Illusions drove him to Prague on rare occasions.

"We are writing an opera which will interest you," Lorenzo said, smirking. "About Don Juan. The genius of sin."

Casanova's eyes lighted. "You know something about that, Lorenzo, don't you?" he grinned back.

"Well," said Lorenzo modestly. "I gladly recognize your supremacy in that field. I am just a feeble imitation of Casanova for innocent little boys like this . . . Cheer up, child, it'll be all right," he encouraged Wolfgang, who had sunk back into his gloom. . . . Salieri . . . it wasn't enough that he spoiled Vienna for him . . . he even wouldn't let him alone in Prague. . . .

There are various versions of how it came about, but in fairly recent years two sheets containing the words of the sextet in *Don Giovanni* were found in Casanova's faded manuscripts.

After Lorenzo had left for Vienna, the Mozarts moved out to the villa of their friends, the Duscheks. Rehearsals began while Mozart was still composing, and groups of singers wandered daily to the suburb to receive his instruction.

Franz and Josefa Duschek were musicians, he a composer and pianist, she a concert singer. Mozart had met them in 1777 when they had been visiting at Salzburg, and had written an aria (K. 272) for her. They had remained friends ever since. Josefa, who had been in Vienna during the preparations for *Figaro,* realized Wolfgang's predicament and had been instrumental in bringing him to Prague.

Now the Mozarts and the Duscheks indulged in an orgy of entertainment. There were always big parties or jolly gatherings at taverns. Sometimes his friends worried about *Don Giovanni*. Wolfgang let himself be distracted too easily. How could he possibly compose in the midst of a bowling game? Interrupt himself casually when his turn came and then go back to his work? Someone once told Constanze about it. She was surprised. She was so used to her husband's unusual working habits that they seemed natural to her. "Why," she said, "he is only copying." "Copying what?" "He has it all ready in his head, and just writes it down. And, you see, he says this is so boring that he must do something else at the same time. Billiards in winter, bowling in the summer. Last year he wrote an entire trio for piano, clarinet, and viola [K. 498] during a bowling party with Gottfried."

Wolfgang came up to them. "What are you talking about?"

"About you. . . ."

". . . your laziness. . . ."

". . . your pleasure-hunting. . . ."

". . . and that *Don Giovanni* won't be finished on time!"

Wolfgang laughed. Didn't they realize that the opera wrote itself, wherever he was, whatever he did?

Rehearsals for *Don Giovanni* met with greater difficulties than Wolfgang had expected. For lack of understudies, Bondini was anxious not to overstrain his singers and to keep them in a good mood. There were no rehearsals on opera days. Moreover, the stage hands were by no means as efficient as those in the Vienna Court theater. Wolfgang saw at once that it would not be possible to have the opera produced on October 14, when Prince Anton of Saxony and Archduchess Maria Theresa of Austria passed through Prague on their honeymoon. *Figaro* was given instead, with Wolfgang conducting, and met with the usual success. Yet Wolfgang was worried. *Don Giovanni* was so different from *Figaro*. Could such a success be repeated? Did not the mere attempt mean challenging fate?

"You can believe me," he told the conductor Kucharz, with whom he strolled along the Moldau after a rehearsal, "I have spared no effort to give my very best." And thoughtfully he added: "People often seem to think that everything comes to me so easily that I only have to grab a pen and put it down. . . . But no one has worked as hard as I have; there is practically no great composer whose work I have not studied with the utmost diligence."

The day of the première approached rapidly. The singers were good, but no more. Often Wolfgang would think longingly of O'Kelly, Nancy, Benucci. Antonio Baglioni, the Don Ottavio, was impossible on the stage. He had to act like a gentleman of a distinguished family—and he did not know how to dance. Wolfgang jumped on the stage and gave his clumsy interpreter a quick dancing lesson. Signora Bondini, the manager's wife and very much in favor with the public, sang Zerlina. She could not be made to utter convincingly the cry of fear and distress which da Ponte had prescribed for the peasant girl at Don Giovanni's backstage attentions. Mozart had the finale repeated and sneaked behind Zerlina in the wings. When this passage came, he seized her suddenly and firmly by the waist. She shrieked . . . and Wolfgang bowed, smiling: "You see, Madame, that is the way an innocent young woman screams when her virtue is in danger. . . ." Up to the last minute there were alterations and additions.

On October 28, the eve of the première, a large party filled the Duscheks' house and gardens. There was much beer, wine and punch, and Wolfgang sat at the clavier to play *Figaro*—and *Don Giovanni*—as dance music. But two men did not share the general cheerfulness: Bondini and Guardasoni, his stage manager. Josefa Duschek watched them whisper excitedly, with an apprehending eye on carefree Wolfgang, and Casanova smirked in his corner. Mischievously Wolfgang clinked glasses with the gloomy visitors. A moment of silence followed. Then Bondini offered a queer toast: "Maestro Mozart! What about the overture, please?"

"Ready!" Wolfgang shouted.

"Where?" Bondini and Guardasoni exclaimed in unison.

"In my head, gentlemen, all up here in my head, everything to the last note."

"Please, Maestro. . . ."

"Finch' han dal vino, Signor Bondino. . . ." Wolfgang paraphrased Don Giovanni's "champagne" aria and was off in a whirl.

Bondini looked imploringly at Constanze.

"Come, Wolfi, you will have to work all night," she begged.

"Surely, and so will you. Come along. Good night, everybody." He grabbed a big bowl of punch and two glasses and preceded her to their room, where he settled himself at the table. "Stanzi-Marini, you are now going to tell me stories, silly stories, please, about Ashenputtel and Cinderella and Rumpelstiltski, and so on, and when I fall asleep, because I am so dreadfully tired and a little drunk too, please wake me up . . . but before you start you better send a note to the copyist to be sure he comes at seven in the morning. . . ."

Constanze sent the message and sat down near her husband. She had a great gift for telling stories, elaborating fantastic passages, inventing little jokes and climaxes. While "Scheherazade" chattered merrily and fed him on punch, Wolfgang, at times screaming with laughter, wrote down the most mysterious piece of music he ever composed. Interrupted only by a two-hour sleep, he wrote until a few minutes of seven, then handed the overture to the copyist and went to bed.

That night the whole of Prague seemed to be on its way to the theater. Diamonds sparkled from boxes reserved weeks in advance, and the galleries were jammed with people who had scraped together their last savings just to get in. It was an act of patriotic duty for good Bohemians to be present. It was *their* opera!

Constanze sat in a box, beautifully dressed, very excited, with her eyes glued to the clock. Duschek secretly glanced at his watch three times a minute. "Don't worry"—Josefa tried to sound reassuring—"they can always substitute the *Idomeneo* overture."

"That wretched copyist," Constanze murmured under her breath. "I hope people won't get impatient."

"They would," Josefa remarked, "with anyone but Mozart."

Torturing minutes dragged. The audience was tense. Any further delay could spoil everything.

Finally, the little door in the pit opened and the orchestra facto-
tum appeared with a bunch of music manuscripts which he hurriedly distributed among the desks. The overture! The three people
in the box relaxed. As the attendant left, he almost collided with
Wolfgang, who was rushing to his place at the clavier. The orchestra
arose and welcomed him with a triple flourish. Wolfgang was more
nervous than ever before. Would they be able to read the overture?
He had hardly looked at the parts.

But when the first chords of *Don Giovanni* filled the theater,
he was reassured. As he conducted, he felt waves of appreciation
behind his back. The spirit of these musicians was wonderful. In
the burst of applause that followed the overture, Wolfgang, between
bows, murmured to the concert master: "Quite a few notes fell
under the desks, but it was all right."

After every number the applause increased. Luigi Bassi was wonderful—a Don after Wolfgang's heart. He made blond-haired,
beardless Giovanni young, unsophisticated—a "boyish demon" with
a bright, flexible voice. With sure artistic instinct, the handsome
but unintellectual singer got across the essentials of the role.

After the final curtain, flowers were thrown to Wolfgang and
people rose to their feet. Even the most dignified among them
lost all self-control—yelled, stamped, clapped. "Speech! Speech!
Speech!" they shouted. *"Evviva il Maestro!* Speech!"

Wolfgang could conduct and play; he could sing to his audiences
in his melodies; he could dance and make the buffoon; but he
had never made a public speech in his life. Only partly conscious
of his gesture, he raised a hand. The noise immediately stopped.
He made a move toward the silent abyss filled with staring eyes—
his arms extended as if he would embrace them all, and a choked
voice said: "My Praguers understand me. . . ."

And a hurricane of love stormed up to him. It went far beyond
his highest expectations.

CHAPTER 26

POVERTY

[1 7 8 8 - 8 9]

T HE PRAGUERS did understand Wolfgang whole-heartedly, but there were many others who did not for quite some time. In Germany, and particularly in Prussia, where *Don Giovanni* was performed later, it was sharply criticized and could not establish itself in the repertoire. Public interest was at its peak before the performance; sensation-hunters vaguely expected something thrilling rather than a work of art. After hearing it, their interest dwindled rapidly.

"Much bombast and noise for the big crowd," a Frankfurt critic wrote, "a dull subject, music great, but too heavy and artificial. Not popular enough to excite general sensation. . . ." The Berlin press was downright rude: "Mozart wanted to write something unusual, inimitably great. . . . The unusual is there, but not the great."

Along with hostile experts came even more hostile moralists, eager to take offense. The subject, they said, was unsuitable, even indecent. Much later, after Mozart's death, the debates went on. Even Beethoven stated angrily that he never would have composed such impossible situations, and he considered his *Fidelio* as a kind of antidote to *Don Giovanni*.

Goethe sided with Mozart's defenders. He was probably thinking of *Don Giovanni* when he said Mozart was the only composer whom he would have permitted to set *Faust* to music. But the

[2 1 6]

prince of poets was never much inclined to have his work set to music, and only made this statement after Wolfgang was dead.

But much worse than these failures and controversies was the undeniable fact that *Don Giovanni* did not please Vienna. Mozart added new numbers to meet the taste of the Viennese and the higher ability of their singers; the last scene was omitted, and this remained the almost unbroken tradition in Austria although this conventionally gay ensemble is needed to restore the proper meaning of the whole as *dramma giocoso*. The Emperor had fixed the date for the première for May 7, 1788. Da Ponte's shrewdness and diplomacy put over fifteen performances during that year. But the public reaction was unsatisfactory and Mozart's enemies rejoiced.

Joseph saw only the last performance. The period of peace had been interrupted by sinister events in Poland, and he had been visiting his troops in the Northeast.

"Divine," he said to da Ponte, "more beautiful than even *Figaro* —but no food for my Viennese."

"Give them time to chew it," Wolfgang replied, when Lorenzo told him about it. But he did not live to see the day of the next performance in Vienna. *Don Giovanni* did not return to the Imperial theater until 1798.

With Salieri's *Azur* the triumph of the season, the anti-Mozart faction had a field day. They boasted that they had always known Mozart was no match for Italian maestri. One man sided fearlessly with Wolfgang—Joseph Haydn. At a party at Count Rosenberg's, he staged a one-man combat on behalf of his friend and terminated the argument with the flat and final statement that he did not feel competent to discuss *Don Giovanni,* but that he considered Mozart the greatest composer of all time.

Gluck had died in November, 1787. The Prague success and the rumors that Wolfgang might leave for England led Joseph to give Mozart Gluck's title as chamber music composer to the Imperial Court. The appointment was not as important as Salieri's, but it meant much prestige, and Gluck had received two thousand gulden a year.

The Emperor's grasp of money questions did not go much beyond the principle that it was necessary to save. Since his advisers obstructed economy in important matters, he tried to apply it to minor ones. He sometimes acted like a housewife who tries to reduce her expenses by cutting salt and pepper out of the meals. The Italian company cost eighty thousand gulden a year, but two thousand for young Mozart seemed too much.

Joseph had not the slightest idea how a man could manage to live with a wife and children on a pittance of two thousand gulden. These simple people probably had some secret recipe for getting along on incredibly small amounts. Mozart might be able to live just as well on, say, twelve hundred, perhaps even one thousand, or, still better, eight hundred. . . .

Expert on such matters was his valet Strack. A valet ought to know such things, and he knew Mozart.

Strack had met Wolfgang years before at the Baroness Waldstätten's. He was a great lover of the arts and never missed Wolfgang's musicales if he could help it. He had the Emperor's ear in matters of music and occasionally he had put small earnings in Wolfgang's way. But he was too cautious to commit himself outright.

The valet was just handing the Emperor his shirt with a ceremonious gesture, when he was asked the delicate question. He hesitated for a moment before replying. Strack did not want to annoy the Emperor. On the other hand, something ought to be done for Mozart. So he answered prudently: "A man in His Majesty's favor can live on very little money. . . ."

"Are the Mozarts modest people?" Joseph went on.

"Yes, very. . . ." And Strack added with a sniff: "Your Majesty knows about Mme. Mozart's family background. . . ."

"So you think. . . ."

"Indeed, Your Majesty, indeed, no doubt they can be quite happy with. . . ."

"... eight hundred gulden ... ?"

The Emperor had said it. So it was eight hundred.

Mozart accepted with sincere joy. He had waited for six years to be taken into the Emperor's service—no, for almost twenty years! He would write plenty of good music for him, and his assignment would attract new pupils and new audiences.

To Nannerl he wrote proudly that it was more than most people at Court drew as a salary. It was, indeed, nearly twice as much as his last pay from the Mufti.

But he did not mention that he already had debts, and that the cost of living in Vienna was steadily rising.

Wolfgang received no substantial order from the Court. He got only crumbs of Imperial commissions—dances. He wrote them by the dozen during the following years, with loving care and more inspiration than the commission warranted. But this was not enough for his ambition. He did not want just the title and the salary.

He had shown himself freely at Court as a successful free lancer, but now, as a minor hanger-on, he hardly ever presented himself. His salary came to him in quarterly installments. Once, when he signed the receipt, he wrote in the margin: "Too much for what I do, too little for what I could do." But this graceful hint produced no response.

Twice Wolfgang was forced to change his lodgings because of his inability to pay the rent. His baby daughter, born on the Tuchlauben in Christmas week, 1787, was very weak. Constanze recovered from her confinement more slowly than usual. Four childbirths within four and a half years, illnesses and misfortunes had shattered her health and spirits and depleted Wolfgang's purse.

The Mozarts had known money troubles many times. But Wolfgang was an optimist and could not help hoping. If the "rain of gold" had failed to appear, there had at least been a shower of silver; debts had been incurred without apprehension. Now there was not even a spray of copper. This meant something Wolfgang had not faced as yet—poverty.

[219]

In the summer of 1788, Wolfgang found himself in the hands of pawnbrokers and pursued by unfriendly butchers and grocers. He was about to move into a shabby little house in the suburb of Währing; there he would at least have a garden in which he could work and his son play, and the quiet of the landscape which he needed so much. But when they were ready to move, their trunks all packed, a messenger came from some former landlord with a note saying that unless Wolfgang paid what he still owed him, he would seize his personal property and send him to jail. Wolfgang gave his all. The Mozarts arrived at their new lodgings without a penny in their pocket.

Wolfgang examined the little garden behind the house and sat down on a bench. It might be a pleasant life if he had less trouble —but how to get money quickly? He had a few subscription concerts, but they hardly paid expenses.

His aristocratic friends were wealthy and spent what seemed to him like a fortune for a single night's entertainment. But were they his friends any longer? Wasn't he already cast aside? New successes might regenerate their interest; petitions for a loan would spoil it forever. And he could not always go on borrowing small sums to pay previous debts. How would he be able to work with his mind so burdened, while Constanze was weeping over the cradle of their little daughter who was not expected to live?

Well, there was Puchberg. Michael Puchberg, a co-Freemason, who had already twice helped him out of a nasty spot, and had even thanked him when, in one of his embarrassed letters only a few days before, Wolfgang had included two tickets for his next concert as a small token of gratitude. Puchberg was no millionaire, but he was a well-to-do merchant who was used to handling money matters. Yet Wolfgang could not see him face to face. He had better write again.

As elaborately as once he had written to Papa, he now explained his situation to Puchberg. Maybe Puchberg could lend him two thousand gulden for a couple of years—or at least two hundred until tomorrow. It was a cry of despair, with all feelings of pride vanquished by the threat of poverty and disgrace. After Wolfgang had sealed the letter, he broke it open again and added a short postscript: "When are we to have a little musical party at your house again? I have composed a new trio!" It was the only thing he could offer in return.

Puchberg sent two hundred gulden immediately. But only ten days later, Wolfgang had to write another letter, and yet a third one at the beginning of July, a hasty little note: "My affairs have become so involved that it is of the utmost importance to raise some money on these two pawnbroker's tickets. In the name of our friendship I implore you to do me this favor. But you must do it immediately. . . ."

The more precarious his financial situation became, the easier some parasites, professing friendship, succeeded in taking from him his last kreutzer with heartbreaking stories about their own need. He knew want so well by now that he was sympathetic to every hard-luck story. Fellow musicians shamelessly exploited this state of mind. The worst of them was Anton Stadler, the clarinetist. Not satisfied with having Wolfgang compose for him the most wonderful pieces of music ever written for his instrument—among them, in 1789, the so-called *Stadler* Quintet (K. 581) for clarinet and strings—he once even cheated him of his last fifty ducats which had been intended to keep the most urgent creditors at bay. Gradually the Mozarts became afraid of every knock at their door. But they were no less afraid of the complete lack of visitors, who might have been messengers of a turn for the better.

Wolfgang led a double existence. One Mozart struggled against misery and humiliation, and for the few pleasures that were left. The other Mozart, free from earthly matters, lived in music and beauty. During June and the first part of July, he wrote among other works two "little" sonatas, one for piano solo (K. 545) and one with violin (K. 547), intended, and still used, for the instruction of beginners; and another piano trio (K. 548). And on June 26, July 25, and August 10, he could enter three symphonies in his catalogue, the three symphonies which ever since have been called the "big," written for concerts that were never given and yet paving the way for the symphonic wealth of the next century: the lyric E flat major (K. 543), the tragic G minor (K. 550), and the powerful C (K. 551) known as *Jupiter*. A farewell to the past, a salute to the future and in between the culmination of earthly tragedy—this is the meaning which has been interpreted into these symphonies by romantic adherents of program music. Mozart, when he wrote them, had no such thoughts in mind. He simply composed, as he had done all his life. And while his piano concertos are considered his most characteristic instrumental works, there is hardly an instrument or a musical form whose use, or whose scope, he did not decisively develop. Having learned the symphonic form from Haydn, he greatly enlivened its score through his novel use of the wind instruments—Haydn later claimed he might have learned it from Mozart if he were not too old.

The entire city of Vienna separated the suburbs of Währing and Landstrasse, and the trip to the center of the town cost ten kreutzer. . . . And perhaps more than ever the Mozarts were eager to see people. So they became closer to Constanze's family. Cäcilia and Sophie, who had married the musician Haibl, lived in the suburb of Wieden, and many an afternoon Wolfgang went to see his mother-in-law with the last pennies he could scrape together to bring her a small package of sugar or coffee or some delicacy.

His other friends were entirely different from the people he had known in the days of prosperity and success. Obscure musicians, talented, careless bohemians, who crowded suburban wineries, the so-called *Heurigen,* where young wine was sold by the vineyard owner for a few kreutzer. Here the soothing landscape of the Vienna woods provided the background for improvised musicmaking and frolicking. This was the way Mozart now spent most of his evenings.

One of his few remaining toeholds in the aristocratic world was his appointment as music director for the private concerts of Baron van Swieten, a post he retained until his death. In his own

sumptuous lodgings, or in the big hall of the Library, or in the palaces of friends in the nobility, the Baron continued his Handel concerts on a large scale. In due course, Wolfgang was asked to orchestrate *Acis and Galathea, Messiah, Alexander's Feast, Ode to Saint Caecilia,* to make up for the lack of an organ. But no remuneration came from this enormous amount of extra work, although van Swieten must have known how poor Wolfgang was. (It was he who, after his death, arranged for his funeral for the equivalent of about—four dollars.)

The fall and winter that followed the writing of the three symphonies was to be the most depressing, the most uninspired period in Mozart's life. His creative power seemed exhausted. Poverty further impaired his already frail health. The strain of the two big operas, together with the restless life in Prague, had damaged his powers of physical resistance and constant worry became too much for him. In sleepless nights he would get up to write pathetic letters, frequently tearing them to pieces before the day dawned. His face grew pale and gray, his skin flabby, his eyes haggard.

Constanze saw nothing of all this. She was expecting another child. Wolfgang in his sadness seemed not too happy about the prospect of another baby. She did not reproach him for that.

CHAPTER 27

VISIT TO BERLIN

[1 7 8 9]

I F ANY of the people around Mozart in the last years of his life deserves credit as a friend in need, it is the merchant Michael Puchberg. Not only had his pockets been generously open to Wolfgang's urgent appeals; he now opened his house to Constanze, which enabled Wolfgang to go on a journey.

Prince Karl Lichnowsky, a relative of Countess Thun and one of Mozart's few male pupils, owned estates in Silesia and had an assignment with the Prussian army which necessitated sporadic trips to Berlin. He was *persona grata* at the Prussian court and thought it would be a good idea for Wolfgang to accompany him there. The prospect of new opportunities helped Wolfgang to overcome his dislike of the Prussians. Leaving Constanze in the care of Puchberg's wife, he left for the North to make some money.

The new King of Prussia, Frederick William II, like the Austrian Emperors, preferred the arts to war. Theaters and concert halls were opened wide to Italian, French, and German opera, to Gluck and Handel, and even to "modernists" like Mozart and Haydn. An excellent cellist himself, the King was familiar with Mozart's chamber music, and the success of *Die Entführung,* still currently given in Berlin, added to his reputation.

The travelers set forth, and their first stop was Prague where Wolfgang was once more filled with hopes when he met Ramm. Ramm reported that the King had asked repeatedly whether it was so that the great Mozart was about to put in an appearance. Next they went to Dresden, the charming capital of Saxony, where they were received with enthusiasm. A concert Mozart gave for the Elector—an unusual honor, for Friedrich August was a melancholy person and hardly anyone could get a hearing—was rewarded with a handsome snuff box containing one hundred ducats. Moreover, he played at the Russian Embassy, and, in a musical duel, finished off an aggressive rival who was locally considered the lion of pianists and organists.

In Leipzig, where they went from Dresden, Mozart met the last surviving pupil of Johann Sebastian Bach, seventy-four-year-old Thomaskantor Doles. When Wolfgang mounted the master's organ before a crowd of listeners, Doles and the organist sat beside him and pulled the stops. Tears ran down the old man's face. "Sebastian Bach has risen again!" he shouted. Then he had his chorus sing a Bach motet.

"This is music from which a man can learn something," Mozart exclaimed joyfully and buried himself in manuscripts of Bach, then gathering dust in the archives, unpublished and unknown. These were revelations to him and their influence is evident in his last quartets and in the Requiem.

The King and Queen of Prussia received Wolfgang kindly, but the resident musicians took a strenuous dislike to him. Duport, the King's 'cello teacher and conductor, was French, and it aroused Wolfgang's anger that "the grinning mounseer" still insisted on speaking his own language. Duport heard of this and resented it deeply, although Wolfgang tried to conciliate him with piano variations (K. 573) on one of his minuets. The King remunerated Wolfgang generously whenever he played at Court, but Potsdam was an expensive place, and Prince Karl Lichnowsky, in a hurry to get home, left Wolfgang there alone. At the last minute the young Prince discovered that he was short of cash and asked Mozart to advance him a hundred gulden. "You must be more delighted with having me back than with the money I shall bring," Wolfgang warned Constanze.

Upon returning from Leipzig, on May 19, where he had gone to give an unprofitable concert, he casually inquired at his inn what they were having at the theater.

"A lovely opera, *Die Entführung*," was the answer. "By general demand."

There was no time for Wolfgang to change. "Short, quick, restless and weak-eyed, an insignificant figure in a gray overcoat," according to the description of an admiring young student, Mozart bustled about the desks in the pit, examined the music placed there, waited for the audience to arrive and, without revealing his identity, talked to this young admirer about his own music. Seated near the orchestra, Mozart annoyed his neighbors by loud, nervous, and unfavorable remarks about the performance until, in Pedrillo's air in the second act, the second violins played D sharp instead of D. This was more than he could stand. "Damn it, play D, will you?" he yelled. The audience became restive and an attendant rushed down the aisle to put the troublemaker out. But someone in the orchestra whispered to the man: "It's Mozart, for Heaven's sake, leave him alone!"

"It's Mozart . . . Mozart is here . . ." the word went around.

"I'm sorry," Wolfgang whispered to the conductor, "please, go on."

Duport's efforts to discredit Mozart did not impress the King of Prussia. Quite unexpectedly he offered him a position for six times his Vienna salary. Wolfgang gasped for breath. There would be no more troubles and privations, no resentful grocers and druggists, no detours through side streets to avoid creditors, no trembling at the doorbell, no pawnbrokers heartlessly evaluating priceless souvenirs.

The Mozart who had worried and wept almost accepted. But then the other Mozart intervened, the Mozart of music and beauty. Look around, the second Mozart warned, look at this stiff, ungraceful Court, look at the streets of Berlin, ugly, cold, uninspiring . . . you will not be Mozart any longer here . . . you will lose contact with living beauty . . . and the music in you will fade . . . and your life will fade with the music. . . .

The King stood waiting. Someone of his escort whispered a few words Wolfgang could not understand, but the heavy Prussian accent again shook his nerves . . . it might have been something unfavorable, an intrigue . . . there would be intrigues here as in Vienna, and Duport might be even worse than Salieri . . . and then the sacrifice would have been in vain. He belonged to Vienna, cruel as it was to him, and Joseph might one day give up Salieri, fire Rosenberg . . . he had always been good to him . . . and all he said was: "But, Your Majesty, would you want me to desert my kind Emperor?"

Frederick William was touched. This unaffected faithfulness, this indifference to money, was unexpected. "Think it over," he said warmly. "I will give you a whole year to make up your mind."

CHAPTER 28

SUMMER NIGHTMARE

[1 7 8 9 - 9 0]

WHEN WOLFGANG left Castle Sans-Souci in Potsdam for the last time, he knew he could never decide to stay in Berlin, either in one year or in his lifetime. But the offer raised his hopes again; if he was so well liked everywhere else—why not in Vienna?

He would be home in the early days of June. Then the suburb of Währing would be filled with the sweet and heavy scent of locust, the huge beds of lilac on the square in front of the Hofburg would be in bloom, a symphony of purple. And, if he was lucky, he might still see the alleys of blooming chestnut trees in the Prater. He thought of the little garden behind their house, with the table on the lawn where he would compose, of the canary twittering in its cage and the dog stretched out in the sun. There Constanze waited for him. He loved her so much. And there was Karl, his only child. He would soon have a little brother or sister, who might perhaps live. Everything would be all right. He remembered an old saying of his mother:

Where there's faith
There is love;
Where there's love,
There is peace;
Where there's peace,

[2 2 9]

There is blessing;
Where there's blessing,
There is the Lord;
And where the Lord is,
There is no need.

He had faith, and there would be no need.

But more bad luck awaited him. Constanze's foot was severely affected by her pregnancy and it was imperative that she take the waters at Baden. Wolfgang was still optimistic, though he had little money left. Then he fell ill. It was late in the season and every day lost meant a lost chance. When, by the end of June, not yet fully recovered, he finally started out to round up subscribers for concerts he found—one. Baron van Swieten.

When he told his friends about the offer of the King of Prussia, they thought he was crazy to have refused. But all they could persuade Wolfgang to do was to put his case before the Emperor, to ask for a higher salary and a chance to earn it.

Joseph listened to Mozart's report about the trip to Berlin and his opportunities there. With a resigned smile in his tired eyes, he interrupted Wolfgang: "And so you are going to leave me, Mozart?" It was as though he had wanted to say: and so you, too, are going to leave me?

Wolfgang, depressed and in urgent need of sympathy as he was, suddenly sensed that the Emperor was also worrying and needed sympathy. And his heart opened wide to offer his sovereign what he needed so badly himself: loyalty. The news from France, Turkey, Belgium . . . Joseph's own people losing confidence in him . . . he looks old and worn, his smile is so sad. . . .

"Only a wretch could have thought of money at such a moment!" he exclaimed indignantly to his friends, who had anxiously awaited the outcome of the audience, and were to learn that Wolfgang had not even mentioned a raise and had simply replied: "I beg Your Majesty's pardon, I will stay."

Joseph had troubles indeed. Alarming reports came from Belgium and Turkey, where problems which he believed had been settled long ago were creating new unrest, but above all from France. Something unprecedented seemed to be in the offing there. Joseph did not think so much of his sister, Marie Antoinette, or her family—he had never quite agreed with her and blamed her more than she really deserved. But the effect of events in France was bound to be felt far beyond the borders of the shaken kingdom.

A single Austrian army corps might be able to smash a French rebellion, if the French army should prove disloyal to the King. But Joseph wondered whether and how a popular monarch, which he considered himself to be, should interfere with a popular uprising in another country. There were the people of Austria to consider too. Would it be wise to let them come in contact with the French rioters, even on the battlefield? The Emperor decided to await further developments. But the people of Austria grew restless. The more the news from France was kept from them, the more they were sure that trouble was brewing. They had known many wars, but never a revolution. This time it would be something different from the usual campaigning, something that would concern them all. Those who had property were afraid of losing it. Those who had nothing wondered how and to what extent a sudden change might improve their situation. There was much tension in Vienna, no sense of enterprise, only a yearning for security—and entertainment.

Entertainment would keep them from worrying, and it was up to the artists to provide it—not to bother people with their own troubles.

The Court was more conservative than it had ever been since Maria Theresa's death. Strict observance of traditional rules should banish the specter of the unknown. Austria tried to escape the threat by ignoring it.

But Mozart could not ignore the growing threat of starvation. For him, the summer developed into a nightmare. Constanze was very ill. The King of Prussia had ordered six string quartets for himself and six piano sonatas for his daughter. If Wolfgang succeeded in furnishing them, his financial crisis might be eased, but he wrote only three quartets and one sonata (K. 576). When the payment for the first quartet (K. 575) arrived, it did not begin to meet his desperate need.

Wolfgang's mental state and the influence of Bach's scores had brought a new quality into his music. No more cataracts of melodies, no more the emotional style of the *Don Giovanni* period. His themes were simpler and fewer than ever. He exhausted all their possibilities, rejoicing, as it were, in his own skill. He no longer cared whether he was understood. Composing had become his recreation, and when he could not afford recreation he did not write at all.

And he wrote little during this summer . . . little music, but many letters. When he saw Puchberg in the Lodge, he did not dare to approach him again. But on July 12 he was at his wit's end. He wrote—and kept the letter lying on his table for two days. July 14, 1789. In Paris, the Bastille fell to the triumphant mob; in Vienna, a harassed little man, with his eyes on his wife who was moaning with pain, broke the seal of the long, desperate letter appealing for help and wrote a postscript: "Oh, God!—I can hardly bring myself to dispatch this letter!—and yet I must! If this illness had not befallen me, I should not have been obliged to beg so shamelessly from my only friend. . . . For God's sake forgive me, only forgive me! and—Adieu!"

His only friend. This was not just a phrase. But the general unrest had had an effect on Puchberg too. In times of emergency a responsible man ought to hoard his money, not lend it away. Puchberg hesitated, and three agonizing days went by. Every knock at the door could bring Puchberg's reply—or the bailiff. Constanze suffered a severe relapse. Wolfgang did not dare to leave her bedside, hardly ate, hardly did any work.

On July 17, he wrote another letter and received a hundred and fifty gulden. Too little and too late.

Finally relief came. Puchberg sent enough money to prevent the worst, and an unexpected invitation dropped in from an unknown admirer, a modest tradesman at Baden, who offered Constanze his house and would pay for her baths.

Wolfgang meanwhile lived on next to nothing. But he had to work despite hunger, heat, and worries. A *Figaro* revival was scheduled for August 29—probably a result of his interview with the Emperor. He had to supervise the rehearsals, and da Ponte's new protégé, who sang Susanna, wanted new arias.

Constanze improved quickly, and as soon as she felt better, she engaged in unrestrained amusement. Wolfgang began to hear gossip about her frivolous and extravagant behavior, and sacrificing some of his meager meals, he rushed to Baden. There was a tempestuous scene between them; Constanze argued with unfettered Weberish temper, Wolfgang scolded and forgave her in the same breath. Exhausted and hardly comforted, he returned to town to get on with the rehearsals, while Constanze stayed in Baden until September.

The renewed success of *Figaro* encouraged the Emperor to commission a new opera from Wolfgang, this time for two hundred ducats. Da Ponte was again to write the libretto. The subject was chosen by Joseph himself. He wanted to see dramatized a real incident in Vienna society: one that had caused much giggling when it happened. Two young cavaliers had bet on their fiancées' faithfulness; each let the other put it to test under the protection of a masquerade, and both had lost their bets within twenty-four hours.

This was *Così fan tutte* (K. 588), a work considered too frivolous in its day, too unreal later. Only a few appreciate it for its fine irony, the naïve charm of the old but never-too-old play of masks —the game for game's sake. Entirely detached from his own sadness—moving again; no money; childbirth; private baptism and a tiny coffin—Mozart revived old *commedia dell' arte* and its smiling characters. In the transparent style which marks this period of creative rest he wrote, shivering with cold and undernourished, a graceful and unreal parody of love.

It has often been alleged that Mozart disliked the subject and wrote the opera hastily and unwillingly. The great number of Italian abbreviations in the score, which he usually did not use, are quoted as proof. But this inference is unwarranted. The opera had to be done very quickly. The Emperor was impatient to have it. Joseph, though a fairly young man, was lonely, unhappy, discouraged, and unwell. People did what they could to give him pleasure.

In his new quarters on the Judenplatz, where Wolfgang moved when even his little refuge in Währing had become too expensive for him, a rehearsal took place on the last day of the year. Only Haydn and Puchberg were present. The invitation to Puchberg had been accompanied by another petition for a loan. Wolfgang was to receive two hundred ducats upon delivery of the opera, but before that, he had to pay off "doctors and apothecaries."

Constanze's health was still impaired. Wolfgang could not rid himself of fear for her. She had been ill for eight months. For a long time visitors were greeted with a "sh," as in the days of her most dangerous condition, and out of habit he even hushed people he met on the street. His household deteriorated. Meals were brought to them from a tavern on the Kärtnerstrasse, the Silver Serpent, where Wolfgang was an habitué in more prosperous days. Fortunately Joseph Deiner, superintendent, was a great admirer of Wolfgang and a most agreeable creditor. Once he even supplied some firewood and "put it on the bill" when he surprised Wolfgang dancing around with Constanze in their room to keep warm on an icy day.

Così fan tutte went very well. The singers were splendid; the critics lauded the work unanimously. The public liked it too, because it was sheer amusement and did not bother them with problems. The opera Wolfgang had written so quickly and lightly promised to become the hit of the season and to solve all his problems for him.

But Mozart's bad luck persisted. The Emperor never saw the opera he had commissioned. The day of the première found him very ill. On February 20, Emperor Joseph died.

CHAPTER 29

THE NEW EMPEROR

[1 7 9 0]

"HERE LIES JOSEPH, unfortunate in all he undertook."
This epitaph the Emperor had drafted for himself. And
Maria Theresa would no more have considered her son
too haughty had she been able to read these lines from his last will:

I beg all those to whom I have not rendered justice to forgive me out
of Christian charity or humanity. The monarch on his throne, like the
poor man in his cabin, is, after all, but a man. . . .

That sentence bridged the gap Joseph had not been able to cross
in his lifetime.

Leopold, his brother and successor to the throne, did not even
try to become a popular ruler. Since childhood he had resented
Joseph's priority. Instead of devoting himself to the Army and
becoming the military leader of the Empire under his brother's
command—as was planned for him—he preferred to become Governor of Tuscany—a comparatively minor post. He lived in Florence with his wife Maria Ludovica, daughter of the King of Spain,
had many children, and never ceased to dream of outliving his
brother and taking his place. Maria Ludovica also felt she deserved
better than the dull life in Florence. When Leopold hastened to
Vienna to take over, he was not so much in a hurry to pilot the
ship of state safely through troubled waters as to abolish what he
disliked—and he disliked almost everything connected with Joseph.

Reforms were revoked and many persons were dismissed.

Among the victims was Count Rosenberg. Leopold did not care much for the theater or music. It took six months and an official event to get him to put in an appearance at the opera. The Empress fancied herself an expert, but she did not like Viennese ways. The reforms she urged on the Emperor had to do with the revival of ballet and old-fashioned Italian opera, and the building of a new theater with boxes equipped for card playing as she knew them from Italy.

The late Emperor's favor and his official title were liabilities to Wolfgang, but he was not prominent enough to be dismissed. Instead, he was completely ignored. He made a formal application for the position of second Court Conductor. Many applications were made in these days and cleared with a promptness unusual in official communications. The answers were mostly turn-downs.

"I have no reply," Wolfgang boasted timidly. "The Emperor has kept my application. It must be under consideration."

The Emperor had retained his application . . . and never replied at all.

Puchberg helped as much as he could, but business was steadily on the decline and even well-to-do merchants had to be careful of their dwindling funds. His loans shrank to low two-figures, just enough to keep the Mozarts from starvation. Wolfgang fell ill again. Toothaches, headaches, rheumatism, painfully reminded him of the symptoms of his mother's fatal disease. He crawled about with his head wrapped in linen. His only chance to earn money was to finish some more of the music for the King of Prussia. Desperately he bowed his aching head over sheets of music paper, but inspiration would not come. The paper remained blank except for some hastily drawn numerals, symbolic of his misery. No inspiration brought no earnings, no earnings brought more trouble, more trouble brought still less inspiration. It was a vicious circle.

He practically begged for pupils. "I now have two pupils and should very much like to raise the number to eight. Do your best to spread the news that I am willing to give lessons," he wrote to

Puchberg. It was as though he had wanted to add "for whatever they want to pay."

Constanze's state of health required no less than sixty baths in Baden, and Wolfgang could not afford to run two households. After painful money-raising, they moved to Baden together, Wolfgang occasionally returning to Vienna when it was unavoidable. Somehow he struggled through two more quartets (K. 589, 590), but in order to raise some cash he had to sell them to his publisher "for a mere song."

There were wealthy and influential people who might still have called themselves his friends. But Wolfgang could not tell them . . . it was imperative for him to keep face. This was another vicious circle. They sponsored the well-groomed young composer, the celebrity from many stages, who did not ask for anything . . . the Mozart who provided enjoyment. They might have turned away for good from the petitioner, the bearer of bad news about himself.

The King of Naples and his family were expected to come to Vienna in the fall, the first royalty to visit Emperor Leopold in his residence. Even before his official assignment, Wolfgang had always been summoned to play on such occasions during Joseph's reign. The festival opera was an opus by young Weigl, a pupil of Salieri. Salieri himself performed, and so did Haydn, the Cavalieri, the two Stadlers. But although Queen Caroline, the Emperor's sister, had known Mozart for over twenty-five years, no one thought of asking him.

By that time Wolfgang was entirely in the hands of money lenders. Already he had a debt of one thousand gulden to one of these gentlemen. They turned a deaf ear to his pleas for additional loans, stating that the order from the Prussian King was no sufficient security and that his furniture was not much better. Wolfgang was desperate enough to consider another offer: a loan of two thousand gulden if he could find a publisher to guarantee the repayment. The proposition sounded all right. It might bring relief until he had rounded up new pupils and subscribers for concerts which he intended to give in the new apartment where they were to move in the fall. This would justify high interest.

But the two thousand gulden existed only in theory. Only half of it was to be paid in cash—just the sum that would be immediately collected—and for the rest he would have to accept cloth. This was a device frequently used to avoid trouble with the law against usury; the money lenders said cloth was easy to sell and well worth the full amount. It was, of course, very hard to sell, and not for anything like a thousand gulden. The unfortunate Wolfgang would be forced to beg his creditor to buy it back himself for half the price or even less, while the debt remained the same.

Mozart did not fully understand the trick. But even if he had understood it, he had no choice.

Wolfgang decided to try a *tour de force*. The Emperor's coronation at Frankfurt was to be celebrated with great ceremony. Salieri was to go there, taking Umlauff as his assistant and fifteen chamber musicians. Mozart applied for a place in one of the musicians' coaches. It was denied to him.

But Wolfgang felt entitled to be present at the Court to which he belonged, with or without Imperial patronage. Frankfurt would be crowded with foreigners of distinction, eager to hear good music and willing to pay for it. A valuable silver plate and some trinkets that had not yet been pawned were sold for what they would fetch to buy a carriage and to raise some cash for the trip. His brother-in-law Hofer would go with him so they could give concerts together.

They left on September 23. While they were gone, Constanze was supposed to move into their new apartment and to bring about the complicated two thousand gulden deal.

With the first turn of the wheels, Wolfgang became optimistic. He was riding again in his own carriage to one of the most splendid events in Europe. A sad chapter seemed to be closed; a new and happier one was opening, or so he thought. The only thing that dampened his mood was the separation from Constanze. Joint sufferings had tied him even more closely to his wife. His letters to her were full of hope and comfort. He promised to work hard—as if he had been an idler all his life!—and he would make a lot of money in Frankfurt. Back in Vienna, he would have many pupils and even more subscribers. It would be a busy and happy life.

The last unproductive year burdened his conscience. Now that his courage had come back, he did not understand why he had let worries keep him from composing. He had a minor commission— the most boring one he could think of—a piece for mechanical organ (K. 594), ordered by the owner of a wax-figure works. As if to prove his zeal to himself and to Constanze, he went to work. It was like a self-imposed penalty for loafing.

But he had no luck in Frankfurt. People there seemed to be "even stingier than the Viennese." The distinguished foreigners were busy with countless amusements, and all halls were taken. Mozart's concert on October 15 (he played among other things his piano concerto in D [K. 537], since called the *Coronation* Concerto), had to be scheduled for eleven in the morning. As some Prince had a breakfast party and the Hessian troops were holding maneuvers, the audience was small. A second concert did not materialize at all, nor did a performance of *Don Giovanni* which had been planned in his honor. *Figaro* was given while he was there, but Wolfgang does not seem to have been much impressed with the performance.

Although much honored socially, his hopes faded, and so did his funds. A letter he wrote Constanze from his next stop, Mainz, was stained with tears of disillusion.

Behind him lay the disappointment of Frankfurt, ahead of him Vienna, city of his frustrated dreams. The old regime had been blind to his needs—the new one was deaf to his music. He would have liked to stay away and go on a concert tour, but he could not stand the thought of a lengthy separation from his family. It was chiefly Constanze who tied him to Vienna now, she and "the few friends who wish me well," as he called those who still seemed to care for him.

Wolfgang met old friends en route: the Wendlings and Lang in Frankfurt, the Cannabichs and Ramm in Munich, and others in

Mannheim. The shortest route back did not go by way of Mannheim, but the place represented for him youth and its hopes. There
he was still Mozart, the young man with the promising future.

He was still Mozart. At Mainz he had played for the Elector of
Erthal and in Munich he had been invited to do what he had failed
to achieve at his own Court—to be heard by the King of Naples.

But those moral successes did not help him to obtain the material
support he needed more and more desperately. Back home, with
only a few pennies left and the carriage much used and depreciated
in value, he learned that the transaction with the money lender had
not materialized. The publisher had refused the guarantee. In vain,
Wolfgang promised to write his full money's worth for him. The
publisher was the same one who years before had warned Wolfgang
about his "modernistic and unpopular" way of composing. He saw
no security in Mozart's music. . . .

CHAPTER 30

"THE MAGIC FLUTE"

[1790-91]

POVERTY, most faithful of his companions, accompanied Wolfgang to his new apartment at Rauhensteingasse 570. The intent to work was still there, but the opportunity was not. The imaginary crowds of pupils and subscribers failed to appear and there were no gratifying orders either.

In those days musicians did not produce freely and try to sell their work afterwards. Music was written to order, or at least for a particular purpose. Demand came before supply. Only later was this situation reversed, after artistic independence was enforced by Beethoven.

It did not occur to Mozart that it might be otherwise. Music was always with him, but it mostly took a specific reason to get it down on paper—commissions, concerts, dedications, souvenirs, presents of gratitude or good-will. Somehow his music had remained attached to the world, to his life, to other people. Now there was little demand. Music roamed in Wolfgang's head, but only rarely did the world force a pen into his fingers.

In December, he wrote the first of two string quintets (K. 593, 614) with the second (his last) to follow in the spring. It sufficed to show him that he could still write. Then came a piano concerto in B flat (K. 595) for himself—his last. Then there were some songs, and other compositions to provide him with bread and butter:

dances and more pieces for mechanical organ. His music was mild, soothing, resigned.

Perhaps he was more resigned than he would admit to Constanze or even to himself. He alone could sense that privation, worry, and penny-hunting were sapping the last shreds of energy which otherwise he might have put into music.

The first premonition of death took shape when Haydn came to say good-by. Prince Esterházy had just died, and the big impresario Salomon had come from London to fetch Haydn for a series of guest appearances. Mozart was to go, too, when Haydn returned.

They spent the last day together, played sonatas and had long talks. When the hour of farewell came, Wolfgang fell sobbing into his friend's arms: "I know, Papa, that this is forever. We won't ever meet again."

Haydn was almost resentful: "Why, I am not that old."

Wolfgang wiped his eyes as though trying to erase a vision.

"I know," he said. "I did not mean it that way."

Haydn did not understand, but he left Wolfgang with a sad heart.

Winter went by. Wolfgang's debts were not reduced, but he at least succeeded in earning enough for a modest living. His steady salary helped a little, but most of his extra money came from dance music. With the political clouds massing ominously, people were more eager than ever for light entertainment. Dance halls were crowded and salon music was consumed like wine. Sometimes, when a few coins tinkled in Mozart's pocket, he could not resist the temptation to buy some little gift for Constanze, which soon after traveled the usual sad road to the pawnbroker.

The high-paying pupils he hoped for did not come. Instead, a young man of twenty-five dropped in early in 1791, timidly asking for lessons in composition—for which he could not pay. Mozart took him on nevertheless. Poor people should help one another and Franz Xaver Süssmayer's talents seemed to be above the average. He could make himself useful in the household, and Wolfgang could teach him by making him his assistant. The young man did well; in fact, so well did he pick up Mozart's style that he could later be safely entrusted with the recitatives for *La Clemenza di Tito* and with the completion of the Requiem after Wolfgang's death.

In the spring, Salieri retired from the opera. He wanted to escape the disgrace of being dismissed. Cavalieri left with him. Salieri's intrigues against Wolfgang stopped from that very moment. Too late. Wolfgang hoped again, and again was disappointed. The vacant post went to Joseph Weigl. Another application had better luck. The magistrate of Vienna graciously accepted Wolfgang's offer to act as an assistant conductor at St. Stephen's—just for the pleasure of a church position and the honor of the title.

Constanze had to go to Baden again. Wolfgang stayed in Vienna, alone, and lonely. From Baden, Constanze wrote sad letters which only increased Wolfgang's depression. He could not get used to living alone. He wrote to Constanze, sometimes twice a day; little about his work, more about himself: "I feel pretty well," or "I am weak from want of food . . ." and ". . . the mental worry and anxiety and the running around connected with it are really exhausting me . . ." but "If I know for certain that you have everything you want, then all my trouble is a joy and a delight. . . ."

Constanze lived comfortably in the quarters which Choirmaster Stoll—for whom Wolfgang wrote the lovely motet, *Ave, verum corpus* (K. 618), in return for his trouble and whom he permitted to perform his *Coronation* Mass—had found for her. Süssmayer made himself useful as best he could. Expenses were kept down to the point of privation for Wolfgang himself.

And in loneliness and sorrow was created what Richard Wagner later called the first German opera and at the same time its most finished masterpiece.

In a courtyard just outside the southern bastions of Vienna stood an inconspicuous building. It was not much more than a barn, but it bore the imposing name of *Theater im Starhembergischen Freihause auf der Wieden*. Here the troupe of Emanuel Schikaneder performed. Schikaneder was still an actor-producer-singer as he had been in the days when Wolfgang knew him in Salzburg. In addition, he was a Freemason.

Schikaneder's fortunes had fluctuated. In 1784, after the collapse of the *Singspiel* company, Emperor Joseph had sponsored a season for his group. Schikaneder stayed on in Vienna and became an actor. He fancied himself a great dramatic performer, but one night he was hissed off the stage and out of the city. While he was seeking his fortune with varying success through Central Europe, bailiffs and prosecutors hunted him. He had always been a gambler, extravagant, imaginative and bombastic. Finally, he staked and lost his all on a single production.

He returned to Vienna in 1789 hoping that in his wife's shabby hut on the *Freihaus,* he would be able to outdo his competitor, Marinelli, whose *Kasperl,* a Viennese variant of Jack Pudding, had been firmly established in the Leopoldstädter Theater for eight years. The Leopoldstädter Theater was hardly an elegant place, but it claimed to be the most elegant among the inelegant stages. And Marinelli was so cocksure about *Kasperl,* that he had nothing but contempt for Schikaneder's undertaking.

But Schikaneder in no time created his own buffoon type: the stupid gardener Anton, about whom he wrote endless serials, playing the part himself. His actors were the companions of his extravagant amusements and were considered the gayest and most irresponsible crowd in Vienna. If they were not quite as bad as people said, they were still bad enough, and certainly not admissible in good society. Mozart no longer felt at ease among the nobility. Somehow the news about his debts had leaked out. In making the rounds, it had picked up an extra cipher, so there was gossip now about the thirty · thousand gulden he was supposed to owe. The sensitive Wolfgang withdrew from contact with these respectable critics. In his masonic Lodge, too, he came to associate more and more with those who did not consider solvency the most important thing in life.

Mozart had met Schikaneder again in his Lodge, and in 1790 had collaborated on a duet for the producer's first attempt at fairy comic opera, which was the big fashion in the suburbs. Wolfgang's friend

Schack, a remarkable tenor and musician, was a member of Schikaneder's group, and so was his sister-in-law, Josefa Hofer.

Freemasonry brought them even closer to each other. The late Emperor Joseph had encouraged the order, but Leopold persecuted it vigorously. The masonic brothers were charged with hostility to the state and to religion. Public opinion accused them of instigating the dreaded French Revolution. Naturally, the Masons adhered strictly to their rules of silence and discipline and became more closely linked to each other than ever before.

One morning in spring, Schikaneder showed up in Wolfgang's apartment.

"I'm in a bad hole," he confessed. "I'll have to close up, unless you help me out of it."

"Me? Help you out of debt?" Wolfgang had to laugh.

"Not the way you mean." Schikaneder remained serious. "Let's talk it over."

He filled Wolfgang's ears with a plan to write an opera together. Wolfgang was reluctant. He did not know Schikaneder's public, and could not predict its reaction to his music. If he consented, it would be a jump in the dark. He might land safely and profit from the experience, but he might just as easily break his neck.

On the other hand, he was always inclined to be helpful. Especially to a Mason.

"I'm lost in Vienna, unless you do the music," he heard Schikaneder say. Lorenzo da Ponte had used almost the same words six years before, he remembered. They had led to *Figaro*. . . . But that had been Lorenzo—and Emperor Joseph . . . it hurt to think of it. Yet, unless he wrote for Schikaneder, Wolfgang would hardly ever have a chance to write an opera again. And it would have to be a German opera, the old cherished dream which he had almost forgotten.

After all, Mozart reflected, he was getting nowhere scraping pennies together from trifles, composing nothing that really gratified him. Wasn't it better to write for the suburbs than not at all, and for a simple public instead of canvassing those who had grown tired of him?

"Say, young man," Schikaneder poked his ribs. "Did you hear what I said?"

"Not all of it," Wolfgang admitted.

"I just told you that I had no money to pay you an advance."

"Never mind," Wolfgang replied. His fascination with the thought of another opera was already so strong that he had characteristically forgotten the main point: that Schikaneder at the moment was almost as poor as he. "We want to help each other. You pay what you can and leave me the original score so I can sell it to other theaters."

"So it's yes?"

"If you have a good libretto, yes."

"Eh, libretto," Schikaneder mimicked. "Of course I have one. An oriental fairy tale," he continued mysteriously, "with a good queen, a wicked magician, a kidnaped princess and an exotic prince who marries her after a number of trials. The prince has a magic flute which protects him and a funny birdman who is afraid of everything as a servant. I've called him Papageno. Imagine me in feathers!"

"It's a tempting idea," Wolfgang laughed. "But it doesn't seem to be very new."

It was not new. But it had been tried out and proven successful. There were no copyright laws to prevent theft and repetition of a synopsis in any number of versions. The main source for *Die Zauber-flöte,* which was to be the name of the opera, was Wranitzky's *Oberon,* which Wolfgang had heard in Frankfurt and which Schikaneder had scheduled. The libretto of *Oberon,* tracing to Wieland's collection of oriental fairy tales, had been written by Ludwig Giesecke, university student, Freemason, actor, and playwright.

Giesecke later disappeared from Vienna. When he returned in his old age, as a renowned professor of mineralogy, he boasted of having written almost all of *Die Zauberflöte* libretto. No other source confirms his statement, and it is hard to understand why he should have waited for so many years to claim the credit if he was really entitled to it. Interesting as this question may be from the standpoint of research, it is immaterial as far as the opera itself is concerned. Whatever Giesecke and Schikaneder wrote was a stock pattern. Whatever the one had written might just as well have been written by the other. Whether and to what extent Giesecke collaborated, it hardly makes any difference to the living opera as it stands.

Wolfgang shook his head at the skeleton of the plot. There was hardly any stage effect omitted: walls of colored fire and water; the sun and the stars; thunder, lightning, storm, and earthquake; flying machines; and an entire zoo. It was good theater, but a manager's rather than a dramatist's theater, with many opportunities for Schikaneder in his feathered costume. The scenes were incoherent. The verses were poor and made Wolfgang regretfully remember Lorenzo's poetical skill.

Then da Ponte himself appeared to say good-by. He preferred England to the Court in Vienna, which had become so unpleasant. "Why don't you come along, Wolfgang?"

As a matter of fact, Wolfgang could have gone. He had been offered a contract by the manager of the Italian company in London to do two operas a year for three hundred pounds. Probably O'Kelly was behind it, and the Storaces. He had refused in one of these spells of discouragement he could not explain to himself. It was as if an evil spirit tied him to Vienna whenever there was an opportunity abroad.

"I have to finish this," he told Lorenzo.

Da Ponte sniffed. "Why, that's easy work—just trash. . . ."

"Not as easy as you think," Wolfgang replied. "But I won't take long." He would finish *Die Zauberflöte* and go to England in perhaps six months. At least that was what he told Lorenzo. . . .

At the beginning, Mozart's work on *Die Zauberflöte* was as disorganized as his whole life had become. Schikaneder was not the person to stick to a regular schedule. He did his work on the libretto, with or without assistance, just in scraps. The composition was done in scraps too, sometimes pressing forward ahead of the script, sometimes developing out of an unrest which Wolfgang called boredom. "Out of sheer boredom I composed an aria today," he wrote Constanze in one of the letters in which he tried tenderly but vainly to conceal his melancholy, and "I cannot tell you what I would not give to be with you in Baden instead of being stuck here." "Stuck here" was the last expression he would normally have thought of using in connection with an opera assignment.

It was not merely the longing for Constanze's company which made his life miserable. His frequent headaches increased. Everything made him nervous and frightened. The apartment was big—having been intended for concerts. The furniture was scanty. The timber was dry and it cracked at night. The noise mixed in a ghostly duet with the sound of mice, the only living creatures that kept Wolfgang company. Darkness brought no relief from the blazing heat in the narrow Rauhensteingasse. The mornings found Wolfgang even more exhausted than the evenings.

When Schikaneder saw Wolfgang's condition, he worried not only on Mozart's account but also on account of his opera. He insisted that Wolfgang must work at a more comfortable place, where he would not mind writing down the music which he claimed was ready anyway. In the courtyard of his theater was a little pavilion, furnished with nothing but a table, two chairs and a sofa. But there were no vermin and there was always a current of fresh air. A few trees stood in front of the windows.

"This is yours," said Schikaneder. "You sit down here and write. Or else I'll lock the door."

"Lock the door?" Wolfgang laughed. "Do you want to know what happened to Josefa Duschek? When I was through with *Don Giovanni* and wanted a good rest, she locked me in a pavilion because I was late in writing down her aria [K. 528]. This made me mad. And when I was through I made the poor thing sing it on the spot, and if she'd made a single mistake she wouldn't have got it at all. I wonder how you'll manage with an entire opera."

"So I won't lock the door," Schikaneder grumbled. "But you're our prisoner just the same."

This little pavilion in which most of the music was written has been preserved. In 1877, it was shipped to Salzburg and

placed on the Kapuzinerberg, a friendly dark green hill facing the
fortress. A steep, narrow path lined with the Stations of the Cross
leads up to it. In front of it are flower beds and a Mozart statue.

The work on *Die Zauberflöte* entered a new phase. Schikaneder
and his singers were around most of the day. There was constant
contact and collaboration. There were Mlle. Gottlieb, Mozart's first

Barbarina, now to sing Pamina; Josefa Hofer and Schack; and the
two Gerls, he, Sarastro, she, Papagena, a pretty young woman who
proudly encouraged the gossip spread about her and Wolfgang.
It was for Josefa with her very particular vocal qualities that he
wrote the arias of the Queen of the Night, which since have been
the cross of casting directors' lives. And it was for Gerl that he led
Sarastro's aria down to the low F. "Can you sing the *'doch'*?"
managers in the 19th century would ask bassos who waited in a
Vienna café for opportunities. The singer would lazily get up from
his chair at the coffee table, sing the note and, if he did well, was
engaged on the spot.

Night after night there were rounds of the taverns. Schikaneder was the ringleader in these escapades, the captain of an army of pleasure-seekers. There was much noise and fun—and Mozart's growing fears were temporarily silenced. Death was already in him and drove him towards the warm pulses of life and the stimulation of alcohol. He no longer cared about his reputation. Those who criticized him were hypocrites trying to find a belated excuse for their neglect.

At the outset, Schikaneder had nothing in mind but to write another magic opera, which were so popular in those days. As a matter of fact, *Die Zauberflöte* was not very different from *Kaspar, der Fagottist,* which Marinelli produced on June 8. But Schikaneder did not mind resemblances. Fairy queens, stolen talismans or daughters, wicked magicians, and instruments to banish evil, were stock characters and props. The same was true of *Hanswurst* who, whatever name he bore, was used in those days of prolific rumors and tightened censorship to put over forbidden topics, to the delight of the audiences. All Schikaneder expected to be unusual in his opera was an abundance of technical tricks. He wrote many plays before and after, and all of them were pretty shallow.

Die Zauberflöte was not going to be shallow, and there is much more sense to it than superficial observers thought and sometimes still think.

The first act was all but written and composed up to the big finale, when the change occurred. Was it that Wolfgang, feeling that his days on earth were growing very short, tended towards the symbolic, towards ultimate truth enveloped in mysticism? Was it the approaching death of Ignaz von Born which so sadly impressed all Freemasons, that brought about a complete reversal of the plot? Or was it that the authors did not want to miss the opportunity of defending Freemasonry from their own special platform—the operatic stage?

Whatever the impulse, the simple fairy opera was turned into a play with masonic meanings. The switch was so sudden and so complete that the first act would have had to be rewritten entirely to preserve dramatic logic. But Schikaneder did not care about logic.

He was in a hurry, and what was already on paper, had to remain. So the fairy queen became a monster of darkness, fighting against light and wisdom as represented by Sarastro, High Priest of the Temple of Isis. The wicked magician was reduced to a pitifully sensual Moor. The conventional pair of lovers, Tamino and Pamina, became symbols of purified marital love, and the buffoons, birdman and birdwoman, symbols of simple human emotions.

The dramatic musician in Mozart knew that he faced the most worth-while task of his life. Schikaneder thought in more realistic terms. If rumors spread that the play had hidden masonic meanings, friend and foe would come to see it without the censors being able to find out what it was all about.

There is no doubt that Wolfgang had a strong hand in the libretto. But he was no literary man and neither was Schikaneder. For all its underlying poetry and symbolism, the language of the text is poor and the workmanship defective. "It takes more education to recognize its value than to condemn it," said Goethe, and began to write a sequel.

Die Zauberflöte was designed to appeal to everybody, not only the spoiled and sophisticated. It was hardly a play for courts and courtiers. Wolfgang's detachment from courts and courtiers had been painful, and not merely for material reasons. In Schikaneder's company he seemed to be down to the lowest rung of the social ladder. But the challenge of this new, strange, and pervasive element in his life developed his genius to its greatest perfection. It was an element that Papa had not taught him and that he had had to discover for himself.

Not even Emperor Joseph could have objected that there were too many notes in *Die Zauberflöte*. Never had Wolfgang composed with so few or worked with such simple devices. He labored hard on it; simple music is more difficult to write than complicated. It was as if Mozart wanted to go back to the roots of his art, to all he had heard and written. There was something in the opera from Italy, Germany, and France, from Handel, Bach, Gluck, and Haydn, and from his own serenades.

It was the music of Mozart's life just as the Requiem was to become the music of his dying. It bears the vital elements of his own well-being: edification, beauty, and comedy. Its pathos is not embarrassing; its drama not frightening; its humor not so coarse as to be disagreeable. It is enjoyable. It smiles. It is the most Viennese of Mozart's works.

More than that, it broke Italian predominance by blazing new trails for German dramatic composers. It became the point of issue for romantic opera. It was the opera of operas to Weber, Wagner, and Richard Strauss.

And from it sprang the Viennese operetta too, which came to have its home in the Theater an der Wien, which Schikaneder built ten years later right across from the wooden barn where *Die Zauberflöte* was first performed.

The earnings of *Die Zauberflöte* financed the new theater. It enabled Schikaneder to have himself painted on the curtain as Papageno, and to order and produce Beethoven's *Fidelio*. There is a Schikaneder Street, and a Papageno Road, in the vicinity of the theater.

What did Wolfgang get out of it? One hundred ducats and a small-type announcement at the bottom of the playbill at the première in the fall: "The music is by Herrn W. A. Mozart, conductor, and real Imperial and Royal Court Composer. Out of reverence to a gracious and venerable public, and friendship for the author of the play, Herr Mozart will conduct the orchestra in person."

CHAPTER 31

THE MESSENGER

[1791]

NIGHTS of hectic entertainment drowned the worry and strain of the days, but also hastened the decline of Wolfgang's weak powers of resistance.

Schikaneder drove him hard. There was no let-up after closer co-operation on *Die Zauberflöte* began.

Money troubles continued. Wolfgang still had to find people who might lend him a few gulden.

Headaches plagued him almost constantly, and he did not know whether they came from overstrain, from the heat, from sleepless nights, or whether he was really ill.

And he began to miss Constanze to the point of madness. Whenever he had a chance he would slip away to Baden, but each time the happiness of seeing his wife again was overshadowed by anticipation of the farewell.

When Wolfgang was at home, he started to play and sing what he had just composed. But often his voice broke off or faded away in a crying spell.

Nothing gave him real pleasure. Blanchard made his first flight in a hot-air balloon, starting in the Prater and coming down somewhere outside the city. The Viennese celebrated the event as a holiday. But Mozart stayed at home. For him, who loved spectacles so much, it was "just the kind of thing one can imagine."

By the first days of July, the vocal parts and the bass of *Die Zauberflöte* were finished. Wolfgang started the instrumentation and the singers began to rehearse.

Constanze returned by the middle of the month. Rauhenstein-gasse 570 was more habitable now that his wife was back, but even so Wolfgang's nervousness was hardly abated. On July 26, Franz Xaver Wolfgang was born.

Constanze was still in bed. The afternoon was unbearably hot. Yellowish clouds forecast a heavy storm. Unable to concentrate on anything, Wolfgang brooded in his room. It grew darker and darker. Perhaps he should light a candle? But even the lighting of a candle seemed too great a physical effort.

There was a heavy knock at the door, then another knock, and a third—like the Commendatore's ghost announcing himself in *Don Giovanni*—and with the third knock came a thunderbolt.

"Come in," Wolfgang said automatically.

The door opened and closed.

It was nearly dark in the room. It took Wolfgang a few breathless moments to realize that a man stood before him, a lean figure, very tall, clad in gray from head to toe, solemn and erect.

A dry voice rang out. "Good evening."

Wolfgang did not hear himself answer. He sat as if paralyzed.

The stranger bowed. Solemnly and stiffly. He took a letter out of his pocket and handed it to Wolfgang. The letter was real, so the messenger must be too.

A flash of lightning . . . then another. It began to rain.

Wolfgang moved to the window. He could read there. He examined the letter. It was plain white, closed with a big black seal. The seal was blank. No initials, no crest.

A torrential cloudburst battered the windows. It grew lighter.

Wolfgang broke the seal hastily, looked for the signature. There was none. It was all like a weird dream.

The letter began with a long eulogy of Mozart. Then came a

formally phrased question as to how much he would charge and how long it would take him to write a Requiem Mass for someone who could not reveal his name.

Wolfgang blanched. A Mass for the Dead. For an unknown . . . for a man who was to die soon . . . how long would he still live? Or was he already dead . . . ? Who was he?

From the bedroom came weak cries.

They reminded him that this was a house of life. In the other room were Constanze and their infant. They had buried four children but this one had to live, would live, and he, too, would live.

He had to see Constanze and his son, the living.

He went to the other room. The messenger waited motionless.

Constanze gazed happily at her husband. Her cheeks were red with sleep.

"Stanzi, there is someone outside who wants me to . . . write . . . a Requiem. . . . What do you think?" He tried to make it sound casual.

"But that's wonderful," Constanze exclaimed. "You always wanted to do church music again!"

She was not afraid. The baby stirred in her arms. This is life, Wolfgang thought.

The storm had subsided. There remained only a slight sprinkle of rain from reddish clouds. Gray as the twilight, the messenger stood waiting.

"Can you tell me for whom I am supposed to write the Requiem?" Wolfgang asked.

"That I cannot tell you, Sir, and I must ask you not to inquire."

"But where am I to send the music?"

"I shall call for it," came the answer in a monotone.

"It will be a long job. I have to finish an opera before . . . (I die, he wanted to say, he did not know why). . . ."

"We shall wait."

"I shall have to charge fifty ducats." Money was something real. The most real thing on earth.

"You shall have them." And, stiffly bowing, the gray messenger left. The door opened and closed.

Wolfgang was wondering whether the appearance of the stranger had not been one of his childhood nightmares resulting from over-tension, when the phantom reappeared a few days later, stiff and ceremonious as before, handing him the fifty ducats, promising more when the work was finished, leaving behind the breath of mystery.

As a very small child, Wolfgang had been afraid of ghosts. Later he had been so busy living that he had nearly forgotten his fears. Now he had again become the little boy of bygone days, who cried bitterly at the slightest sadness and who once had fainted at the sound of a trumpet. Little things, and greater shocks later, had created a deep-rooted fear which now found a dreadful invocation in the gray man.

He couldn't tell anyone. He had to fight it through alone. Fight? You couldn't fight off death. So he would become acquainted with death by writing for death.

As if pressed by a magic power, Mozart started to work. He was afraid and at the same time eager to do the Requiem to his own satisfaction and to the satisfaction of Mystery.

In the middle of August a letter came from Prague. It called Wolfgang back to life and reality. It was an invitation to write an opera for the coronation of Emperor Leopold as King of Bohemia.

The Praguers were certainly loyal to him. They must have had quite a struggle to force him on the Viennese music-bureaucrats for an event of such importance. So he would finally be noticed by his Court? But he had to finish *Die Zauberflöte* and then concentrate on the Requiem. The message of life had come after the message of death. Too late. . . .

The coronation was to take place on September 6. It was almost impossible to write a whole opera on such short notice. And he would have no influence on the libretto. It was already finished. *La Clemenza di Tito* (K. 621) by Metastasio, had been modernized by the Saxon Court Poet Mazzolà, da Ponte's friend. An *opera seria* —forgotten dream of his youth. Mozart had not written one since *Idomeneo*. He had lived a lifetime in those ten years. He had fulfilled his mission as a dramatic musician. Once he had longed to write *opera seria*. It had been inextricably linked with his life and love. But man could not reverse the hands of the clock. Too late. . . .

So Wolfgang's reaction, with crowning irony, was profound annoyance at an opera contract and at the prospect of returning to Prague!

But he could not afford to lose two hundred ducats. The children were boarded out and Constanze packed in a hurry. The carriage, battered by the trip to Frankfurt but not yet sold, came in handy. Süssmayer would go with them to help with the writing. Stadler came along, too, to play in the orchestra, as the clarinet would be given an important role.

Wolfgang's foot was already on the step, when he felt that someone was looking at him sharply. A strange power forced him to turn around.

There stood the gray man, like a nightmare come to life.

"So you are leaving, Maestro?" The voice was without expression, and yet Wolfgang felt some supreme mockery as if it wanted to say: you cannot escape.

"I must," Wolfgang stammered. "Something came up. . . . For the Emperor."

The monotone responded: "How about our Requiem, Maestro?"

"I'll get at it when I return. Right away!" There was a plea in Mozart's voice.

"Very well, Maestro, don't be too long!"

Constanze, Süssmayer, and Stadler looked on indifferently as if this were just an ordinary parley. Wolfgang fell back against the cushion. The coachman whipped the horses and the carriage moved. Wolfgang glanced back. The gray man stood motionless. His shadow fell on the Mozarts' house. . . . Wolfgang, shuddering, closed his eyes, forcing himself to open them only much later, well outside the city walls.

"Don't you feel well?" Constanze's anxious voice called him back to reality.

"Just tired," he answered. "But I feel better now. Let's get to work."

They worked hastily on *Tito*. Süssmayer did the recitatives. Wolfgang wrote the arias and ensembles. The opera progressed with amazing speed, but real inspiration would not come.

Prague was overcrowded with people attending the coronation. The Mozarts stayed with the Duscheks. But this time there were no parties or rounds of taverns. There was no time to waste. Wolfgang felt worse than ever before and lived on medicines. Sometimes he tried to show a pathetic kind of good humor. Let them believe that he was only in a hurry to get the opera finished on time. His impatience had other motives. He had to return to Vienna, to answer the call of death.

On September 2, the Imperial family heard *Don Giovanni*. *Tito,* presented on September 6—it had been written in eighteen days— did not please. It bored the audience as it bored Wolfgang himself. Elaborate settings and famous singers could not help it very much. After the première Wolfgang had a nervous breakdown and the Empress, forgetting royal tact, summarized her impression in the words *porcheria tedesca,* meaning "German swinishness."

In vain, friends insisted that *Tito* was a marvelous opera. Since Mozart had written it, how could it be otherwise? For Wolfgang it was a failure. Failure in opera! Failure in Prague! Was this the gray man's work?

Taking leave of the Duscheks, he cried like a little boy, just as if he knew that it was a final farewell. Farewell to the fond witnesses of his most fortunate days; farewell to this friendly old city disappearing in the mists of fall as the carriage drove southward; farewell to the trees and milestones along the road, each of them becoming dear to him when the mist of oblivion swallowed it. Farewell forever.

THE MESSENGER

The messages Stadler sent from Prague, after Mozart had returned to Vienna, came out of the mist. During subsequent repetitions of *La Clemenza di Tito,* the audience had become increasingly responsive. Stadler asked Mozart for a clarinet concerto (K. 622). He wrote it side by side with the Requiem (K. 626).

CHAPTER 32

LIFE WAS SO BEAUTIFUL

[1 7 9 1]

THE IMAGE of this unknown man is ever before my eyes. . . . He entreats me, presses me, impatiently demands the work. . . . The hour strikes! I am going to die. I have come to an end before I have even enjoyed my talent. And yet life was so beautiful. My career began under such fortunate auspices! But one cannot change one's destiny. . . . And so I am going to finish my funeral song. I must not leave it incomplete." So Mozart wrote on September 7, the day after the first performance of *La Clemenza di Tito.*

The next message from the phantom was another letter, again with a blank black seal and without a signature, urging him to work at the Requiem—and to name his price for a certain number of quartets to be produced every year.

Mozart nearly awoke from his evil dreams. The stranger wanted him to write music remote from death? So there was a hereafter? But he dismissed this logical conclusion. Death was friendly. Death wanted to comfort him. That was all.

His vitality declined. His nervousness increased. Frequent fainting spells depressed him. The slightest noise made his nerves shriek.

Schikaneder was worried. Although Mozart had entered *Die Zauberflöte* in his catalogue as finished in July, there were still a few numbers to be done for the priests, and, most important of all, Papageno's songs . . . also, as usual, the overture.

Schikaneder fed Wolfgang on wine and coffee, trying to keep him in condition to work. He watched his composer like a race horse on the eve of a sporting event.

The première was given September 30. When he conducted the overture, Wolfgang felt a sort of chill behind his back. The public was too startled by the novelty of the music to know whether they liked it or not. Would this be another failure?

Something touched Mozart's hand. Young Schenk, who was later to become a popular *Singspiel* composer and Beethoven's teacher, and who now played in the orchestra, had crept forward to the conductor's seat, seized Wolfgang's hand and kissed it.

The applause after the first act was sparse. Wolfgang rushed backstage and refused to take a bow. Schikaneder comforted him: "Give them time to warm up. It's something new to them around here." After the second act, the opera caught on. At least it was no failure, although its great success was still to come.

It took no more than a week for the opera to exceed all expectations. Schikaneder gave it every day. People started talking about it, and the talk did not stop short of the palaces of the nobility. The most elegant carriages in the capital drove up before the wooden barn. It became most fashionable to see *Die Zauberflöte*.

Salieri and Cavalieri hastened to attend a performance—as Wolfgang's guests. The Italian had a bravo for every number and opined that this was the most delightful show he had ever seen. One would have thought he and Wolfgang had always been the most cordial of friends.

Everything seemed to go well. Poverty, already somewhat relieved by recent earnings, might soon disappear permanently when the score of the big hit was sold to other theaters. New pupils would come, new subscribers, and old ones too. Optimistically, Wolfgang suggested that Constanze should go to Baden for another cure. He hoped that she would refuse, but she needed little urging. Karl remained in a boarding school at Perchtoldsdorf, eight miles from Vienna.

In the lonely apartment, furniture still creaked and mice frisked at night—and there was a score, hardly begun but ever present. The specter lived like a haunting shadow in the shadow of the merry birdman.

"The opera was as crowded as ever," Wolfgang wrote to Constanze on October 7. "As usual the duet 'Mann und Weib' and Papageno's Glockenspiel in Act I had to be repeated, and also the trio of the genii in Act II. But what always gives me most pleasure is the silent approval. . . . I sold my nag for fourteen ducats [probably he was already too weak to go out riding]. . . . I told Joseph to get Primus to fetch me some black coffee with which I smoked a splendid pipe of tobacco, and then I orchestrated almost the whole of Stadler's rondo. . . . What do I see? What do I smell? Why, here is Don Primus with the cutlets! Che gusto! Now I am eating to your health!" He continued the letter the next day: "You should have seen me at supper yesterday! I couldn't find the old tablecloth, so I fished out one as white as a snowdrop and put in front of me the double candlestick with a wax candle. . . ." He had always rejoiced in luxury and had prepared a little feast for himself. And the next morning: "I have slept very well and . . . have just enjoyed thoroughly my half of a capon. . . ." (at 7 A.M.!)

Even so, he grew increasingly pale, gaunt, nervous. He did not tell Constanze about it. He had to write this Requiem. He had to be alone with it. He even refused pupils. Nothing should disturb his conversation with death.

He would get up at six o'clock and work all day. The evenings drove him to the theater. There he played pranks backstage, or he would go from box to box where he saw friends, and call their attention to interesting passages in the dialogue. The gray man dominated the days, Papageno, the nights.

Constanze remained in Baden only for a week. Hofer had written her in unmistakable terms that Wolfgang needed nursing more than she. At the first glimpse of her husband, she knew he was right. "He worked so much," Constanze said later, "and with such rapidity that it seemed as though he wanted to put an end to the pains of the material world by taking refuge in the creation of the spirit. He

Frank

overdid it to such an extent that he forgot not only the world that surrounded him but even his own fatigue; quite suddenly he would fall down exhausted and have to be carried to his bed."

But what alarmed her most were his strange talks about death. Whatever the subject, he would say, "it's no use anyway," or "after I'm dead" or something like that. When he was casual about it, it was fully as frightening as when such allusions ended in uncontrolled crying spells.

When he was too weak to work alone, Süssmayer would help according to his instruction, and Constanze would join them in singing what had been written.

Constanze loathed the Requiem. She tried hard to keep Wolfgang from working and saw to it that he had congenial company. Once, on an unseasonably warm November day with a pale sun in a pale sky, she hired a carriage and went with him to the Prater.

They strolled about over the withering grass and through the alleys, and finally sat down on a fallen tree trunk.

"Isn't the Prater wonderful in the fall?" asked Constanze.

"Yes," Wolfgang affirmed. "And it is still more wonderful in spring. . . . And I won't live to see another one." He buried his head in his hands and burst into tears.

"But, Wolfi, our troubles will be over. Everything will be all right."

"Look, Stanzi, there is no use pretending. This gray man . . . I know I am writing my own death song." He didn't look at her but stared at the ground, while his toe played with a rotting chestnut. His voice was clear and terrifyingly calm. "Death is already in me. I know it. Somebody could not wait. I was in his way. He had to poison me."

"Who? How?"

"Italians know all about poisoning."

"You mean . . . ?"

"Of course." Wolfgang did not raise his voice.

The thought of having been poisoned by Salieri became an obsession. Wolfgang never mentioned his name, but talked constantly about it in such plain allusions that there could be no doubt about whom he meant.

When Salieri learned of it, he was deeply shocked. He certainly had not poisoned Mozart's body—but hadn't he poisoned his life? The thought of this accusation haunted Salieri for the rest of his days. On his own deathbed, in spells of delirium, he charged himself with the crime, only to recant the confession desperately in his last lucid moment.

Constanze was now terribly afraid. It's insanity, she thought. They say it starts like this . . . this look . . . these casual statements about the most awful things. All at once it came back to her: his distraction, his absent-mindedness, his fluctuation between extremes of jollity and sadness. . . .

She packed him into the coach, and when they were home, she immediately took the Requiem out of his reach and called Dr. Klosset. Wolfgang was too weak to care. Perhaps at Constanze's instigation, his masonic brothers insisted that he compose and conduct a cantata (K. 623), which Schikaneder had written for the consecration of a Lodge. Some improvement in his health accompanied the work. The music is blissful, almost gay. When Wolfgang came home from its first performance, he was so pleased that he seemed to be himself again.

"Please, Stanzi, give me the Requiem," he begged. "I am all right. After all, I've been paid for it."

Wolfgang seemed to feel so much better that she saw no risk in it. She handed him the fateful manuscript, and he buried himself in the score.

The recovery was very brief. The somber thoughts returned . . . poison, death. When friends came in, he seemed to enjoy them, but after a few moments he stared into blank space, went back to his writing table and worked.

CHAPTER 33

TOO LATE. . . .

[1791]

MOZART liked to drop into the large room of the Silver Serpent in the afternoon, where he found congenial artists in an atmosphere thick with beer and tobacco. On November 19, he came there as usual.

The smells seemed to suffocate him. The mere thought of beer nauseated him. The voices grated on his nerves. There were new faces which he could not seem to endure.

Wolfgang went to the small back room. He all but fell down on a chair. His head ached. His back was cold, his forehead hot. I'm ill, he thought, very ill . . . I won't die before the Requiem is finished . . . but I shall die right after that . . . I could work more slowly to live longer . . . but it's driving me . . . I must get through with it, with the Requiem and with life. . . .

"No beer today," he answered the waiter's question. "Some wine, please."

. . . I have to repay a debt to the Church . . . I have written so little church music in these last years . . . (the feverish thought rolled on) . . . I must pay with the Requiem . . . with life. . . .

"He's so absent-minded," the waiter told Joseph Deiner. "He hardly answered my question, then asked for wine instead of beer . . . and now he doesn't drink it."

Deiner went over to Wolfgang's table. They talked for a few minutes. Mozart complained about his health. Then he rose sud-

denly, staggering: "You drink my wine, Joseph . . . I'm so chilly
. . . please come to see me tomorrow morning, we need some
wood. . . ."

It was a three-minute walk to the Rauhensteingasse, but he could
hardly manage it. Constanze was helpless in her despair. Fortunately
her sister Sophie was there. Together they put Wolfgang to bed.

When Deiner called the next morning, Wolfgang blinked at him
with dull eyes: "Nothing today, Joseph, we are busy with doctors
and apothecaries." His voice was hardly audible.

His hands and feet were swollen and he could hardly move them.
The headache became unbearable and he vomited heavily. Dr.
Klosset was in doubt about the diagnosis, but pessimistic about the
outcome.

Between spells of paralyzing pain, Wolfgang clung to the
Requiem. He had to finish it . . . his salvation might depend on it.
. . . There were many musical thoughts that still roamed in his
aching head and were never to take shape, but those connected with
the Requiem had to remain—even through vanishing consciousness.

At his bedside, Süssmayer tried to read his thoughts when
Wolfgang's voice faltered and his gestures were hampered by pain.
Süssmayer did not understand everything, but one thing he knew:
that the Requiem must be finished.

Wolfgang dictated. Süssmayer wrote. When friends dropped in,
Wolfgang asked them to sing what had been written.

The voices sang the *Dies irae,* the hymn of the day of judgment,
while Mozart prepared himself to appear at the Lord's throne. He
had composed it in trembling fear, but now the song left him
comforted and resigned.

Still his companions spoke of recovery. Sometimes he was deceived
by their optimism. "Tell your mother that I feel better and that I
shall come and congratulate her on her name-day," he said to Sophie,
who spent most of her time in the Rauhensteingasse to help. Constanze was so ill from worry that she had to have treatments herself.

Such encouraging spells did not last long. Death marched on, and
ahead of it came the sound of its song, the Requiem. A soprano

sang of the light prevailing over darkness, the hope beyond the grave.

There was no hope on earth. Dr. Sallaba, head of the General Hospital, who was called in for consultation on November 28, had no word of comfort.

The pains grew worse. The swelling increased. Wolfgang's kidneys, affected by the scarlet fever attack of his childhood days, ached terribly. The singing of his canary caused him physical pain. But only with difficulty could Wolfgang be persuaded to let the bird be removed from his room. Impatient in life, Mozart was infinitely patient in his ordeal.

He hardly complained.

The Requiem bowed before God's omnipotence in *Rex tremendae*. But life was persevering. It sent messengers of prosperity. From Hungary came an offer of a thousand gulden a year for a few pieces of music annually. Too late. . . .

Kindly Jesu, recollect me, though Thy cross with shame affect me . . . the Requiem countered the call of life.

Schikaneder had already collected eight thousand gulden on *Die Zauberflöte*. Wealth was around the corner. But death was ahead of wealth.

Salva me. . . . implored the Requiem.

An offer from Holland dropped in, more favorable even than the one from Hungary. Too late. . . .

The *Recordare* sang eternal peace.

The Requiem was hardly removed from his bed. Burning lashes of fever drove Wolfgang to work on it. Süssmayer sat nearby, listening to Wolfgang's hurried advice about its further execution. Sometimes the sick man's voice was barely audible but his eyes were eloquent. His feeble gestures, the expression of his pale, over-anxious face . . . they spoke in tunes, and Süssmayer understood.

But thoughts of life, like small patches of blue in a stormy sky, still bobbed up. "I should have liked to hear my *Zauberflöte* once more," he murmured, and hummed Papageno's tune almost inaudibly. Kapellmeister Roser, one of Schikaneder's men, went to the piano to play and sing it and Wolfgang seemed to enjoy it. But the birdman's song was soon drowned again in the song for the gray man.

Minutes and hours passed with solemn slowness. It was Sunday, December 4, 1791, 2 P.M. Performers at Schikaneder's theater came, as they did almost every day, bringing some of the fragrance of the stage into his moldy sickroom. Wolfgang wanted them to perform his Requiem.

They grouped around his bed. The parts were handed to them. Schack sang the soprano, Hofer the tenor, and Gerl the bass, with Wolfgang himself taking the alto part. His voice was thin, but there was something sublime in it. Slowly the voices rose, proceeding from note to note as if on the path of death.

They had reached the *Lacrimosa* when Wolfgang suddenly stared beyond the group towards a corner of the room. His fevered fantasy showed him a huge shadow, not unlike the birdman's, slowly rising, smoothly but firmly advancing towards his bed, step by step, in the rhythm of the *Lacrimosa* . . . and he knew it was death. . . .

What was still earthbound in Mozart was too weak to struggle, could do nothing but weep . . . weep. . . .

The voices broke off. Quietly, the visitors left.

The weeping gradually stopped. Wolfgang grew calmer. The dark shadow had gone, but had left a strange taste. "The taste of death is already on my tongue," he told his sister-in-law. "I taste death. . . ."

Constanze had lost nearly all that was left of her scanty self-control. "Since you left he has been so ill, I never expected him to live through the day. If he is that way again, he will die tonight," she had greeted her sister.

Sophie hurried away to inform her mother—and to look for a priest. It was a desperate search.

Süssmayer did not leave Wolfgang's bedside, and from time to time, Wolfgang gave advice about the Requiem. Suddenly he called Constanze: "Promise to keep my death a secret until Albrechtsberger has applied for my post at St. Stephen's." Again, tears came into his eyes: "Didn't I tell you I was writing it for myself?" Süssmayer knew there was no answer.

Dr. Klosset paid a visit later, after the theater, and ordered cold compresses for the dying man's burning head. That was all he could do. A new delirium set in—and with the delirium came the shadow again, mild and soft . . . the body did not struggle any longer. No sound came from the colorless lips, the swollen hands hardly moved, perspiration covered the fading face—but this face reflected faraway tunes. Süssmayer could no longer understand them. They were no more from this world. The Requiem wrapped the dying genius in the mantle of its tunes to fly painlessly to eternal life. He still breathed but he no longer wept. His last song greeted Heaven, and Heaven must have greeted the blessed singer too, with mighty chords. The wax-pale cheeks inflated as if he was to blow the trumpet . . . the trumpet of the angels. . . .

It was 12:55 A.M. of December 5.

CHAPTER 34

PETTY MORTALS

DEINER helped to dress Mozart in the black death-shirt of the masonic brothers, while Constanze hysterically threw herself on the death-bed, hoping to catch Wolfgang's disease and die.

Van Swieten, hastily informed, arrived. He sent Constanze to friends and advised her not to go to the funeral. He, himself, arranged for the burial for eleven gulden thirty-six kreutzer.

December weather was at its worst when the simple fir coffin, after it had been blessed in the Kreuzkapelle at St. Stephen's, was carried to St. Marx cemetery. It stormed. Rain fell, mixed with snow. The few men who followed the carriage—van Swieten, Salieri, Süssmayer, Deiner, and a few members of Schikaneder's troupe—turned back at the Stubentor.

"Another pauper," remarked the grave-diggers. They hurried to get the coffin down in a mass grave. "What weather!"

When Constanze asked much later for her husband's resting place, it could not be found. The grave-digger in charge had died and nobody could remember.

Schikaneder went about Vienna, crying that Wolfgang's image was ever before his eyes. But he did nothing for Constanze's support.

Wolfgang left only two hundred gulden in cash and five hundred gulden worth of furniture. His debts amounted to three thousand. Puchberg refused to be repaid. The Emperor showed himself more gracious to Mozart dead than to Mozart living. He sponsored an all-Mozart concert, and his generous contribution enabled Constanze to pay her debts and to put some money in the bank. Her application for a pension was granted, after Leopold's death in 1792, by his son and successor Emperor Francis II. Constanze received 266 gulden 40 kreutzer a year, arranged occasional benefit concerts, and developed an astonishing skill in dealing with publishers.

Süssmayer bravely finished the Requiem. Two months after Mozart's death, the gray messenger reappeared and Constanze handed him the completed work. The puzzle was solved much later. The mysterious stranger was the major-domo of Count Walsegg zu Stuppach. The Count wanted to be considered a great composer and used to pay generously for music ghost-written for him by first-rate but needy artists. It was at his castle near Wiener Neustadt that the Requiem, ordered in memory of his wife, was first performed.

Constanze rented rooms in her lodgings. One of her boarders was Georg Nikolaus von Nissen, a councilor of the Danish Embassy in Vienna. He married her in 1809 and became Mozart's first biographer.

The two boys were educated in Prague. Karl Thomas later held a minor governmental position in Milan and died there in 1859, while Franz Xaver Wolfgang—later rechristened Wolfgang Amadeus—had musical ambitions but was unable to overcome the handicap of his name. As a music teacher, pianist, and unnoticed composer, he led a dreary life in Lwow and Vienna, and died in 1844 in Karlsbad. There are no descendants of Mozart.

Constanze moved to Copenhagen with her husband and they returned to Austria after his retirement, settling down at Salzburg. Nissen died there in 1826. Constanze, together with widowed Sophie, led a highly respected life in Mozart's birthplace until her death in 1842.

Nannerl, too, had come to live in Salzburg again when she became a widow. But Baroness Berchtold zu Sonnenburg and Mme. von Nissen hardly ever spoke to each other.

APPENDICES

GLOSSARY
BIOGRAPHICAL NOTES
MOZART WORKS AND RECORDINGS
THE WORLD THAT MOZART LIVED IN

The list of Mozart Works and Recordings and "The World That Mozart Lived In" were prepared by Elizabeth C. Moore

GLOSSARY

AUT CAESAR AUT NIHIL. Either Caesar or nothing.

BÄSLE. A dialect diminutive of the German word for cousin.

BEL CANTO. Literally, beautiful singing. The traditional Italian style of singing, characterized by smoothness of sound.

CONCERTS SPIRITUELS. Earliest subscription concerts in Europe, started in 1725 to provide musical entertainment during the Lenten season when there were no opera performances.

COSÌ FAN TUTTE. *They All Do It.*

DA CAPO. Repeat from the beginning.

DAS VEILCHEN. *The Violet.*

DER RAUCHFANGKEHRER. *The Chimney Sweep.*

DER SCHAUSPIELDIREKTOR. *The Impresario.*

DIE ENTFÜHRUNG AUS DEM SERAIL. *The Abduction from the Seraglio.*

DIE ZAUBERFLÖTE. *The Magic Flute.*

DRAMMA GIOCOSO. Literally, gay drama. Operas of a transitionary type, containing elements from both opera buffa and opera seria.

EIN MUSIKALISCHER SPASS. *A Musical Joke.*

EVVIVA IL MAESTR(IN)O. Long live the (little) master.

FINCH' HAN DAL VINO. *When we'll have wine . . .*

FIORITURA. From fiore, flower. Vocal embellishment.

GRADUS AD PARNASSUM. *A Step Toward Parnassus.* For a long time the standard textbook on composition, written by Johann Joseph Fux (1660-1741), outstanding musical authority in Vienna.

GYMNASIUM. In German usage, the most ambitious educational system for teen-agers. An eight-year curriculum stresses old languages and mathematics. Graduation is required for enrollment at a university.

IL RÈ PASTORE. *The Shepherd King.*

IL SOGNO DI SCIPIONE. *Scipio's Dream.*

KÄRNTNERTHOR. Literally, Gate to Carinthia.

KASPAR, DER FAGOTTIST. *Caspar, the Bassoonist.*

LA FINTA GIARDINIERA. *The Disguised Gardener* (feminine).

LA FINTA SEMPLICE. *Disguised Simplicity.*

LE DEVIN DU VILLAGE. *The Village Soothsayer.*

LE NOZZE DI FIGARO. *The Marriage of Figaro.*

LE PREMIER COUP D'ARCHET. The first stroke of the bow, delivered by the violins in unison fortissimo. A favorite orchestral device in France just then.

GLOSSARY

LIBRETTO. Literally, little book. Term used for opera text.

L'OCA DEL CAIRO. *The Goose of Cairo.*

LO SPOSO DELUSO. *The Deceived Husband.*

MELODRAMA. Combination of rhapsodic speech and instrumental music, very popular as a complete dramatic work in Mozart's day.

MISERERE. From "Miserere mei deus" ("Be the Lord gracious to me"), the opening words of the 50th Psalm—the 51st in Protestant liturgy. Three musical settings of it, among them Allegri's, are still being performed in the Sistine Chapel during Holy Week.

MÖNCHSBERG. Literally, Monk's Mountain—the hill against which old Salzburg was built, with St. Peter's at its foot and the fortress on top.

MOZARTEUM. Salzburg musical association comprising a conservatory and a library.

NAME-DAY. The day dedicated to a person's patron saint and celebrated in Catholic families.

NON PIÙ ANDRAI. *You will no more* (play the part of a lover) . . . Figaro's aria in the first finale, addressing Cherubino.

NON SO D'ONDE VIENE. *I don't know where Thou comest from* . . .

OPERA BUFFA. Italian comic (popular) opera which emerged from comic intermezzi in serious opera, leaning toward simple melody, ensemble singing, and fast-moving recitative.

OPÉRA COMIQUE. French "comic" opera, mainly characterized by spoken dialogue. It was often serious in contents, but received its name to distinguish it from the competitive grand opera with recitatives.

OPERA SERIA. Old Italian serious opera, its plot drawn from history, legend, or myth, containing arias requiring an unusual standard of voice culture, elaborate ballets, and complicated stage settings. It declined during the rational 18th century and received its decisive blow through Gluck's reform, though it still lingered on for some time.

RUBATO. Literally, robbed, meaning robbed time. Temporary abandonment of strict tempo for the benefit of expression.

SINGSPIEL. Light opera in German, with spoken dialogue. The Viennese variety drew strongly on opera buffa and native folk comedy.

THEATER IM STARHEMBERGISCHEN FREIHAUSE AUF DER WIEDEN. Literally, theater in the privileged house of Prince Starhemberg, in the suburb of Wieden—"privileged" meaning exempt from municipal duties and taxes.

UNA COSA RARA. *A Rare Thing.*

VICE-KAPELLMEISTER. Assistant musical director.

ZUM AUGE GOTTES. *To the Eye of God.*

BIOGRAPHICAL NOTES

ABEL, Karl Friedrich (1725-1787), German composer and the last great viola da gamba player, pupil of his father and Johann Sebastian Bach. He went to England in 1759, and in 1765 was appointed director of chamber music to the Queen. He lived with Johann Christian Bach and shared with him in directing the so-called Bach-Abel concerts. These were the first public subscription concerts in England, and brought many new works, including Haydn's, before the London public. His compositions include concertos, chamber music, and symphonies; Mozart was particularly impressed with them during the first part of his stay in London. He copied for practice one of Abel's symphonies, an early example of the use of the clarinet in a symphonic score which, found among Mozart's manuscripts, was long mistaken for one of his youthful compositions.

ALBRECHTSBERGER, Johann Georg (1736-1809), Austrian organist, composer of church and instrumental music, and a particularly famous theorist. He started with minor appointments in rural churches, became Court organist in Vienna in 1772, and, as Mozart had wished on his deathbed, his successor at St. Stephen's Cathedral. His textbook on composition has been translated into English. He taught Weigl, Hummel, and Beethoven.

ANFOSSI, Pasquale (1727-1797), Italian composer of about seventy operas of wide but short-lived success. He was pushed up to fame by a faction opposing his teacher and friend Piccini, causing the latter's withdrawal from Rome. For a time Anfossi directed Italian opera in London. During the last years of his life he was a chapel-master at the Lateran, in Rome, and abandoned secular for sacred composition.

ATTWOOD, Thomas (1765-1838), Mozart's prize pupil, became a prominent English composer and organist. Prior to his visit to Vienna he was a chorister at the Royal chapel and, upon the good offices of the Prince of Wales, a student in Italy. Returning to England in 1787, he became attached to the royal household in various musical capacities. He was a co-founder of

[277]

the Philharmonic Society and a friend of Mendelssohn. Among his works are operas, songs, piano sonatas, and church music.

BACH, Johann Sebastian (1685–1750), greatest German Protestant composer. He was a member of a large family of Thuringian musicians and after various Court appointments became a cantor and organist at the old Thomas Church in Leipzig. Among his compositions are some two hundred vocal cantatas, four Passions, a Catholic Mass, and many works for instrumental solo and combinations for which he used both old and new forms. Bach was a supreme master of the organ and of the fugue, and with him contrapuntal composition reached its climax and end. During his lifetime, however, he was mostly appreciated as an organist and teacher; his music, eclipsed by the advent of classical style, was only scantily known until its rediscovery in the Romantic nineteenth century.

Five of Bach's sons were musicians; two of them, Carl Philip Emanuel (1714–1788) and Johann Christian (1735–1782) rate among the most influential masters of the preclassic era and were early promoters of the modern pianoforte. Carl Philip Emanuel held high positions at the Prussian Court and the Hamburg Cathedral, and made consequential innovations in the structure of instrumental music. Among his many disciples were Haydn and Beethoven. Mozart also admired him, but had more natural affinity with Johann Christian who had gone to study with Padre Martini, become an organist at Milan and a Catholic, and established himself in England in 1762. There he was appointed music master to the Queen, a post that had been vacant since Handel's death. Idolized by the British public, he wrote a quantity of Italian operas, symphonies, chamber music, and compositions for the piano, filled with the flavor of Italian melody and new instrumental colors. He was also highly successful as a musical organizer (see Abel).

BARRINGTON, Daines (1727–1800), son of the first Viscount of Barrington, a judge by profession, a naturalist and antiquary besides. He approached the child Mozart from a scientific point of view. He made him sight read and sing with his father, and improvise arias of love and of anger. He noted the self-assurance with which the boy corrected Leopold, making no mistake himself, and the correctness of the improvisations as to tempo, construction, and expression. Already half assured of Leopold's veracity about Wolfgang's age by the boy's childish behavior outside of music, he corroborated it by writing for a copy of his birth record. His observations, including information on young Mozart received by Johann Christian Bach, were laid down in a later report to the Royal Society for Natural Sciences in London.

BEAUMARCHAIS, Pierre Augustin Caron de (1732–1799), French

author, son of a watchmaker. Successful speculations enabled him to buy himself into public office and noble rank. After having lost a much publicized lawsuit against a business partner's heirs, Beaumarchais made himself an advocate of the Third Estate against the ruling class, being simultaneously in the King's secret service. In the 1770's he used his position and wealth to procure French help for the American colonists. His plays were satirical comedies on French noble society, which the nobles, headed by Queen Marie Antoinette, found very amusing while King Louis XVI considered their implications dangerous. During the Revolution he was accused of shady dealing and forced to seek temporary refuge abroad. His last years, spent in Paris, were uneventful.

BEETHOVEN, Ludwig van (1770–1827), greatest German instrumental composer, of Dutch ancestry, settled in Vienna in 1792. Like Mozart, he became a favorite among the aristocracy because of his piano playing, but his independent attitude toward his sponsors established the acceptance of the artist as an equal in society. He was greatly interested in social problems and literature, and loved nature. His deafness which began in his thirtieth year was partially responsible for his ultimate isolation. Beethoven's work forms the transition from the classical to the romantic period in music, that is, from impersonal beauty to emotional self-expression. Although his opera *Fidelio* and his *Missa Solemnis* are unique masterpieces of their kind, his influence was due to his instrumental works. His sonatas, concertos, chamber music and nine symphonies are still the center of concert repertories all over the world. The *Ode to Joy* referred to in the story is his setting for vocal quartet and chorus of Schiller's poem of that name in the last movement of his Ninth Symphony. It was the first convincing instance of the use of the human voice in a symphonic score.

CANNABICH, Christian (1731–1798), a pupil of Stamitz and Jommelli, representative of the second generation of Mannheim symphonists. In 1759 he became concert master of the orchestra and in 1775 its conductor, together with Holzbauer. His compositions show the decline of the Mannheim school into what Leopold Mozart termed "mannerisms," but Cannabich was an excellent orchestra leader and teacher.

CLEMENTI, Muzio (1752–1832), one of the most celebrated pianists and teachers of his time. Born in Rome, he was an organist at nine, and at fourteen created a sensation as a composer-virtuoso in England, where he made his home between tours. Later in life he concentrated on composition and a publishing enterprise. As a writer of piano sonatas he established the final classical shape of that form; his studies, *Gradus ad parnassum,* are still being used for piano instruction. Mozart made some biting remarks about Clementi's playing, but the theme of the sonata he heard him perform at Court crept into the *Zauberflöte* overture ten years later.

DITTERSDORF, Karl Ditters von (1739–1799), Austrian composer, gaining early fame as a violinist, became one of the most successful representatives of preclassical symphony and chamber music. Twelve of his 115 symphonies are based on Ovid's *Metamorphoses,* very early examples of program music. From 1769 until a few years before his death he was the musical director of the Prince-Bishop of Breslau, at Johannisburg in Silesia, where a special theater was built for the production of his *Singspiele.* His best works in that form, however, were written for Vienna. In 1770 he was made a Knight of the Golden Spur, and in 1773 obtained his title of nobility from Emperor Joseph.

DUPORT, Jean-Pierre (1741–1818), one of two brothers who were considered the most prominent French 'cellists of their time and influenced the development of 'cello virtuosity. He played in the Court orchestra at Potsdam from 1773 and later became the director of Court concerts.

GASSMANN, Florian Leopold (1729–1774), Bohemian musician with initial experience in Italy, Court Conductor in Vienna from 1764. There he founded in 1772 the first welfare agency for widows and orphans of musicians. He wrote operas, church and instrumental music; his string quartets particularly impressed Mozart.

GLUCK, Christoph Willibald Ritter von (1714–1787), born in Germany, raised in Bohemia and Italy, and widely traveled, became Court Conductor in Vienna in 1754, and later (1774) Court Composer. Influenced by Viennese intellectuals he decided to lead opera back to the ideals of Greek drama, chorus and all. His "reform" operas were trail-blazers in the development of German music drama even though they were not written to German words. The Viennese gave *Orfeo ed Euridice* (1762), *Alceste* (1767), and *Paride ed Elena* (1770), a cool reception; Gluck's ambitions were more readily understood in France, although the first Paris performance (*Iphigénie en Aulide,* 1774) had to be enforced by order of the Queen. Then the admirers of Italian melody opera rallied around Piccini, and journalists, speculators, and sensation-hunting society built the argument into an excited quarrel that lasted for many years. After 1779, Gluck remained in Vienna, highly esteemed but of failing health.

Mozart, as a child, heard *Orfeo* and *Alceste* in Vienna and was deeply impressed. He kept studying the score of *Alceste* for many years. Later his artistic credo developed into the very opposite from Gluck's. Gluck says: "When I write an opera I try to forget that I am a musician." Mozart says: "In an opera, poetry must by necessity be the obedient daughter of music." However, Mozart could not fail to notice the significance of Gluck's reform and some of it found echoes in his own work.

GOETHE, Johann Wolfgang von (1749–1832), greatest German man of letters. Scion of a distinguished family, he studied law in Leipzig and Strassburg, and in 1775 moved to Weimar, where the Grand Duke, an ardent admirer of his outstanding genius, named him a minister of state and later director of the Court theater. Travels abroad, particularly those to Italy, had a profound effect on his approach to universal questions, which, in turn, influenced all European thinking. He wrote poetry, drama, novels, philosophy, memoirs, travelogues, and treatises on natural sciences. His greatest work was *Faust,* an elaborate dramatic poem in which his life's experience and philosophy are set against the background of the old legend of Dr. Faustus and the devil. Goethe's interest in music centered around melodrama and songs, and he wrote a couple of *Singspiel* libretti. He befriended some composers connected with the Potsdam Court, ignored Schubert, but was kind to young Mendelssohn.

HANDEL, George Frederick (1685-1759), German composer who, following experience at the Hamburg opera, studied in Italy and later settled in England, where he wrote operas to Italian and oratorios to English words. A former employer, the Elector of Hanover, again became his patron as King George I. Handel was in due course music master to the royal family, director of the new Royal Academy of Music, and an opera impresario. He became a British subject in 1726, anglicized his name, and England considers him one of her greatest musicians.

Handel's epoch-making achievements were his thirty-two oratorios and among them *The Messiah* (1742) has remained the most widely known. They were first planned to replace opera during the Lenten season. His operas, cantatas, and *concerti grossi* are highly perfected specimens of their kind, but do not deviate from the then current patterns.

HASSE, Johann Adolph (1699–1783), first a tenor, later (like Handel and Johann Christian Bach) a celebrated German composer of Italian opera. He studied in Naples, and in 1731 went to Dresden where he and his wife, the prima donna Faustina Bordoni, held prized musical appointments at Court. Later he produced operas in Vienna in successful rivalry with Gluck and spent the last years of his life at Venice. Hasse's word carried great weight in musical circles and his support was of utmost value to the Mozarts. In a letter of recommendation, Hasse wrote about Wolfgang in 1769: ". . . he has done things which would be remarkable in a grown-up man . . . is beautiful, lively, charming, and behaves in such a way that one cannot help loving him . . . if his development keep pace with his age something wonderful will come of it. . . ."

HAYDN, (Franz) Joseph (1732–1809), grew up in a village near the Austro-Hungarian border and was a choir boy in St. Stephen's Cathedral. After a miserable adolescence he found employment with the wealthy Hungarian Princes of Esterházy, later was placed in full charge of their musical entertainment and remained connected with them for the rest of his life. He visited Vienna frequently and England twice in the 1790's. The opportunity to work at leisure and try his compositions with a full orchestra enabled Haydn to carry out substantial experiments; and his love for the countryside and its songs, on which he drew for much of his work, helped him to emancipate instrumental music from foreign models. He is credited with the standardization of symphony and string quartet in their classical forms, and ranks as the oldest among the classical masters, and the oldest representative of the so-called Viennese School in which he shares honors with Mozart, Beethoven, and Schubert. The contact with Mozart greatly enriched his music as illustrated by the last of his hundred-odd symphonies, and his oratorios, *The Creation* and *The Seasons*. He also composed the Austrian National Anthem.

His brother (Johann) Michael (1737–1806) was also a choir boy in Vienna and is considered by many Joseph's equal in talent. He may have deprived himself of a career almost as spectacular when he decided to remain at Salzburg in 1762. He twice refused an offer to join his brother and persistently declined the publication of his works. His religious music was valued by Joseph more highly than his own, and strongly influenced young Mozart. Among his pupils was Carl Maria von Weber.

HOLZBAUER, Ignaz (1711–1783), Court Conductor in his native Vienna, Stuttgart, and Mannheim, with occasional visits to Italy where he produced operas. He was a cofounder of the Mannheim school (see Stamitz) and wrote valuable instrumental music. His *Günther von Schwarzburg,* highly praised by Mozart, contributed to the hitherto short-lived experiments on grand opera in German.

HUMMEL, Johann Nepomuk (1778–1837), Mozart's pupil, became one of the most celebrated pianists of his day and was considered Beethoven's rival in improvisation. He first appeared as assisting artist at one of Mozart's concerts and thereafter started on his first professional tour. After Mozart's death he received musical guidance from Albrechtsberger, Haydn, and Salieri. Some of his compositions still survive as salon music, and his textbook on piano playing was among the first to give intelligent instructions on fingering.

JOMMELLI, Niccolò (1714–1774), one of the leading Italian opera composers of his day, called "the Italian Gluck" for his departure from convention and his attempts at orchestral color. He is credited with having brought the Italian vocal crescendo, transferred to the orchestra, to Germany, while he was a Court Conductor in Stuttgart (1753–1769), an innovation which did not pass unnoticed by the orchestra leaders of nearby Mannheim. His own music, however, took on a German harmonic flavor and was thereafter considered ponderous and unmelodious in Italy.

MARTÍN Y SOLAR, Vicente (1756–1806), born in Spain, became a successful rival of noted opera composers in Italy and of Mozart in Vienna. Later he became a conductor of Italian opera in St. Petersburg, Russia. From his most popular opera, *Una Cosa rara,* which then triumphed over *Figaro,* Mozart quoted in the last act of *Don Giovanni*. It was also the first opera to include a waltz.

METASTASIO, Pietro Antonio Bonaventura (1698–1782), Italian writer of poetry and drama, Court Poet in Vienna from 1730. His gift of melodious verse made him the most coveted supplier of opera texts. Of his thirty-four libretti many were set several times—some as many as forty—by the musical celebrities of a few generations. Mozart used his lyrics for *La Betulia liberata, Il Sogno di Scipione, Il Rè pastore, La Clemenza di Tito,* and for some twenty compositions for voice and instruments.

MOLIÈRE, Jean Baptiste Poquelin (1622–1673), French actor and playwright, the greatest French writer of satirical comedy. He quit his law studies in 1643 to join a players' troupe touring France. In 1655 he assumed directorship and began to write his own plays. Three years later he won the support of the Court, the group then becoming known as the King's Comedians. The clergy, however, resented Molière's tendency to expose human weakness and hypocrisy. His satires were aimed at certain types, almost invariably featured in the title roles, such as the bluestocking, the misanthropist, the miser, the hypocrite, the parvenu, the hypochondriac. It was supreme irony that he was fatally taken by a stroke while enacting the latter character.

PAISIELLO, Giovanni (1740–1816), Italian opera composer, trained in Naples. After establishing his reputation with fifty operas written in twelve years, he held prized appointments at the Courts of Russia, Naples, and France (under Napoleon). His *Il Barbiere di Siviglia* (1782) remained so popular that it caused the initial failure of Rossini's masterpiece of the same name, twenty-four years later.

PICCINI, Niccolò (1728–1800), Italian opera composer, a leading musical figure in his day. He had his first successes in Naples and Rome, and thereafter went to Paris where he was appointed head of an Italian opera troupe and voice teacher to Marie Antoinette. Unwittingly made the figurehead of the faction opposing the innovator Gluck, whom he highly respected, Piccini felt uneasy at the use of his name in the spectacular verbal war and took no active part in it. After Gluck's death he tried, though vainly, to raise a fund for yearly memorial performances. He spent his last years in reduced circumstances and ill health.

ROUSSEAU, Jean Jacques (1712–1778), Swiss philosopher and author, living mostly in France, whose writings were decisive contributions to the conception of revolutionary doctrines. His advocacy of simple living (expressed in the famous slogan "return to nature") and his socialistic ideas were considered exciting novelties in French society and made him a center of attention. He composed music and wrote about it. *Le Devin du village,* the pastoral opera on which Mozart based *Bastien und Bastienne,* was his best composition and held the stage for over sixty years.

SAMMARTINI, Giovanni Battista (1701–1775), often confused with his older brother Giuseppe who lived in London and was director of chamber music to the Prince of Wales. The younger Sammartini whom Mozart met in Milan was an organist and chapel-master there and had taught Gluck. His some two thousand works include much chamber music and twenty-four symphonies which show him as a pioneer in these forms.

SARTI, Giuseppe (1729–1802), Italian composer of very successful operas. Prior to his trip to Russia he had held appointments with the Danish Court and the Milan Cathedral. Mozart wrote a set of eight piano variations on one of his operatic airs and later quoted from the same opera in *Don Giovanni.* Their

friendly relations in Vienna, however, did not prevent Sarti from referring to Mozart's string quartets as "barbarian."

SCHOBERT, Johann (*c.* 1720–1767), a native of Silesia, raised in Strassburg, settled in Paris in 1760 as a chamber musician to the Prince de Conti. Schobert was a prominent disciple of the Mannheim school, particularly cultivating emotional contrasts. He was first to discover the possibilities of chamber music with harpsichord. Mozart, whose earliest piano concertos were but arrangements of sonata movements by older composers, used one of Schobert's for his second concerto (1767).

SCHWEITZER, Anton (1735–1787), a theatrical conductor and highly successful *Singspiel* composer at the Court theater in Weimar. He and Wieland were commissioned to write a grand opera, *Alceste* (1773), the first serious opera in German. Its success resulted in a similar order from the Elector of the Palatinate (*Rosamunde*), on which the authors were working when Mozart met them in Mannheim. With his melodrama *Pygmalion,* to words by Rousseau, Schweitzer introduced another type of dramatic composition in Germany (1772).

STAMITZ, Johann Wenzel Anton (1717–1757), son and pupil of a Bohemian village cantor, first attracted attention as a violin virtuoso at the coronation festivities of Emperor Charles VII in 1742. From 1745 until his death he was the leader of the Mannheim Court orchestra. His bold and sometimes eccentric experiments in tone color and instrumental form made him one of the most spectacular pioneers of classical style, and the group of his associates and disciples has become known as the Mannheim School. His brother and two sons also were musicians; the latter settled in Paris where they knew Mozart in 1778.

STORACE, Stephen (1763–1796), son of a double bass player, was an accomplished violinist at ten, and a student at the Naples Conservatory at twelve. Back in England after 1787, he wrote for the leading theaters a number of operas whose orchestral treatment echoes the influence of Mozart and the Italians.

SUESSMAYER, Franz Xaver (1766–1803), primarily remembered for his association with Mozart, became a theater conductor in 1792 and two years later second conductor at the opera. His many works for the stage were very successful. He also composed church and instrumental music.

UMLAUFF, Ignaz (1746-1796), Austrian composer, a member of the Court orchestra since 1772, and in 1778 musical director of the new National Theater for which he wrote a number of successful *Singspiele*. After 1789 he worked under Salieri as deputy conductor of the Imperial chapel and under Weigl at the Court opera.

VOLTAIRE, François Marie Arouet (1694–1778), French writer, historian, philosopher, and famous satirist. Among his writings are tragedies, philosophical poems and novels (*Candide*), and historical works. For satirical and slanderous writings he was imprisoned twice in the Bastille and later forced into fifteen years of retirement. In 1750 he accepted an invitation of Frederick II, who was anxious to bring elements of progressive *kultur* to his Court, but in 1753 he had to leave Prussia in disgrace. In Switzerland where he sought refuge he made himself unpopular with the clergy and withdrew to Ferney near the French and Swiss border. There the Mozarts unsuccessfully tried to see him on their way home from their grand tour.

WAGENSEIL, Georg Christoph (1715–1777), Austrian composer and keyboard virtuoso, Court Composer from 1739, music teacher of the Imperial family. He also wrote operas and oratorios, but is primarily known as an important representative of pre-classical symphony and piano concerto.

WEBER, Carl Maria von (1786–1826), the son of Fridolin Weber's brother—a poor musician posing as an impoverished aristocrat—was born lame. He became a conductor in Prague and Dresden and, as a composer, the first full-fledged Romanticist. Riding the wave of German nationalism which was surging high after the Napoleonic wars, he created the German romantic folk opera (*Der Freischütz*), and wrote the first German grand opera of consequence (*Euryanthe*), fifty years after Schweitzer's and Holz-bauer's short-lived attempts. He died in London shortly after the première of *Oberon*. He was also a brilliant pianist and an erudite music critic.

WEIGL, Joseph (1766–1846), son of a 'cellist in Prince Esterházy's orchestra, godchild of Haydn, pupil of Albrechtsberger and Salieri, composed a score of operas in Italian and German, ballets, cantatas, chamber music, and songs. He succeeded Salieri at the opera in 1790 —in rivalry with Mozart—and at the Imperial chapel in 1825—with Schubert as his competitor for the post. From then on he wrote almost exclusively church music.

WIELAND, Christoph Martin (1733–1813), German man of letters, son of a clergyman, studied law and after 1772 lived mostly in Weimar, center of literary activity. He began with romantic love poetry, then switched to satirical novels aimed at German provincialism, which brought him the surname of "the German Voltaire." His output was enormous and included dramas, epics, and romances in verse, literary criticism, and the first German translation of Shakespeare's plays. He introduced classical forms into German poetry, which largely accounts for his inclusion in the group of the six German classical poets. Wieland enjoyed a great reputation and was called upon to lend his name and talent to opera in German which was sponsored by some courts (see Schweitzer).

WRANITZKY, Paul (1756–1808), one of two brothers, Moravian musicians living in Vienna, both composers and violinists. He first played in Prince Esterházy's orchestra under Haydn and in 1785 became concert master of the Vienna opera orchestra. He was particularly successful with musical stage works in the light vein.

MOZART WORKS AND RECORDINGS

Note.—*Mozart's works are always distinguished and identified by their "Köchel numbers," assigned to them by the musicologist Köchel of Vienna and Salzburg in his Mozart catalogue of 1862. This explains why, for in-stance, the* Turkish *Violin Concerto is referred to as K. 219, the* Jupiter *Symphony as K. 551, etc.*

In the following list, however, the works are arranged not in the order of their Köchel numbering but—for the sake of easy finding—in groups accord-ing to type of composition and in the order of their writing.

The phonograph recordings available in the early autumn of 1946 are entered under such works as have been recorded. In the past a number of Mozart recordings have been made that are not listed here because they are European and for some time have not been available here. But these works are steadily being recorded in this country, so that it will pay the collector to ask his dealer about new recordings.

I—INSTRUMENTAL

A—FOR ORCHESTRA

1. Symphonies

RECORD NO.

K. 16, E-flat major. Composed in London, 1764–65.
K. 19, D major. London, 1765.
K. 22, B-flat major. The Hague, 1765.
K. 76, F major. Vienna, 1767.
K. 45, D major. Vienna, 1768.
Anh. 221, G major. Vienna, 1768.
Anh. 214, B-flat major. Vienna, 1768.
K. 48, D major. Vienna, 1768.
K. 81, D major. Rome, 1770.
K. 97, D major. Rome, 1770.
K. 95, D major. Rome, 1770.
K. 84, D major. Milan and Bologna, 1770.
K. 74, G major. Milan, 1770.
Anh. 216, B-flat major. Salzburg, 1771.
K. 75, F major. Salzburg, 1771.
K. 73, C major. Salzburg, 1771.
K. 110, G major. Salzburg, 1771.
K. 96, C major. Milan, 1771.
K. 112, F major. Milan, 1771.
K. 114, A major. Salzburg, 1771.
K. 124, G major. Salzburg, 1772.

K. 128, C major. Salzburg, 1772.
K. 129, G major. Salzburg, 1772.
K. 130, F major. Salzburg, 1772.
K. 132, E-flat major. Salzburg, 1772.
K. 133, D major. Salzburg, 1772.
K. 134, A major. Salzburg, 1772.
K. 161 and 163, D major. Salzburg, Milan, 1772.
K. 162, C major. Salzburg, 1773.
K. 199, G major. Salzburg, 1773.
K. 181, D major. Salzburg, 1773.
K. 184, E-flat major. Salzburg, 1773.
K. 182, B-flat major. Salzburg, 1773.
K. 200, C major. Salzburg, 1773.
K. 183, G minor (No. 25, the "little G minor"). Salzburg, 1773.
    N. Y. Philharmonic-Symphony Orch., Barbirolli   CX-217
K. 201, A major. Salzburg, 1774.
K. 202, D major. Salzburg, 1774.
Anh. 9 (297b), E-flat major (*Sinfonia Concertante*). Paris, 1778.
K. 297, D major (No. 31, *Paris*). Paris, 1778.
    London Philharmonic Orch., Beecham   CM-360
Anh. 8, B-flat major. Paris, 1778.
*K. 318, G major. Salzburg, 1779.
K. 319, B-flat major. Salzburg, 1779.
K. 338, C major (No. 34). Salzburg, 1780.
    London Philharmonic Orch., Beecham   CM-548
K. 385, D major (No. 35, *Haffner*). Vienna, 1782.
    N. Y. Philharmonic Symphony Orch., Toscanini   VM-65
    London Philharmonic Orch., Beecham   CM-699
K. 425, C major (*Linz*). Linz, 1783.
    B.B.C. Symphony Orch., Busch   VM-226
    London Philharmonic Orch., Beecham   CM-387
K. 444, G major (really by Michael Haydn, Mozart having written the *Introduction* only). Linz, 1783.
K. 504, D major (No. 38, *Prague,* or Symphony without a Minuet). Vienna, 1786.
    London Philharmonic Orch., Beecham   CM-509
    Chicago Symphony Orch., Stock   CM-410
    Vienna Philharmonic Orch., Walter   VM-457

* The original manuscript of this symphony, in Mozart's hand, is in the New York Public Library.

K. 543, E-flat major (No. 39). Vienna, 1788.
    B.B.C. Symphony Orch., Walter   VM-258
    London Philharmonic Orch., Beecham   CM-456
K. 550, G minor (No. 40). Vienna, 1788.
    Chicago Symphony Orch., Stock   VM-109
    London Philharmonic Orch., Koussevitzky   VM-293
    London Philharmonic Orch., Beecham   CM-316
    Berlin State Opera Orch., Walter   CM-182
K. 551, C major (No. 41, *Jupiter*). Vienna, 1788.
    B.B.C. Symphony Orch., Boult   VM-203
    London Philharmonic Orch., Beecham   CM-194
    N. Y. Philharmonic-Symphony Orch., Walter   CM-565

2. SERENADES, DIVERTIMENTI, ETC.

K. 62, Cassation, D major. Salzburg, 1769.
K. 99, Cassation, B-flat major. Salzburg, 1769.
K. 100, Serenade, D major. Salzburg, 1769.
K. 63, Divertimento, G major. Salzburg, 1769.
K. 113, Divertimento, E-flat major. Milan, 1771.
K. 131, Divertimento, D major. Salzburg, 1772.
K. 136, Divertimento, D major. Salzburg, 1772.
    Boyd Neel String Orch.   D-25536/8
K. 137, Divertimento, B-flat major. Salzburg, 1772.
K. 138, Divertimento, F major. Salzburg, 1772.
    Boyd Neel String Orch.   D-25536/8
K. 166, Divertimento, E-flat major. Salzburg, 1773.
K. 185, Serenade, D major. Vienna, 1773.
K. 186, Divertimento, B-flat major. Milan, 1773.
K. 187, Divertimento, C major. Salzburg, 1773.
K. 205, Divertimento, D major. Vienna, 1773.
K. 203, Serenade, D major. Salzburg, 1774.
K. 204, Serenade, D major. Salzburg, 1775.
K. 213, Divertimento, F major. Salzburg, 1775.
Anh. 226, Divertimento, E-flat major. Munich, 1775.
Anh. 227, Divertimento, B-flat major. Munich, 1775.
K. 101, Serenade, F major. Salzburg, 1776.
K. 188, Divertimento, C major. Salzburg, 1776.
K. 239, *Serenata notturna,* D major. Salzburg, 1776.
    Vox Chamber Orch., Fendler   Vox-161
K. 240, Divertimento, B-flat major. Salzburg, 1776.
K. 247, Divertimento, F major. Salzburg, 1776.
K. 250, Serenade, D major (*Haffner*). Salzburg, 1776.
K. 251, Divertimento, D major (*Septett*). Salzburg, 1776.

K. 252, Divertimento, E-flat major. Salzburg, 1776.

K. 253, Divertimento, F major. Salzburg, 1776.

K. 286, Divertimento, D major (*Notturno*). Salzburg, 1776-77.

K. 270, Divertimento, B-flat major. Salzburg, 1777.

K. 287, Divertimento, B-flat major. Salzburg, 1777.
    A. Fiedler's Sinfonietta   VM-434
    Szigeti, Chamber Orch., Goberman   CM-322

K. 288, Divertimento, F major. Salzburg, 1777.

K. 289, Divertimento, E-flat major. Salzburg, 1777.

K. 320, Serenade, D major. Salzburg, 1779.
    Two movements: Concertante and Rondo, Vox Chamber Orch., Fendler   Vox-161

K. 334, Divertimento, D major. Salzburg, 1779.
    London Philharmonic Orch., Harty   CM-207

K. 361, Serenade, B-flat major (*Gran Partita*). Munich and Vienna, 1781.
    E. Fischer and Chamber Orch.   VM-743

K. 375, Serenade, E-flat major. Vienna, 1781.

K. 388, Serenade, C minor. Vienna, 1782.
    A. Fiedler's Sinfonietta   VM-433

K. 525, Serenade, G major (*Eine kleine Nachtmusik*). Vienna, 1787.
    Minneapolis Symphony Orch., Ormandy   V-8588/9
    Symphony Orch., Walter   C-68016/7D
    (See also under String Quartets)

K. 563, Divertimento, E-flat major. Vienna, 1788.
    Heifetz, Primrose, Feuermann   VM-959

3. DANCE TUNES FOR ORCHESTRA

K. 25a, Minuet.

K. 64, Minuet, D major. 1769.

K. 65a, 7 Minuets for strings. 1769.

K. 103, 19 Minuets. 1769.

K. 104, 6 Minuets. 1769.

K. 105, 6 Minuets. 1769.

K. 61g, 2 Minuets. 1769.

K. 61h, 6 Minuets. 1769.

K. 122, Minuet. 1770.

K. 123, Kontretanz. 1770.

K. 164, 6 Minuets. 1772.

K. 176, 16 Minuets. 1773.

K. 267, 4 Kontretänze. 1777.

K. 300, Gavotte. 1778.

RECORD NO.

K. 363, 3 Minuets. 1780.
K. 446, Music for a Pantomime. 1783.
K. 461, 6 Minuets. 1784.
K. 462, 6 Kontretänze. 1784.
K. 463, 2 Quadrilles. 1784.
K. 509, 6 German Dances. 1787.
K. 510, 9 Kontretänze. 1787.
K. 534, *Das Donnerwetter* (The Thunderstorm). 1788.
    Fischer Chamber Orch.   V-18029
K. 535, Kontretanz, *The Battle.* 1788.
K. 535a, 3 Kontretänze. 1788.
K. 536, 6 German Dances. 1788.
K. 565, 2 Kontretänze. 1788.
K. 567, 6 German Dances. 1788.
K. 568, 12 Minuets. 1788.
K. 571, 6 German Dances. 1789.
K. 586, 12 German Dances. 1789.
K. 587, Kontretanz, *The Hero of Coburg.* 1789.
K. 106, Ouverture and 3 Kontretänze. 1790.
K. 599, 6 Minuets. 1791.
K. 600, 6 German Dances. 1791.
    Minneapolis Symphony Orch., Ormandy   V-1722/3
      (Recording incl. Nos. 1-5 from K. 600; No. 3 from
        K. 602; and Nos. 2 and 3 from K. 605)
K. 601, 4 Minuets. 1791.
K. 602, 4 German Dances (for recording see under K. 600).
    1791.
K. 603, 2 Kontretänze. 1791.
K. 604, 2 Minuets. 1791.
K. 605, 3 German Dances. 1791.
    Vienna Philharmonic Orch., Walter (all 3)   V-4564
    (See also above under K. 600)
K. 606, 6 Ländler. 1791.
    Nos. 1 and 3 arr. for violin and piano. Schmidt and
      Eaver   V-24528
K. 607, Kontretanz. 1791.
K. 609, 5 Kontretänze. 1791.
K. 610, Kontretanz, *The Malicious Girls.* 1791.
K. 611, Dance. 1791.

4. MARCHES, SYMPHONIC MOVEMENTS, MINOR ORCHESTRATION

K. 189, March, D major. 1773.
K. 214, March, C major. 1775.

K. 215, March, D major. 1775.

K. 237, March, D major. 1774.

K. 248, March, F major. 1776.

K. 249, March, D major. 1776.

K. 290, March, D major. 1773.

K. 335, Two Marches, D major. 1779.
    No. 1 from K. 335 and No. 2 from K. 408, Paris Con-
    servatory Orch., Fendler   V-4549

K. 445, March, D major. 1779.

K. 408, Four Marches. 1782.
    (For recording, see above, K. 335)

K. 477, Masonic Dead March, C minor. 1785.

K. 544, March, D major. 1788.

K. 32, Galimathias musicum (*Quodlibet*), D major. 1766.

K. 120, Finale for the symphony of *Ascanio in Alba.* 1771.

K. 161 and 163, *Allegro* and *Andante* for a symphony,
D major. 1772.

K. 102, Finale for a symphony or divertimento, C major.
1775.

K. 121, Finale for a symphony or divertimento, D major.
1775.

Anh. 103, *La Chasse,* A major. 1779.

K. 409, Symphony Minuet, C major. 1782.

K. 410, *Adagio* for bassoon and 2 basset horns, F major.
1783.

K. 411, *Adagio* for 2 clarinets and 3 basset horns, B-flat
major. 1783.

K. 522, *Ein musikalischer Spass* (A Musical Joke), sextet
for strings and horns, F major. 1787.

K. 594, *Adagio* and *Allegro* for organ, A-flat major. 1790.

K. 616, *Andante* for a small organ, F major. 1791.

B—CONCERTOS

1. FOR VIOLIN AND ORCHESTRA

Anh. 294a, D major (*Adelaide*). Paris, 1766.
    Menuhin and Paris Symphony Orch., Monteux   VM-246

K. 190, Concerto for two violins, C major. Salzburg, 1773.

K. 207, B-flat major. Salzburg, 1775.

K. 211, D major. Salzburg, 1775.

K. 216, G major. Salzburg, 1775.
    Menuhin and Paris Symphony Orch., Enesco   VM-485

MOZART WORKS AND RECORDINGS

K. 382, Concerto Rondo, D major. Vienna, 1782.

K. 386, Concerto Rondo, A major. Vienna, 1782.

K. 413, F major. Vienna, 1782-83.

K. 414, A major. Vienna, 1782.

    Kentner, London Philharmonic Orch., Beecham — CM-544

K. 415, C major. Vienna, 1782-83.

K. 449, E-flat major. Vienna, 1784.

    Serkin, Busch Chamber Players — VM-657

    K. Long, Boyd Neel Orch. — D-25532/4

K. 450, B-flat major. Vienna, 1784.

    Elly Ney and Orch., Hoogstraten — VM-365

K. 451, D major. Vienna, 1784.

K. 453, G major. Vienna, 1784.

    Dohnanyi, Budapest Philharmonic Orch. — CM-111

    Edwin Fischer and Chamber Orch. — VM-481

K. 456, B-flat major. Vienna, 1784.

K. 459, F major. Vienna, 1784.

    A. Schnabel, London Symphony Orch., Sargent — VM-389

K. 466, D minor. Vienna, 1785.

    E. Fischer, London Philharmonic Orch. — VM-223

    Iturbi, Rochester Philharmonic Orch. — VM-794

K. 467, C major. Vienna, 1785.

    A. Schnabel, London Symphony Orch., Sargent — VM-486

K. 482, E-flat major. Vienna, 1785.

    E. Fischer and Orch., Barbirolli — VM-316

K. 488, A major. Vienna, 1786.

    Rubinstein, London Symphony Orch., Barbirolli — VM-147

    M. Long and Orch., Gaubert — CM-261

K. 491, C minor. Vienna, 1786.

    Casadesus, Paris Symphony Orch., Bigot — CM-356

    E. Fischer, London Philharmonic Orch., Collingwood — VM-482

K. 503, C major. Vienna, 1786.

    K. Long, Boyd Neel Orch. — DX-229/32

K. 537, D major (*Coronation*). Vienna, 1788.

    W. Landowska and Chamber Orch., Goehr — VM-483

K. 595, B-flat major. Vienna, 1791.

    Casadesus, N. Y. Philharmonic-Symphony Orch., Barbirolli — CM-490

    A. Schnabel, London Symphony Orch., Barbirolli — VM-240

3. For Wind Instrument and Orchestra

RECORD NO.

K. 191, for bassoon, B-flat major. Salzburg, 1774.
    Oubradous and Orch., Bigot   VM-704
    Camden, Hallé Orch., Harty   CM-71
K. 299, for flute and harp, C major. Paris, 1778.
    M. Moyse, L. Laskine, and Orch., Coppola   VM-141
K. 313, for flute, G major. Mannheim, 1778.
    M. Moyse and Orch., Bigot   V-12123/5
K. 314, for flute, D major. Mannheim, 1778.
    M. Moyse and Orch., Coppola   VM-589
K. 315, *Andante* for flute and orchestra, C major. Mannheim, 1778.
    Berlin Philharmonic Orch., Blech   V-11407
K. 371, Rondo finale for horn concerto, E-flat major. Vienna, 1781.
K. 412, for horn, D major. Vienna, 1782.
K. 293, for oboe, F major. Vienna, 1783.
K. 417, for horn, E-flat major. Vienna, 1783.
K. 447, for horn, E-flat major. Vienna, 1783.
    A. Brain, B.B.C. Symphony Orch., Boult   VM-829
K. 495, for horn, E-flat major. Vienna, 1786.
K. 622, for clarinet, A major. Vienna, 1791.
    R. Kell, London Philharmonic Orch., Sargent   VM-708

C—CHAMBER MUSIC

1. Duo Sonatas for Piano and Violin

K. 6, C major. Salzburg, Brussels, Paris, 1762-4.
K. 7, D major. Paris, 1763-4.
K. 8, B-flat major. Paris, 1763-4.
K. 9, G major. Paris, 1764.
K. 10, B-flat major (for violin or flute). London, 1764
  ("*âgé de huit ans*").
K. 11, G major (for violin or flute). London, 1764.
K. 26, E-flat major. The Hague, 1766.
K. 27, G major. The Hague, 1766.
K. 28, C major. The Hague, 1766.
K. 29, D major. The Hague, 1766.
K. 30, F major. The Hague, 1766.
K. 31, B-flat major. The Hague, 1766.

K. 55, F major.
K. 56, C major.
K. 57, F major.
K. 58, E-flat major.   Date and place
K. 59, E-flat major.   uncertain
K. 60, E minor
K. 61, A major.

K. 296, C major. Mannheim, 1778.
K. 301, G major. Mannheim, 1778.
K. 302, E-flat major. Mannheim, 1778.
K. 303, C major. Mannheim, 1778.
K. 304, E minor. Paris, 1778.
    Szigeti and Magaloff   C-LX604
K. 305, A major. Paris, 1778.
K. 306, D major. Paris, 1778.
K. 376, F major. Vienna, 1781.
K. 377, F major. Vienna, 1781.
K. 378, B-flat major. Salzburg, 1779.
    Heifetz and Bay   VM-343
K. 379, G major. Vienna, 1781.
K. 380, E-flat major. Vienna, 1781.
K. 402, A major. Vienna, 1782.
K. 403, C major. Vienna, 1782.
K. 454, B-flat major. Vienna, 1784.
    Heifetz and Bay   VM-343
K. 481, E-flat major. Vienna, 1785.
K. 526, A major. Vienna, 1787.
    Yehudi and Hephzibah Menuhin   V-8412/3
Anh. 50, A major. Vienna, 1787.
Anh. 47, G major. Vienna, 1788.

K. 359, Variations on *La Bergère Célimène*. Vienna, 1781.
K. 360, Variations on *Hélas, j'ai perdu mon amant*. Vienna,
    1781.
K. 372, *Allegro,* B-flat major, for a duo sonata. Vienna,
    1781.
K. 396, *Adagio,* C minor, for a duo sonata. Vienna, 1782.
K. 404, *Andante* and *Allegretto,* C major, for a duo sonata.
    Vienna, 1783.
Anh. 48, *Allegro,* A major, for a duo sonata. Vienna, 1785.
K. 547, Sonatina, F major. Vienna, 1788.

2. Duos and Trios for Strings and for Wind

K. 46d, Duo for violin(?) and violoncello, or for clavier, C major. Vienna, 1768.

K. 46e, Duo for violin(?) and violoncello, or for clavier, F major. Vienna, 1768.

K. 423, Duo for violin and viola in G major. Salzburg, 1783.

K. 424, Duo for violin and viola in B-flat major. Salzburg, 1783.

    Goldberg and Hindemith   CMX-46

    Heifetz and Primrose   VM-831

K. 292, Sonata for bassoon and violoncello, B-flat major. Munich, 1775.

K. 266, Trio for 2 violins and violoncello, B-flat major. Salzburg, 1777.

K. 404a, Six 3-voice (J. S.) Bach fugues arr. for violin, viola, violoncello. Vienna, 1782.

K. 443, Fugue for violin, viola, violoncello, G major. Vienna, 1783.

Anh. 229 and 229a, Five Divertimenti for clarinets and bassoon, B-flat major. Vienna, 1783.

K. 487, Twelve duos for horns, C major. Vienna, 1786.

3. String Quartets (2 violins, viola, violoncello) *

K. 80, G major. Lodi and Vienna, 1770, 1773 (or Salzburg, 1774).

K. 155, D major. Bozen, 1772.

K. 156, G major. Milan, 1772.

K. 157, C major. Milan, 1772.

K. 158, F major. Milan, 1773.

K. 159, B flat major. Milan, 1773.

K. 160, E-flat major. Milan and Salzburg, 1773.

K. 168, F major. Vienna, 1773.

K. 169, A major. Vienna, 1773.

K. 170, C major. Vienna, 1773.

K. 171, E-flat major. Vienna, 1773.

K. 172, B-flat major. Vienna, 1773.

K. 173, D minor. Vienna, 1773.

* A number of Mozart's works are called either String Quartets or Divertimenti—e.g., K. 136, 137, and 138, listed above as Divertimenti, are sometimes played by the four instruments of a quartet, and sometimes by a larger number.

K. 387, G major. Vienna, 1782.
    Lener String Quartet   CM-144

K. 421, D minor. Vienna, 1783.
    Lener String Quartet   CL-1965/7
    Flonzaley Quartet   V-7607/8

K. 428, E-flat major. Vienna, 1783.
    Pro Arte Quartet   VM-375

K. 458, B-flat major (*Hunting*). Vienna, 1784.
    Lener String Quartet   CM-134
    Budapest Quartet   V-9290/2

K. 464, A major. Vienna, 1785.
    Roth Quartet   CM-222

K. 465, C major (*Dissonant*). Vienna, 1785.
    Budapest Quartet   VM-285
    Gordon String Quartet   CM-219
    (Note—The six quartets above, 387 through 465, are those dedicated to Haydn.)

K. 499, D major. Vienna, 1786.
    Budapest Quartet   VM-222

K. 525, G major (*Eine kleine Nachtmusik*). Vienna, 1787.
    Lener Quartet   CL-1729/30
    (See also K. 525 under Serenades and Divertimenti above.)

K. 575, D major (*'Cello*). Vienna, 1789.
    Kolisch Quartet   CM-X53

K. 589, B-flat major. Vienna, 1790.
    Kolisch Quartet   VM-407

K. 590, F major. Vienna, 1790.
    Budapest Quartet   VM-348
    (Note—The three quartets above, K. 575, 589, and 590, are those dedicated to King Frederick William II of Prussia.)

K. 405, Five 4-voice (J. S.) Bach fugues arr. for string quartet. Vienna, 1782-83.

K. 546, *Adagio* and Fugue, E-flat major, for string quartet. Vienna, 1788.

4. QUARTETS FOR STRINGS AND WIND

K. 285, D major, flute and strings. Mannheim, 1777.

Anh. 171, Allegro and Andantino, C major, flute and strings. Mannheim, 1778.

RECORD NO.

K. 298, A major, flute and strings. Paris, 1778.
K. 370, F major, oboe and strings. Munich, 1781.
    L. Goossens and members of the Lener Quartet   CX-21

5. Quintets and Sextet for Strings, and for Strings with Wind

K. 174, B-flat major, quartet with 2d viola. Salzburg, 1773.
K. 406, C minor, quartet with 2d viola. Vienna, 1787.
K. 407, E-flat major, quartet and horn. Salzburg, 1773.
K. 515, C major, quartet with 2d viola. Vienna, 1787.
    Pro Arte Quartet with Hobday   VM-270
K. 516, G minor, quartet with 2d viola. Vienna, 1787.
    Budapest Quartet with Katims   CM-526
    Pro Arte Quartet with Hobday   VM-190
K. 522, Sextet, F major (*A Musical Joke*), quartet with 2 horns. Vienna, 1787.
    Kolisch Quartet with Caputo and Barrows   VM-432
K. 546, C minor, *Adagio* and Fugue, quartet with double-bass. Vienna, 1788.
    Busch Chamber Players   V-12324
    Hallé Orch., Heward   CDX-1056
K. 581, A major (*Stadler*), quartet with clarinet. Vienna, 1789.
    Budapest Quartet with Goodman   VM-452
    Roth Quartet with Bellison   CM-293
K. 593, D major, quartet with 2d viola. Vienna, 1790.
    Pro Arte Quartet with Hobday   VM-350
K. 614, E-flat major, quartet with 2d viola. Vienna, 1791.

6. Piano Trios, Quartets, Quintets

K. 12, Trio, A major, piano and strings. London, 1764.
K. 13, Trio, F major, piano and strings. London, 1764.
K. 14, Trio, C major, piano and strings. London, 1764.
K. 15, Trio, B-flat major, piano and strings. London, 1764.
K. 254, Divertimento, B-flat major, piano and strings. Salzburg, 1776.
K. 442, Trio, D minor, piano and strings. Vienna, 1783.
K. 452, Quintet, E-flat major, piano, oboe, clarinet, horn, bassoon. Vienna, 1784.
    Schulhoff and Taffanel Wood Wind Ensemble   VM-137
K. 478, Quartet, G minor, piano and strings. Vienna, 1785.
    A. Schnabel and members of the Pro Arte Quartet   VM-251

K. 493, Quartet, E-flat major, piano and strings. Vienna, 1786.

K. 496, Trio, G major, piano and strings. Vienna, 1786.

K. 498, Trio, E-flat major, piano, clarinet, viola. Vienna, 1786.

K. 502, Trio, B-flat major, piano and strings. Vienna, 1786.

K. 542, Trio, E major, piano and strings. Vienna, 1788.

K. 548, Trio, C major, piano and strings. Vienna, 1788.

K. 564, Trio, G major, piano and strings. Vienna, 1788.

K. 617, *Adagio* and Rondo, C minor, harmonica, flute, oboe, viola, violoncello. Vienna, 1791.

D—PIANO COMPOSITIONS

1. SONATAS AND FANTASIAS

K. 279, Sonata, C Major. Salzburg, 1774.

K. 280, Sonata, F major. Salzburg, 1774.

K. 281, Sonata, B-flat major. Salzburg, 1774.

K. 282, Sonata, E-flat major. Salzburg, 1774.

K. 283, Sonata, G major. Salzburg, 1774.

K. 284, Sonata, D major (*Dürnitz*). Munich, 1775.

K. 309, Sonata, C major. Mannheim, 1777.

K. 311, Sonata, D major. Mannheim, 1777.

K. 310, Sonata, A minor. Paris, 1778.

K. 330, Sonata, C major. Paris, 1778.

K. 331, Sonata, A major (with the *Rondo alla turca*). Paris, 1778.

K. 332, Sonata, F major. Paris, 1778.

K. 333, Sonata, B-flat major. Paris, 1778.

K. 395, Capriccio, C major. Paris, 1778.

K. 394, Fantasia with a Fugue, C major. Vienna, 1782.

K. 396, Sonata movement, C minor. Vienna, 1782.
   E. Fischer   V-8696

K. 397, Fantasia, D minor. Vienna, 1782.
   W. Landowska   V-15607

K. 457, Sonata, C minor. Vienna, 1784.

K. 475, Fantasia, C minor. Vienna, 1785.

K. 545, Sonata, C major. Vienna, 1788.

Anh. 135 and 138a, Sonata, F major. Vienna, 1788.

K. 570, Sonata, B-flat major. Vienna, 1789.

K. 576, Sonata, D major. Vienna, 1789.

2. Variations

K. 24, Eight Variations, G major, on a Dutch song. The Hague, 1766.

K. 25, Seven Variations, D major, on *Willem van Nassau.* Amsterdam, 1766.

K. 180, Six Variations, G major, on *Mio caro Adone.* Vienna, 1773.

K. 179, Twelve Variations, C major, on a Minuet by Fischer. Salzburg, 1774.

K. 354, Twelve Variations, E-flat major, on the aria *Je suis Lindor* from Beaumarchais's opera *The Barber of Seville.* Paris, 1778.

K. 265, Twelve Variations, C major, on *Ah, vous dirai-je, Maman.* Paris, 1778.

    Miliza Korjus   V-13826

K. 353, Twelve Variations, E-flat major, on *La belle Françoise.* Paris, 1778.

K. 264, Nine Variations, C major, on *Lison dormait.* Paris, 1778.

K. 352, Eight Variations, F major, on the March from Grétry's opera *Les Mariages Samnites.* Vienna, 1781.

K. 398, Six Variations, F major, on *Salve tu, Domine,* from Paisiello's opera *The Astrologers.* Vienna, 1783.

K. 460, Eight Variations, A major, on the aria *Come un' agnello* by Sarti. Vienna(?), 1784.

K. 455, Ten Variations, G major, on *Unser dummer Pöbel meint* from Gluck's opera *The Pilgrim of Mecca.* Vienna, 1784.

K. 500, Twelve Variations, B-flat major, on an *Allegretto.* Vienna, 1786.

K. 573, Nine Variations, D major, on a Minuet by Duport. Potsdam, 1789.

K. 613, Eight Variations, F major, on the song *Ein Weib ist das herrlichste Ding.* Vienna, 1791.

3. Duets for One or Two Pianos

K. 19d, Sonata, C major, for 4 hands. London, 1765.

K. 381, Sonata, D major, for 4 hands. Salzburg (?), 1772.

K. 358, Sonata, B-flat major, for 4 hands. Salzburg, 1774.

K. 448, Sonata, D major, for 2 pianos. Vienna, 1781.

K. 401, Fugue, B-flat major, for 2 or 4 hands. Vienna, 1782.

K. 426, Fugue, C minor, for 2 pianos. Vienna, 1783.

K. 357, Sonata, G major, for 4 hands. Vienna, 1786.

K. 497, Sonata, F major, for 4 hands. Vienna, 1786.

K. 501, *Andante* with five variations, G major, for 4 hands. Vienna, 1786.

K. 521, Sonata, C major, for 4 hands. Vienna, 1787.

4. OTHER PIANO COMPOSITIONS ("EINZELSTUCKE")

K. 1, Minuet and Trio in G major. Salzburg, 1761 or 1762 (Mozart aged 5 or 6).
   E. Fischer   G-1693

K. 2, Minuet in F major. Salzburg, 1762.

K. 3, *Allegro,* B-flat major. Salzburg, 1762.

K. 4, Minuet in F major. Salzburg, 1762.

K. 5, Minuet in F major. Salzburg, 1762.

K. 9a, *Allegro,* C major. 1763.

K. 9b, *Andante,* B-flat major. 1763.

K. 15a, *Allegro* for clavier. London, 1764.

K. 312, *Allegro* for a clavier sonata, G minor. Salzburg, 1774.

K. 315a, Eight Minuets with trios. Salzburg, 1779.

K. 400, *Allegro* for a clavier sonata, B-flat major. Vienna. 1781.

K. 153, Beginning of a fugue, E-flat major. Vienna, 1782.

K. 154, Fugue, B-flat major. Vienna, 1782.

K. 154a, Two little fugues for clavier or organ.

K. 399, Piano suite, C major. Vienna, 1782.

K. 453a, Little funeral march, C minor. Vienna, 1784.

K. 485, Rondo, D major. Vienna, 1786.

K. 494, Rondo, F major. Vienna, 1786.

Anh. 136, Clavier sonata, B-flat major. Vienna, 1786.

K. 511, Rondo, A minor. Vienna, 1787.

K. 511a, Rondo (Beethoven), B-flat major.

K. 533, *Allegro* and *Andante,* F major. Vienna, 1788.

K. 540, *Adagio,* B minor. Vienna, 1788.

K. 574, Little gigue, G major. Leipzig, 1789.
   R. Casadesus   C-11702D
   E. Joyce   CDX-1055

K. 236, *Andantino,* B-flat major. Vienna, 1790.

K. 355, Minuet, D major. Vienna, 1790.
   R. Casadesus   C-11702D
   E. Joyce   CDX-1055

K. 356, *Adagio,* C major, for harmonica. Vienna, 1791.

K. 624, Cadenzas for the piano concertos, 1768-91.

E—ORGAN COMPOSITIONS

K. 67, Church Sonata, E-flat major, for organ and strings. Salzburg, 1767.

K. 68, Church Sonata, B-flat major, for organ and strings. Salzburg, 1767.

K. 69, Church Sonata, D major, for organ and strings. Salzburg, 1767.

K. 144, Church Sonata, D major, for violins and organ (or violoncello). Salzburg, 1772.

    E. Power Biggs with Fiedler Sinfonietta   VM-1019

K. 145, Church Sonata, F major, for violins and organ (or violoncello). Salzburg, 1772.

K. 212, Church Sonata, B-flat major, for organ and strings. Salzburg, 1775.

K. 241, Church Sonata, G major, for organ and strings. Salzburg, 1776.

K. 224, Church Sonata, F major, for organ and strings. Salzburg, 1776.

K. 225, Church Sonata, A major, for organ and strings. Salzburg, 1776.

K. 244, Church Sonata, F major, for organ and strings. Salzburg, 1776.

    E. Power Biggs with Fiedler Sinfonietta   VM-1019

K. 245, Church Sonata, D major, for organ and strings. Salzburg, 1776.

    E. Power Biggs with Fiedler Sinfonietta   VM-1019

K. 263, Church Sonata, C major, for organ, violins, trumpets. Salzburg, 1776.

K. 274, Church Sonata, G major, for organ and strings. Salzburg, 1777.

K. 278, Church Sonata, C major, for organ, strings, oboes, trumpets, bassoon. Salzburg, 1777.

    E. Power Biggs with Fiedler Sinfonietta   VM-1019

K. 329, Church Sonata, C major, for organ, strings, oboes, horns, trumpets, bassoon. Salzburg, 1779.

K. 336, Church Sonata, C major, for organ and strings. Salzburg, 1780.

    E. Power Biggs with Fiedler Sinfonietta   VM-1019

K. 608, Organ Fantasia, F minor. Vienna, 1791.
    G. D. Cunningham on organ of King's Way Hall,
    London   C-69009D

II—VOCAL

A—CHURCH MUSIC

1. MASSES

K. 49, Missa brevis, G major. Vienna, 1768.
K. 65, Missa brevis, D minor. Salzburg, 1769.
K. 66, Missa (*Dominicus*), C major. Salzburg, 1769.
K. 116, Missa brevis, F major. Salzburg, 1771.
K. 139, Missa [solemnis], C minor. Salzburg, 1772.
K. 115, Missa brevis, C major. Salzburg, 1773.
K. 167, Missa in honorem SSmae Trinitatis, C major. Salzburg, 1773.
K. 192, Missa brevis, F major. Salzburg, 1774.
K. 194, Missa brevis, D major. Salzburg, 1774.
K. 220, Missa brevis in C major. Munich, 1775.
K. 257, Missa [*Credo*], C major. Salzburg, 1776.
K. 258, Missa brevis, C major. Salzburg, 1776.
K. 262, Missa [longa], C major. Salzburg, 1776.
K. 259, Missa brevis (*Organ Solo*), C major. Salzburg, 1776.
K. 275, Missa brevis, B-flat major. Salzburg, 1777.
K. 317, Missa (*Coronation*), C major. Salzburg, 1780.
K. 337, Missa solemnis (*Fagottsolomesse*), C major Salzburg, 1780.
K. 427, Missa, C minor (unfinished), Vienna, 1782-83.
    Agnus Dei, Chorus (Les Disciples de Massenet), Marcelle Denya, and Montreal Festivals Orch. under W. Pelletier   V-18512
    Kyrie eleison
      D. Labette, Leeds Festival Chorus, and London Philharmonic Orch., Beecham   CLB-19
    Et incarnatus est
      Ria Ginster   D-25167
    Qui tollis
      Leeds Festival Chorus and London Philharmonic Orch., Beecham   C-68385D
    Laudamus te
      Johanna Egli   D-20406

K. 626, *Requiem,* D minor. Vienna, 1791 (finished by Süssmayer).

    Complete recording by Univ. of Penna. Choral Society
and Philadelphia Orch.   VM-649

    (Note—The so-called "Twelfth Mass" is now known
to be by a minor composer and not by Mozart.)

2. LITANIES AND VESPERS

K. 109, Litaniae de B. M. V. (*Lauretanae*), B-flat major.
Salzburg, 1771.

K. 125, Litaniae de venerabili altaris sacramento, B-flat major. Salzburg, 1772.

K. 195, Litaniae Lauretanae, D major. Salzburg, 1774.

K. 243, Litaniae de venerabili altaris sacramento, E-flat major. Salzburg, 1776.

K. 193, *Dixit* and *Magnificat,* C major. Salzburg, 1774.

K. 321, Vesperae de Dominica, C major. Salzburg, 1779.

K. 339, Vesperae solennes de confessore, C major. Salzburg,
1780.

3. KYRIES, OFFERTORIES, ETC.

K. 33, Kyrie, F major, for voices and orchestra. Paris, 1766.

K. 89, Kyrie for 5 sopranos. Rome, 1770.

K. 90, Kyrie, D minor, for voices and organ. Salzburg, 1771.

K. 91, Kyrie, D major, for voices, strings, organ. 1774.

K. 221, Kyrie, C major, for voices and basso continuo. Salzburg, 1771.

K. 322, Kyrie, E-flat major, for voices, orchestra, organ.
Mannheim, 1778.

K. 323, Kyrie, C major, for voices, orchestra, organ. Salzburg, 1779.

K. 340, Kyrie, C major, for solo voices. 1780.

K. 341, Kyrie, D minor, for voices, orchestra, organ. Munich,
1781.

K. 20, Motet, D minor, *God Is Our Refuge.* London, 1765.

K. 34, Offertorium in festo S. Benedicti, *Scande coeli limina,*
for voices, orchestra, organ. 1766-7.

K. 44, Introit *Cibavit eos* for voices and organ. Bologna,
1770.

K. 47, *Veni Sancte Spiritus,* for voices and organ. Vienna,
1768.

K. 72, Offertorium pro festo S. Joannis Baptistae, *Inter natos mulierum,* for voices, strings, organ. Salzburg, 1771.

K. 85, *Miserere,* C major. Bologna, 1770.

K. 86, Antiphon *Quaerite primum regnum Dei.* Bologna, 1770.

K. 92, *Salve Regina,* F major, for voices, orchestra, organ. 1769(?).

K. 93, Psalm *De profundis,* E-flat major, for voices and organ. Salzburg, 1771.

K. 108, *Regina Coeli,* C major, for voices, orchestra, organ. Salzburg, 1771.

K. 117, Offertorium [pro omni tempore], *Benedictus sit Deus; Introibo; Jubilate.* Voices, orchestra, organ. Salzburg, 1769.

K. 127, *Regina Coeli,* B-flat major, for voices, orchestra, organ. Salzburg, 1772.

K. 141, *Te Deum,* C major, for voices, strings, organ. Salzburg, 1769.

K. 142, *Tantum ergo,* B-flat major, for voices, orchestra, organ.

K. 143, Soprano aria *Ergo interest* and *Quaere superna,* with strings and organ. Milan, 1770.

K. 165, Soprano motet, F major, *Exsultate, jubilate,* with orchestra and organ. Milan, 1773.

> The *Alleluia* from this motet:
> S. Onegin   V-1367
> R. Ginster   D-25167
> L. Pons   CM-518

K. 197, *Tantum ergo,* D major, for voices, orchestra, organ.

K. 198, Offertorium for soprano and tenor, *Sub tuum praesidium,* F major, with strings and organ. Milan, 1773.

K. 222, Offertorium de tempore, *Misericordias Domini,* F major, for voices and organ. Munich, 1775.

K. 223, *Osanna,* C major, for voices, strings, organ. 1773(?)

K. 260, Offertorium de venerabili sacramento, *Venite, populi,* D major, for two choirs, strings, organs. Salzburg, 1776.

K. 273, Graduale ad festum B. M. V., *Sancta Maria,* F major, for voices, strings, organ. Salzburg, 1777.

K. 276, *Regina Coeli,* C major, for voices, orchestra, organ. Salzburg, 1779.

K. 277, Offertorium de B. M. V., *Alma Dei creatoris,* F major, for voices, strings, organ. Salzburg, 1777.

K. 326, Hymns, *Justum deduxit Dominus* and *O sancte,* for voices and organ. Salzburg, 1771.

K. 327, Hymn, *Adoramus te,* for voices and organ.
Strasbourg Cathedral Choir, with orch. and organ   C-69488D

K. 343, Two hymns, *O Gottes Lamm* and *Als aus Aegypten,* solo with bass accompaniment. Salzburg, 1779.

K. 618, Motet, *Ave, verum corpus,* D major, for voices, strings, organ. Baden near Vienna, 1791.
Strasbourg Cathedral Choir   C-69488D
Les Disciples de Massenet, Goulet   VM-844
Wienersängerknaben and organ   D-25281

B—CANTATAS

K. 42, Passion Cantata with accompaniment of strings and horns. Salzburg, 1767.

K. 118, *La Betulia liberata,* oratorio in 2 parts, text by Metastasio. Salzburg, 1771.

K. 429, *Dir, Seele des Weltalls,* cantata for tenors and bass with orchestra. Vienna, 1783.

K. 469, *Davidde penitente,* cantata for 3 solo voices, chorus, orchestra. Text by da Ponte(?). Vienna, 1785.

K. 471, *Sehen, wie dem Starren Forscherauge,* short Masonic cantata for tenor and men's chorus with orchestra. Vienna, 1785.

K. 623, *Laut verkünde unsre Freude,* short Masonic cantata for tenors and bass with orchestra. Vienna, 1791.

C—OPERAS

K. 35, *Die Schuldigkeit des ersten Gebotes* (The Observance of the First Commandment), sacred opera in 3 parts, only the first part by Mozart. Salzburg, 1767.

K. 38, *Apollo et Hyacinthus,* a Latin comedy. Salzburg, 1767.

K. 50, *Bastien et Bastienne,* a one-act operetta. Vienna, 1768.

K. 51, *La finta semplice,* opera bouffe in 3 acts. Vienna, 1768.

K. 87, *Mitridate, Rè di Ponto,* opera in 3 acts. Milan, 1770.

K. 111, *Ascanio in Alba,* dramatic serenade in 2 acts. Milan, 1771.

K. 126, *Il sogno di Scipione,* dramatic serenade, text by Metastasio. Salzburg, 1772.

K. 135, *Lucio Silla,* drama with music in 3 acts. Salzburg, 1772.

K. 196, *La finta giardiniera,* opera bouffe in 3 acts. Salzburg and Munich, 1774-5.

K. 208, *Il Rè pastore,* drama with music in 2 acts. Salzburg, 1775.

    "*L'amerò, sarò constante,*" E. Rethberg   V-7472

Anh. 10, Ballet music for the pantomime *Les Petits Riens.* Paris, 1778.

    Overture and Nos. 6, 10, and 12, London Symphony Orch., Blech   V-11445

K. 344, *Zaide,* opera in 2 acts. Salzburg, 1779.

K. 345, Choruses and incidental music for *Thamos, King of Egypt.* Salzburg, 1779.

    Two Entr'actes, Minneapolis Symphony Orch., Mitropoulos   C-11578D

K. 366, *Idomeneo, Rè di Creta,* opera in 3 acts. Salzburg and Munich, 1780-81.

K. 367, Ballet music for *Idomeneo.* Munich, 1781.

K. 384, *Die Entführung aus dem Serail* (The Abduction from the Seraglio), comic opera in 3 acts. 1781-82.

    Overture, Vienna Philharmonic Orch., Krauss   V-11142
    "*Ach, ich liebte*" and "*Welche Wonne,*" L. Pons   CM-518

K. 422, *L'oca del Cairo,* opera bouffe in 2 acts. Salzburg, 1783.

K. 430, *Lo sposo deluso,* opera bouffe in 2 acts. Salzburg, 1783.

K. 486, *Der Schauspieldirektor* (The Impresario), one-act comedy with music. Vienna, 1786.

    Overture, B.B.C. Symphony Orch., Boult   V-11659

K. 492, *Le Nozze di Figaro* (The Marriage of Figaro), opera bouffe in 4 acts. Vienna, 1786.

    Complete recording (in Italian) by the Glyndebourne Opera Co., Fritz Busch   VM-313/14/15
    Overture, London Philharmonic Orch., Beecham   C-LX639
    Overture arr. for 2 pianos, Luboschutz and Nemenoff   V11-8455
    "*Se vuol ballare,*" E. Pinza and E. Rethberg   V10-1104
    "*La Vendetta,*" S. Baccaloni   C-71193D
    "*Non so più cosa son*"
        Risë Stevens   C-17298D
        E. Schumann   V-1431
    "*Non più andrai,*" E. Pinza   V-18015

RECORD NO.

"Porgi amor"
   T. Lemnitz   V-15178
   E. Rethberg   V-2155
   L. Lehmann (in German)   D-25817

"Voi che sapete"
   R. Ginster   V-7822
   E. Schumann   V-7076
   Risë Stevens   C-17298D
   L. Pons (in French)   CM-518

"Crudel! perchè finora," E. Rethberg and E. Pinza   V-2155

"Dove sono"
   T. Lemnitz   V-15178
   E. Rethberg   V-18015

"Deh, vieni, non tardar"
   Bidu Sayao   V-18496
   L. Bori   V-17614

K. 527, *Don Giovanni*, opera bouffe in 2 acts. Prague, 1787.
Complete recording (in Italian) by the Glyndebourne
   Opera Co., Fritz Busch   VM-423/24/25
Overture
   London Philharmonic Orch., Beecham   C-70365D
   London Symphony Orch., Wood   C-68410D
"Madamina, il catalogo," S. Baccaloni   C-71048D
"La ci darem la mano"
   Rethberg and Pinza   V-2154
   Perras and Hüsch   V-4374
   Bettendorf and Hüsch   D-20010
"Or, sai chi l'onore," R. Bampton   V11-8466
"Dalla sua pace"
   T. Schipa   V-1308
   H. Nash   C-9880
   B. Gigli   V-15601
" 'Finch' han dal vino," E. Pinza   V-1467
"Batti, batti"
   Bidu Sayao   C-71557
   E. Schumann   V-7076
   E. Rethberg   V-7472
   L. Bori   V-14614
   E. Steber   V11-9114
Minuet, W. Landowska (harpsichord)   V-1199
"Deh, vieni alla finestra," E. Pinza   V-1467
"Vedrai, carino"
   Bidu Sayao   C-71557
   L. Bori   V-1846

"*Ah, pietà*," Baccaloni	C-71048D
"*Il mio tesoro*"	
R. Crooks	V-15235
B. Gigli	V-15601
T. Schipa	V-1308
D. Lloyd (in English)	CDX-983
"*Mi tradì*," M. Licette	C-9911
"*Non mi dir, bell' idol mio*," Bampton	VII-8466

K. 588, *Così fan tutte*, opera bouffe in 2 acts. Vienna, 1790.

Complete recording (in Italian) by the Glyndebourne Opera Co., Fritz Busch	VM-812/13/14
Overture	
B.B.C. Symphony Orch., Boult	V-18084
N. Y. Philharmonic-Symphony Orch., Walter	CM-565

K. 620, *Die Zauberflöte* (The Magic Flute), grand opera in 2 acts. Vienna, 1791.

Complete recording by the Berlin State Opera with Berlin Philharmonic Orch., Beecham	VM-541/42
Overture	
B.B.C. Symphony Orch., Toscanini	V-15190
Symphony Orch., Walter	C-67660D
"*Der Vogelfänger*," G. Hüsch	D-20036
"*Bei Männern*"	
Pinza and Rethberg	V10-1104
Hüsch and Perras	V-4374
"*O Isis and Osiris*"	
A. Kipnis	V-1738
Ivar Andrésen	D-25233
E. Pinza (in Italian)	V-6642
"*Der Hölle rache*" (Queen of the Night Aria)	
L. Pons	CM-518
Miliza Korjus	V-11921
"*In diesen heil'gen Hallen*"	
A. Kipnis	V-8684
Ivar Andrésen	D-25233
"*Ach, ich fühl's*"	
D. Maynor with Boston Symphony Orch., Koussevitzky	V-15826
E. Steber with Victor Orch., Leinsdorf	VII-9114
L. Lehmann	D-20279
L. Pons (in French)	V-8733
Priests' Chorus, Metropolitan Opera Chorus	V-4027
"*Ein Mädchen oder Weibchen*," G. Hüsch	D-25443

K. 621, *La clemenza di Tito,* grand opera in 2 acts. Vienna
and Prague, 1791.
Overture, Vienna Philharmonic Orch., Walter   V-12526

K. 311a, Overture in B-flat major.
Paris Conservatory Orch., Fendler   V-12327

D—SONGS FOR ONE OR MORE VOICES WITH PIANO (OR ORGAN) ACCOMPANIMENT

K. 53, *To Joy* ("*Freude, Königin der Weisen*").

K. 52, *Daphne, deine Rosenwangen.*

K. 147, *Wie unglücklich bin ich nit.*

K. 148, *O heiliges Band.*

K. 149, *Die grossmütige Gelassenheit* ("*Ich hab' es längst gesagt*").

K. 150, *Geheime Liebe* ("*Was ich in Gedanken küsse*").

K. 151, *Die Zufriedenheit im niedrigen Stande* ("*Ich trachte mich nach solchen Dingen*").

K. 152, Canzonetta, *Ridente la calma* ("*Der Sylphe des Friedens*").

K. 307, Arietta, *Oiseaux, si tous les ans* ("*Wohl tauscht ihr Vögelein*").

K. 308, Arietta, *Dans un bois solitaire* ("*Einsam ging ich jüngst*").

K. 349a and b, *Die Zufriedenheit* ("*Was frag ich*")—two versions.

K. 351, *Komm, liebe Zither.*

K. 390, *An die Hoffnung* ("*Ich würd auf meinem Pfad*").

K. 391, *An die Einsamkeit* ("*Sei du mein Trost*").

K. 392, *Verdankt sei es dem Glanz* and *Mich locket nicht der Schall.*

K. 393, *Solfeggien.*

K. 441, *Das Bandel* ʌ"*Liebes Mandel, wo is 's Bandel?*").

K. 468, *Gesellenreise* ("*Die ihr einem neuen Grade*").

K. 472, *Der Zauberer* ("*Ihr Mädchen, flieht Damöten ja*").

K. 473, *Die Zufriedenheit* ("*Wie sanft*").

K. 474, *Die betrogene Welt* ("*Der reiche Tor*").

K. 476, *Das Veilchen* ("*Ein Veilchen auf der Wiese stand*").

K. 506, *Lied der Freiheit* ("*Wer unter eines Mädchens Hand*").

K. 517, *Die Alte* ("*Zu meiner Zeit*").

K. 518, *Die Verschweigung* ("Sobald Damoetas Chloen sieht").

K. 519, *Das Lied der Trennung* ("Die Engel Gottes weinen").

K. 520, *Als Luise die Briefe ihres ungetreuen Liebhabers verbrannte* ("Erzeugt von heisser Phantasie").

K. 523, *Abendempfindung* ("Abend ist's").

K. 524, *An Chloe* ("Wenn die Lieb'").

K. 529, *Des kleinen Friedrichs Geburtstag* ("Es war einmal").

K. 530, *Das Traumbild* ("Wo bist du, Bild?").

K. 531, *Die kleine Spinnerin* ("Was spinnst du").

K. 552, *Beim Auszug in das Feld* ("Dem hohen Kaiser-Worte treu").

K. 596, *Sehnsucht nach dem Frühlinge* ("Komm, lieber Mai").

K. 597, *Im Frühlingsanfang* ("Erwacht zum neuen Leben").

K. 598, *Das Kinderspiel* ("Wir Kinder, wir schmecken").

K. 619, *Die ihr der unermesslichen Weltalls Schöpfer ehrt,* a little German cantata, solo.

K. 441c, *Ständchen,* trio for 2 sopranos (or tenors) and bass.

Anh. 5, *Caro mio Druck und Schluck,* comic quartet for soprano, 2 tenors, bass.

K. 483, *Zerfliesset heut', geliebte Brüder,* song for 3-part chorus with organ.

K. 484, *Ihr unsre neuen Leiter,* song for 3-part chorus with organ.

E—CANONS

K. 89, *Canon,* A major, for 4 voices (no text).

K. 89a, Five riddle-canons.

K. 228, *Ach, zu kurz ist unsers Lebens Lauf,* double canon for 4 voices.

K. 229, *Sie ist dahin,* 3 voices.

K. 230, *Selig, selig alle,* 2 voices.

K. 231, *Leck mich im Arsch,* 6 voices.

K. 232, *Lieber Freistädtler, lieber Gaulimauli,* 4 voices.

K. 233, *Leck mir den Arsch,* 3 voices.

K. 234, *Bei der Hitz im Sommer ess ich,* 3 voices.

K. 347, *Lasst uns ziehn,* 6 voices.

K. 348, *V'amo di core teneramente,* three 4-voice choruses.

K. 507, *Heiterkeit und leichtes Blut,* 3 voices.

K. 508, *Auf das Wohl aller Freunde,* 3 voices.

K. 508a, Eight canons (no text).

K. 553, *Alleluja,* 4 voices.

K. 554, *Ave Maria,* 4 voices.

K. 555, *Lacrimoso son' io,* 4 voices.

K. 556, *G'rechtelt's enk,* 4 voices.

K. 557, *Nascoso è il mio sol,* 4 voices.

K. 558, *Gehn ma in 'n Prada,* 4 voices.

K. 559, *Difficile lectu mihi mars,* 3 voices.

K. 560a and b, *O du eselhafter Peierl* and *O du eselhafter Martin,* 4 voices.

K. 561, *Bona nox, bist a rechta Ox,* 4 voices.

K. 562, *Caro, bell' idol mio,* 3 voices.

K. 562a, Canon for 4 voices (no text).

K. 562b, Study for a canon, 4 voices.

Anh. 191, Canon for 4 voices.

F—ARIAS, DUETS, TRIOS, QUARTETS, AND CHORUSES

K. 23, Soprano air, *Conservati fedele.* 1766.

K. 21, Tenor air, *Va, dal furor portata.* 1765.

K. 36, Tenor recitative and air, *Or che il dover* and *Tali e cotanti sono.* 1766.

K. 70, Soprano recitative and air, *A Berenice* and *Sol nascente.* 1769.

K. 71, Tenor air, *Ah, più tremar non voglio.* 1769-70.

K. 74b. Soprano air, *Non curo l'affetto.* 1771.

K. 77, Soprano recitative and air, *Misero me* and *Misero pargoletto.* 1770.

K. 78, Soprano air, *Per pietà, bell' idol mio.* 1770.

K. 79, Soprano air, *O temerario Arbace* and *Per quel paterno amplesso.* 1770.

K. 82, Soprano air, *Se ardire, e speranza.* 1770.

K. 83, Soprano air, *Se tutti i mali miei.* 1770.

K. 88, Soprano air, *Fra cento affanni.* 1770.

K. 119, Soprano air, *Der liebe himmlisches Gefühl.* 1782.

K. 146, Soprano air, *Kommet her, ihr frechen Sünder.* 1779.

K. 178, Soprano air, *Ah, spiegarti, o Dio.* 1772.

K. 209, Tenor air, *Si mostra la sorte.* 1775.

K. 210, Tenor air, *Con ossequio, con rispetto.* 1775.

K. 217, Soprano air, *Voi avete cor fedele.* 1775.

K. 255. Alto recitative and air, *Ombra felice* and *Io ti lascio, e questo addio.* 1776.

K. 256, Tenor air, *Clarice cara mia sposa.* 1776.

K. 272, Soprano recitative and air, *Ah, lo previdi* and *Ah, t'invola agl' occhi mei.* 1777.

K. 294, Soprano recitative and air, *Alcandro, lo confesso* and *Non so d'onde viene.* 1778.

K. 295, Tenor air, *Se al labbro mio non credi* and *Il cor dolente.* 1778.

K. 316, Soprano recitative and air, *Popoli di Tessaglia* and *Io non chiedo, eterni dei.* 1778.

K. 368, Soprano recitative and air, *Ma, che vi fece, o stelle sperai vicino il lido.* 1781.

K. 369, Soprano scene and air, *Misera dove son!* and *Ah! non son' io che parlo.* 1781.

K. 374, Soprano recitative and air, *A questo seno deh vieni* and *Or che il cielo a me ti rende.* 1781.

K. 383, Soprano air, *Nehmt meinen Dank, ihr holden Gönner!* 1782.

K. 416, Soprano scene and rondo, *Mia speranza adorata* and *Ah, non sai, qual pena.* 1783.

K. 418, Soprano air, *Vorrei spiegarvi, oh Dio* and *Ah conte, partite.* 1783.

K. 419, Soprano air, *No, no, che non sei capace.* 1783.

K. 420, Tenor air, *Per pietà, non ricercate.* 1783.

K. 432, Bass recitative and air, *Cosi dunque tradisci* and *Aspri rimorsi atroci.* 1783.

K. 433, Bass air, *Männer suchen stets zu naschen.* 1783.

K. 434, Tenor recitative and air, *Misero! o sogno* and *Aura, che intorno.* 1783.

K. 435, Tenor air, *Müsst ich auch durch tausend Drachen.* 1783.

K. 440, Soprano air, *In te spero, o sposo.* 1782.

K. 486a, Soprano recitative and air, *Basta, vincesti* and *Ah non lasciarmi, no.* 1778.

K. 490, Soprano scene with rondo, *Non più, tutto ascoltai* and *Non temer, amato bene.* 1786.

K. 505, Soprano scene with rondo, *Ch'io mi scordi di te* and *Non temer, amato bene.* 1786.

K. 512, Bass recitative and air, *Alcandro, lo confesso* and *Non so, d'onde viene.* 1787.

K. 513, Bass air, *Mentre ti lascio, o figlia.* 1787.

K. 528, Soprano scene, *Bella mia fiammi* and *Resta, o cara.* 1787.

K. 538, Soprano air, *Ah se in ciel, benigne stelle.* 1788.

K. 539, A German war song, *Ich möchte wohl der Kaiser sein*. 1788.

K. 541, Bass air, *Un bacio di mano*. 1788.

K. 569, Air, *Ohne zwang, aus eignem Triebe*. 1789.

K. 577, Soprano rondo, *Al desio, di chi t' adora*. 1789.

K. 578, Soprano air, *Alma grande e nobil core*. 1789.

K. 579, Soprano air, *Un moto di gioia mi sento*. 1789.

K. 580, Soprano air, *Schon lacht der holde Frühling*. 1789.

K. 582, Soprano air, *Chi sà, chi sà, qual sia*. 1789.

K. 583, Soprano air, *Vado, ma dove?—oh Dei!* 1789.

K. 584, Bass air, *Rivolgeti a lui lo sguardo*. 1789.

K. 584a, Soprano air, *Donne vaghe*. 1789.

K. 612, Bass air, *Per questa bella mano*. 1791.

Anh. 245, Bass air, *Io ti lascio, o cara, addio*. 1791.

K. 389, Duet for 2 tenors, *Welch angstliches Beben*. 1782.

K. 436, Duet (Notturno) for soprano and bass, *Ecco quel fiero istante*. 1783.

K. 437, Duet (Notturno) for soprano and bass, *Mi lagnerò tacendo*. 1783.

K. 489, Duet for soprano and tenor, *Spiegarti non poss' io*. 1786.

K. 625, Comic duet for soprano and bass, *Nun, liebes Weibchen, ziehst mit mir*. 1790.

K. 346, Trio (Notturno) for 3 voices, *Luci care, luci· belle*. 1783.

K. 438, Trio (Notturno), *Se lontan, ben mio, tu sei*. 1783.

K. 439, Trio (Notturno) for 2 sopranos and bass, *Due pupille amabile*. 1783.

K. 480, Terzett (Trio), *Mandina amabile*. 1785.

K. 532, Trio for soprano, tenor, bass, *Grazie agl' inganni tuoi*. 1787.

K. 549, Canzonetta for 2 sopranos and bass, *Più non si trovano*. 1788.

K. 479, Quartet for soprano, tenor, 2 basses, *Dite almeno, in che mancai*. 1785.

K. 615, Final Chorus, *Viviamo felici in dolce contento*. 1791.

THE WORLD THAT MOZART LIVED IN

MOZART'S LIFE	MUSICAL EVENTS	WORLD EVENTS
1756 Born on Jan. 27 at Salzburg.	1756 B., Prince Carl Lichnowsky, friend of Mozart and Beethoven. Mozart's father Leopold publishes his *Violin Method*.	1756 B., "Light-Horse Harry" Lee, Aaron Burr. In Europe, Seven Years' War declared (in America, the French and Indian War).
	1757 D., Domenico Scarlatti, J. W. Stamitz. B., Ignaz Pleyel.	1757 B., Lafayette, Wm. Blake. Franklin goes to England to represent the Pennsylvania Colonial Assembly. British wars in India begin.
	1759 D., Handel. Joseph Haydn composes his First Symphony and is apptd. cond. of Count Morzin's orchestra.	1759 B., Burns, Pitt, Schiller. G. Washington marries Mrs. Custis. British take Quebec; Generals Montcalm and Wolfe killed.
1760 Begins clavier lessons with his father.	1760 B., Cherubini, Dussek, Rouget de Lisle. In Vienna, Gluck's opera *Tetide* is produced.	1760 George II d., George III succeeds. French surrender Canada to British. Macpherson's *Ossian* (Pt. I) pub.
1761 Composes first clavier pieces.	1761 Haydn enters service of Prince Esterházy at Eisenstadt. Gluck produces *Don Juan* ballet in Vienna.	1761 D., Samuel Richardson. B., Sir John Moore, Albert Gallatin.
1762 With his father and sister, visits Munich, Vienna, and Pressburg.	1762 J. C. Bach (the "English Bach") goes to London to live. Gluck's finest opera, *Orfeo*, produced in Vienna.	1762 B., George IV, Fichte. Catherine II usurps Russian throne on death of Elizabeth Petrovna. In London, the "Cock Lane Ghost" affair.

1763 Returns to Salzburg. Some little clavier pieces are published. Concert tour as far as Paris.

1764 At Versailles (Court of Louis XV) where he plays. Then to London, meeting J. C. Bach and playing at court. Composes syms. and sonatas.

1765 The Mozarts give concerts in London. On ending their visit they go on to Holland.

1766 Concerts in Holland. Visits to Versailles, Paris. Family returns home by way of Switzerland.

1767 Second visit to Vienna.

1768 Another Vienna visit. Comp. the opera *La Finta semplice*, and has *Bastien and Bastienne* produced in Dr. Mesmer's private theater.

1769 *La Finta semplice* is produced in Salzburg. In December, sets out for Italy with his father.

1763 B., Méhul. At Esterházy, Haydn prod. his *Acis and Galatea* and writes first clavier sonata.

1764 D., Rameau, Leclair, Mattheson, Locatelli. Haydn's six "Paris" symphonies pub. In Vienna, *La Rencontre imprévue*, by Gluck.

1765 B., Thomas Attwood, pupil of Mozart (1785) and organist at St. Paul's. Gluck's ballet *Semiramide*, Vienna.

1766 D., Porpora. Haydn becomes conductor of the Esterházy orchestra.

1767 D., Telemann. In Vienna, Gluck's opera *Alceste* is produced.

1768 Fire at Esterházy destroys much of Haydn's music. His opera *Lo Speziale* produced. In Paris, Grétry's opera *Le Huron*.

1769 B., Benjamin Carr, comp. of early American operas. Grétry produces *Le Tableau vivant* in Paris.

1763 B., "Jean Paul" Richter, Wm. Cobbett, Fouché. End of Seven Years' War in Europe, and of French and Indian in America.

1764 D., Hogarth. Goldsmith's *Traveller*, Walpole's *Castle of Otranto*, Voltaire's *Dictionnaire philosophique*.

1765 B., Robt. Fulton, Eli Whitney. Watt inv. steam engine. Stamp Act passed. Blackstone's *Commentaries* pub.

1766 Franklin goes to England to fight Stamp Act; it is repealed. Goldsmith's *Vicar of Wakefield* published.

1767 B., Andrew Jackson, John Quincy Adams. Britain imposes tea and other duties on American colonies.

1768 D., L. Sterne. B., Tecumseh, Charlotte Corday, Chateaubriand. Genoa cedes Corsica to France. Sterne's *Sentimental Journey* published.

1769 B., Napoleon Bonaparte, Humboldt, Cuvier, Wellington, DeWitt Clinton. In Phila., Rittenhouse erects telescope to observe transit of Venus.

MOZART'S LIFE

1770 Italian triumphs. Studies with Martini. Opera *Mitridate, Re di Ponto* is prod. in Milan, Wolfgang conducting.

1771 Salzburg again. The Mozarts return to Milan in August, where *Ascanio in Alba* is produced.

1772 Salzburg. Wolfgang composes much. In October, he and his father go to Italy. *Lucio Silla* produced in Milan.

1773 From Salzburg goes to Vienna in vain quest of court position. Composes first string quintet.

1774 Salzburg. Visits Munich in December.

1775 In Munich, he produces *La Finta giardiniera,* January; and in April *Il Re pastore* at Salzburg.

MUSICAL EVENTS

1770 D.,Tartini. B., Ludwig van Beethoven. In Vienna, Gluck's opera *Paris and Helen.* Parts of *Messiah* (Handel) first heard in America.

1771 B., J. B. Cramer. In Paris, Grétry's *Zémire et Azor.* Dr. Burney's *Present State of Music in France and Italy* published.

1772 D., Daquin. Haydn writes *Farewell* Symphony. Gluck makes his first visit to Paris to produce opera.

1773 In Paris, Grétry's *Le Magnifique* and *Céphale et Procris.* Gossec reorganizes the Concerts Spirituels. Burney pub. *The Present State of Music in Germany.*

1774 D., Jommelli. B., Spontini. Gluck goes to Paris to live; prod. *Iphigénie en Aulide* and (revised) *Orfeo.*

1775 D., Giovanni Sammartini. B., Boieldieu. In London, J. C. Bach starts the Bach-Abel Concerts. Haydn's oratorio *Il Ritorno di Tobia* is performed in Vienna.

WORLD EVENTS

1770 B., Wordsworth, Hegel. Boston Massacre. Capt. James Cook, on first circumnavigation, discovers Australia. Goldsmith's *Deserted Village* pub.

1771 B., Walter Scott, Sydney Smith, Robert Owen, Mungo Park. Smollett's *Humphry Clinker* published.

1772 D., John Woolman. B., Coleridge. First partition of Poland among powers. Cook's 2d voyage begins.

1773 D., Lord Chesterfield. B., Metternich, Wm. Henry Harrison. Boston Tea Party. Daniel Boone moves to Kentucky. Publication of Cook's *Voyage Round the World, 1768-71.*

1774 D., Louis XV, Goldsmith, Clive. First Continental Congress meets at Phila. British close port of Boston. Goethe's *Sorrows of Werther* pub. Warren Hastings made Governor of India.

1775 B., Charles Lamb, Jane Austen, J. M. W. Turner, Lyman Beecher. Battles of Lexington, Concord, Bunker Hill; and Washington takes command of continental armies. Edmund Burke's speech on conciliation of the colonies.

1776 Salzburg. *Haffner* Serenade comp. for wedding in friend's family. Increasing friction with the Archbp. of Salzburg.

1777 With his mother, starts on another tour. At Mannheim meets the Weber family.

1778 Goes on to Paris, where his mother falls ill and dies. Comp. music for ballet, *Les petits riens*. Home by way of Mannheim and Munich.

1779 In Salzburg, composing actively.

1780 Salzburg. Receives commission for opera *Idomeneo* from Munich, where he goes in November.

1776 Vienna Natl. Theater founded. Gluck produces *Alceste* in Paris. Feud begins between his followers and Piccinni's. Haydn composes opera *La vera costanza*.

1777 D., G. C. Wagenseil. Gluck produces *Armide* in Paris. Erard makes first French pianoforte.

1778 D., Thomas Arne. B., J. N. Hummel. Vienna National Singspiel is founded.

1779 Gluck's *Iphigénie en Tauride* establishes his supremacy over Piccinni. At Esterházy, Haydn prod. opera *L'isola disabitata*.

1780 D., J. L. Krebs. B., famous stage soprano Angelica Catalani. Grétry's opera *Andromaque* in Paris.

1776 Declaration of Independence. Benj. Franklin goes to Paris for 9 years. Battles of Long Island and Trenton. Nathan Hale executed. Adam Smith's *Wealth of Nations* published.

1777 B., Henry Clay, T. Campbell, Taney, Hallam, Mme Récamier. Battle of Saratoga; Burgoyne surrenders. Washington at Valley Forge. Articles of Confederation signed, creating the U. S. A.

1778 D., Voltaire, Rousseau, Piranesi, elder Pitt, Linnaeus. B., Brougham, Brummell, Hazlitt, Robt. Emmet, Gay-Lussac. Alliance signed between U. S. and France. Burney's *Evelina* pub.

1779 Capt. Cook killed in Hawaii by natives. B., Zebulon M. Pike, Decatur, Thomas Moore, Lord Melbourne. Naval battle between *Bonhomme Richard* and H.M.S. *Serapis*. Col. George Rogers Clark seizes British Northwest.

1780 D., Empress Maria Theresa. B., Francis Scott Key, Béranger, Mary Somerville. Rochambeau arrives in U. S. Benedict Arnold's treason; John André hanged. British defeated at King's Mountain.

MOZART'S LIFE	MUSICAL EVENTS	WORLD EVENTS
1781 January, *Idomeneo* is produced in Munich. Mozart goes to Salzburg and Vienna. Quarrels with Archbp. and leaves his service. Contest with Clementi. Meets Haydn.	1781 B., Diabelli. Haydn publishes his *Stabat Mater.* His friendship with Mozart begins. Beethoven starts lessons in organ, violin, and composition.	1781 D., Lessing, Turgot. Battle of the Cowpens, siege of Yorktown, surrender of Cornwallis. Pub. of Kant's *Critique of Pure Reason,* Schiller's *The Robbers,* Rousseau's *Confessions.*
1782. In Vienna. *Die Entführung aus dem Serail* is produced in July. On August 4 he marries Constanze Weber.	1782 D., Metastasio (librettist), J. C. Bach. B., Paganini, Auber, John Field. Rousseau's collected writings on music are published.	1782 B., Daniel Webster, John C. Calhoun, Martin Van Buren, Thomas Hart Benton. Lord North resigns. Britain signs prelim. peace with U. S. Publication of Fanny Burney's *Cecilia.*
1783 Takes his wife to Salzburg to meet his father and sister. Begins and abandons *L'Oca del Cairo.* Returns to Vienna.	1783 D., Johann Adolf Hasse, Caffarelli, Kirnberger, Padre Soler. Beethoven, aged 13, is appointed to the court orchestra at Bonn.	1783 D., Dr. Wm. Hunter, D'Alembert, Mme d'Epinay. B., Bolivar, Iturbide, Washington Irving, Stendhal, Nancy Hanks. European powers recog. independence of U. S. Treaty of Paris signed. Pitt becomes prime minister.
1784 In Vienna. Meets Paisiello and Sarti.	1784 D., Wilhelm Friedemann Bach (J. S. Bach's eldest son), Padre Martini. B., Spohr, Ferdinand Ries, Fétis. Beethoven made deputy court organist. Gossec establishes Ecole Royale de Chant in Paris.	1784 D., Diderot, Dr. Johnson. B., Leigh Hunt, Lord Palmerston. "Affair of the Diamond Necklace" begins, Paris. King's College, N. Y., becomes Columbia College. Jefferson's *Notes on the State of Virginia* published.
1785 In Vienna. Visited by his father. Is called by Haydn "the greatest composer known to him." Begins *Le Nozze di Figaro.*	1785 D., Galuppi. In Vienna, J. H. Hummel becomes Kapellm. at Schikaneder Theater; his son takes lessons from Mozart.	1785 B., Audubon, Oliver Hazard Perry, De Quincey, the Dauphin ("Louis XVII"). Napoleon Bonaparte is commissioned lieutenant of artillery.

1786 In Vienna. In February, *Der Schauspieldirektor* is produced at Schönbrunn. On May 1, *Le Nozze di Figaro* is produced.

1786 D, Michael Arne. B, Sir Henry Bishop, Carl Maria von Weber. Cherubini leaves Italy to live in Paris.

1786 D, Fredk. the Great. Impeachment of Warren Hastings begins. World's first steamboat built by Symington at Edinburgh. Burns's *Poems* pub.

1787 Visits Prague; *Prague* Symphony given, *Don Giovanni* commissioned. In Vienna visited by Beethoven. *Don Giovanni* produced on Oct. 29, Prague.

1787 D, Gluck, Mozart's father Leopold. Haydn composes "King of Prussia" Quartets.

1787 Assembly of Notables at Versailles. U. S. Constitution signed. Shays's Rebellion in Mass. *Federalist Papers* start publication.

1788 *Don Giovanni* (revised) introduced to Vienna. During the summer composes last three Symphonies—E-flat major, G minor, and C major (*Jupiter*).

1788 D, Karl Philipp Emanuel Bach. Beethoven apptd. violist in court orchestra, Bonn; friendship with the Breunings and Waldstein begins. Haydn writes *Oxford* Symphony.

1788 D, Gainsborough, Buffon, the Young Pretender (Charles Edward Stuart). B, Byron, Schopenhauer, Sir Robt. Peel. London *Times* started. Penal settlement founded in Australia.

1789 With Prince Lichnowsky, visits Dresden, Leipzig, and Berlin. In Vienna, is commissioned by Emperor Joseph II to write *Così fan tutte.*

1789 In Paris, Sarrette forms the Natl. Guard Band. Cimarosa succeeds Paisiello in St. Petersburg as court composer.

1789 B, Jas. Fenimore Cooper, Daguerre. Washington elected President. Mutiny on the *Bounty.* Paris mob seizes Bastille, French Revolution opens.

1790 *Così fan tutte* produced. At Emperor's coronation, at Frankfort, plays *Coronation* Pf. Concerto.

1790 On death of Esterházy, Haydn retires on a pension. He meets the young Beethoven at Bonn.

1790 D, Franklin. B, Lamartine. Galvani discovers current electricity. Louis XVI accepts new Constitution.

1791 Vienna. Meets Schikaneder, composes *Die Zauberflöte.* Mysterious stranger commissions a *Requiem. La Clemenza di Tito* prod. in Prague. Though ill, he conducts prem. of *Die Zauberflöte.* On Dec. 5 dies, leaving *Requiem* unfinished.

1791 D, Paradies. B, Czerny, Meyerbeer. Haydn makes first visit to England; comp. new symphonies for London and Oxford performance.

1791 D, Mirabeau. B, Faraday, S. F. B. Morse. Congress passes first ten amendments (Bill of Rights). Flight of French king and queen to Varennes. Boswell's *Johnson,* Paine's *Rights of Man,* pub. Bank of U. S. founded.

INDEX OF NAMES

INDEX OF NAMES

INDEX TO MOZART'S WORKS